W9-CKI-503

BUFFALO
CALF ROAD WOMAN

**Center Point
Large Print**

**This Large Print Book carries the
Seal of Approval of N.A.V.H.**

BUFFALO
CALF ROAD WOMAN

The Story of a Warrior of the Little Bighorn

ROSEMARY AGONITO
AND JOSEPH AGONITO

CENTER POINT PUBLISHING
THORNDIKE, MAINE

This Center Point Large Print edition
is published in the year 2007 by arrangement with
Globe Pequot Press.

Copyright © 2006 by Rosemary Agonito and Joseph Agonito.

All rights reserved.

The text of this Large Print edition is unabridged. In other
aspects, this book may vary from the original edition. Printed in
Thailand. Set in 16-point Times New Roman type.

ISBN: 1-58547-898-9
ISBN 13: 978-1-58547-898-9

Library of Congress Cataloging-in-Publication Data

Agonito, Rosemary.
   Buffalo Calf Road Woman : the story of a warrior of the Little Bighorn
/ Rosemary Agonito and Joseph Agonito.--Center Point large print ed.
      p. cm.
   ISBN-13: 978-1-58547-898-9 (lib. bdg. : alk. paper)
   1. Road Woman, Buffalo Calf. 2. Cheyenne women--Biography. 3. Cheyenne
Indians--Wars, 1876. 4. Little Bighorn, Battle of the, Mont., 1876. 5. Large type
books. I. Agonito, Joseph. II. Title.

E99.C53R633 2007
973.8'2'092--dc22
[B]

2006023799

To our son and daughter,
John and Mae Lee,
who made the journey with us to discover
Buffalo Calf Road

CONTENTS

CONTENTS

AUTHORS' NOTE

An intriguing reference to a Cheyenne woman fighting at the 1876 Battle of the Rosebud in Dee Brown's *Bury My Heart at Wounded Knee* first sparked our interest. Who was she? Why was she in battle? That reference led to a search that spanned years and thousands of miles.

We understood how women's history is forgotten, neglected, trivialized, and even deliberately concealed. Indeed, Dee Brown, unable to account for Buffalo Calf Road's presence among warriors in battle, mistakenly assumed she had come to help with the horses.

In resurrecting Calf's story, several difficulties emerged. The nomadic Northern Cheyenne lacked a written language, thus leaving no records, diaries, or letters. A limited number of Northern Cheyenne narratives from the period exist, recorded by white interpreters. With two exceptions, they are provided by men, who seldom speak of women. In accounts of battle, for example, Cheyenne warriors seldom mention Buffalo Calf Road, despite a battle being named for her. Anthropologists and historians who interviewed Plains Indians seldom spoke with women or showed interest in them beyond domestic roles. Similarly, photographers captured hundreds of images of the Northern Cheyenne but rarely focused on women

9

except while doing domestic chores or as "wife of" a prominent man.

Despite these limitations, we slowly pieced together the story of Buffalo Calf Road. The richest contemporary Cheyenne narratives referring to Calf come from two women, Iron Teeth and Kate Bighead, as well as a warrior, Wooden Leg. Having lived through many of the same events, they provide a picture of Calf's bravery in battle and aspects of her personal life. A number of secondary sources from the oral tradition (see Bibliography) also provide some information on Calf's life. As is the case with oral accounts passed through time, contradictions emerged, sometimes forcing us to choose.

We also examined visual materials—sketches, paintings, photographs—providing a vivid record of Plains Indian life, culture, and military exploits. Many are colored pencil drawings in ledger books obtained from whites. Since men produced this ledger book art, it focuses on military exploits and occasionally on scenes of everyday life. Here we found two sketches of Buffalo Calf Road; one depicts her riding into battle with her brother and another saving her brother at the Rosebud. We found no photos of Calf, not surprising since she spent most of her life as a "hostile," far from the agencies where many Plains Indian portraits were taken.

The National Archives contain another rich source on Plains Indians, especially the records of the Bureau of Indian Affairs and Department of War. Correspondence from military officials in the field, reports, official accounts of events, and census data provided some information on Calf and her husband, Black Coyote. The Smithsonian and National Museum of the American Indian in New York provided additional material.

We also searched newspaper accounts of the period. Reporters covering the Indian wars who write about battles Calf fought failed to mention her. We did find accounts of Black Coyote's trial.

Our pursuit of Buffalo Calf Road included a lengthy trip through Cheyenne country on the Northern Plains to do research and explore the land Calf traveled. We visited typical terrain the Cheyenne roamed, battle sites, forts, the Sand Hills where Calf and her people hid, the area where Calf died, and the Cheyenne reservation at Lame Deer, Montana. Here we searched tribal census rolls, looked for Calf's descendants (we found none) and interviewed older Cheyenne likely to know Calf's story. (For clarification on Cheyenne names and familial reationships, see the Glossary in the back of the book.)

Museums, galleries, and libraries also featured prominently in our travels. A special place was the University of Nebraska, which houses the papers of Mari Sandoz, who wrote *Cheyenne Autumn*, a study of the flight from Indian Territory. Unlike others, Sandoz interviewed Cheyenne women, including Old Cheyenne Woman, who lived through many of the events in Calf's life. So it is not surprising that Calf and other women figure prominently in Sandoz's account.

11

Sadly, much of Calf's story has been lost and we had to fill in the gaps. This involved a good bit of detective work, such as unearthing clues that placed her at various events. It included studying Northern Cheyenne culture to accurately represent daily life, physical features of camp, and religion. It meant learning about regional terrain, weather, plant life, and animals. It involved examining artifacts and dress of the Cheyenne in various museums in Montana, Wyoming, and Nebraska and studying period photos. Combining these elements with factual data, we were able to create an authentic, although partially fictionalized, version of Buffalo Calf Road's life.

We all know that the telling of history is a continual unfolding of the past. It is never static, never finished. After this book had gone to press, we learned that the Northern Cheyenne had announced they were prepared to break a one-hundred-year vow of silence taken immediately after the Battle of the Little Bighorn in 1876. At a public gathering on June 28, 2005, in Helena, Montana, Cheyenne elders made the startling claim that Buffalo Calf Road (also known as Buffalo Calf Trail Woman) delivered the final blow that knocked General George Armstrong Custer from his horse and killed him. The Cheyenne promise to release more information in time. This is a new and exciting turn of events which we will follow closely. However this controversy plays out in the months and years ahead we are pleased to bring this forgotten great woman's story to light.

A nation is not conquered
Until the hearts of its women
Are on the ground.
Then it is done, no matter
How brave its warriors
Or how strong its weapons.

Traditional Cheyenne saying

THE STORY OF BUFFALO CALF ROAD WOMAN

CHAPTER 1

The end of the world began that day. Not slowly or quietly, not piece by piece or by degrees, but as a calamity that brings another and another and another.

A heavy mist hung over the sleeping village wrapped in cottonwoods against the biting winter cold. As the first gray light moved uncertainly over the haze, a lone, hungry jackrabbit in the distance scuttled across the snow in search of a naked patch of yellow grass. The distant neighing of a horse in the cloistered pony herd interrupted its furtive movements. It crouched, long ears erect, listening. But the hunger of the lean winter moons soon pushed the starving animal past its fear, and it darted forward again, searching. Suddenly, out of the dense brush leapt a coyote, heavy with its burden of unborn pups, its yellowish eyes wild and full of fire. The rabbit's hind legs propelled it through the snow, swift and straight, the hot eyes tight against its back. The swollen coyote circled, pressing its desperate prey toward the distant bluffs, then fell back. Glimpsing a chance to escape, the rabbit ran some more, but the grateful moment passed as quickly as it began. The coyote's mate, patient and cunning and sure, jumped from a waiting rock. The rabbit's futile flight home ended on the bloodied snows.

17

In the village, the day began as ordinary as any day. Strands of light spread slowly across the eastern sky as Buffalo Calf Road opened her eyes. She glanced at Little Seeker asleep under her blanket, then to the empty space beside her where Black Coyote normally slept. She ran her fingers over the soft warm fur, wishing he had not gone hunting. Her nose could almost smell the fresh musky scent of his body. She could see his lean powerful frame and imagined his hard stomach pressing against hers as his body settled on her. The Coyote was always a gentle lover, warm in his caresses. Calf smiled at the thought of Black Coyote, but soon a small cloud moved across the smile. Sometimes it seemed to her there were two Coyotes, one generous and caring, full of life's joys, and another, dark and brooding, full of life's pain.

Calf pulled her robe tightly around her tall slender body against the cold dawn, reluctant to leave its soft warmth. The slicing winds and volleys of snow that roared through the huddled camp the night before had left behind a frigid stillness. Faint sounds of rushing water broke the silence. She loved listening to the stream beyond her lodge as it moved swiftly over the rocks and boulders, veering off the banks, diving under exposed roots clinging to land. Nothing stopped it, not even the cold of many winter moons.

The Moon of the Light Snows had arrived at Old Bear's camp and soon the hard winter would end, Calf thought. The pony herd would grow strong again feasting on the green grass, and they would move camp in search of the life-giving buffalo. In her mind she could see the herds of elk, antelope, and buffalo grazing along the Tongue and Powder Rivers and the newborn colts swelling the pony herd. She pictured the women cutting thin strips of meat to dry and preparing the rich buffalo hides, renewing their weather-battered lodges and replenishing their stores of food.

Huddled in the dark, Calf longed for spring, with its promise of warmth, life, and freedom of movement. In her mind, Black Coyote returned from the hunt with stores of buffalo meat and Little Seeker played in the sun with the children of camp. With the deep snows gone, she imagined the balmy wind blowing through her hair as she rode her pony across the plains.

Most of the camp still slept as Calf sluggishly rose in the morning cold to force the dying embers of last night's fire back to life. Only Box Elder, the blind prophet of the Cheyenne, had already ventured out. The stars still dotted the black sky while he carefully made his way, walking stick in hand, through the crunching snow toward the mesa where he offered his morning prayers to Maheo, Father and Creator of the Universe, and Grandmother Earth. He prayed, as he always did, that the Holy Persons protect his people from the strangers carving their way over the land of the Cheyenne. As Box Elder finished his prayers the black sky above him slowly grayed till the colors of dawn slid across the horizon to the east.

Suddenly the morning calm exploded. Box Elder

had barely reached the edge of camp when unfamiliar sounds struck his ears, faint and distant—the noise of a rush of people, of hushed commands, of rifles banging against the rocks. In an instant he knew. *Veho! The white man called the spider by his people!* The old man quickened his stumbling pace and shouted his warning.

"Soldiers! Soldiers! Run!" the blind man screamed at the village just beginning to stir from its sleep.

Already the attacking troops crowded against the southern edge of camp, cutting off access to the main pony herd down river. Most of the waking villagers barely had time to dress before the soldiers entered camp. Screams and rifle shots carried far through the dry cold air. In the panic to escape, many slashed the walls of their buffalo hide lodges. Children cried as their mothers carried or dragged them away from the gunfire. A few managed to grab packs of food or blankets, but most fled only with their lives. Old people stumbled through the snow as a hail of bullets whizzed through the shivering cottonwoods, searing the lodge skins in their path. Warriors desperately seized their weapons and covered their people's retreat as best they could.

By now another flank of soldiers charged the ravine to the west and a third advanced up the dry creek bed to the south. Calf and the others saw that their only escape lay up the rocky mesa behind their camp.

Everything was chaos and terror. Buffalo Calf Road rushed Little Seeker away from the direction of the charge, her hand on the revolver tucked in her belt. Behind them ran Chicken Woman, Black Coyote's sister. They crouched close to the ground as they hurried frantically through camp. Suddenly Calf stopped, her darting eyes searching the crowd. Everywhere old people, children, men, and women struggled with their special burdens of ill health, infirmity, packs, babies, and fear.

"Please take her," Calf pleaded as she gently thrust five-year-old Little Seeker to Chicken Woman, her sister-in-law. Assured that the two were headed in the direction of safety, she turned and ran back to the lodge of her dear friend, Brave One. Soldiers were already entering the village on foot, moving among the lodges with their carbines drawn before them like menacing arms against the freezing air.

When Calf arrived Brave One had just finished dressing the two frightened orphans in her charge and was frantically lifting one of them in her right arm as the weight of her packs of supplies pulled at the other. Calf grabbed the hand of the other child, but as they turned to rush out, a blue figure, rifle in hand, charged the lodge.

The soldier paused for an instant at the sight of the children and two women. Calf seized the moment of hesitation, raised her revolver, and fired. The man's cap leapt into the air as the force of the bullet grazed the soldier's head, pushing him backward out the opening to the ground.

Clutching the knife she used for digging roots,

21

which always hung from her belt, Buffalo Calf Road ripped a hole through the back of the lodge and the four slipped out into the cold and panic. The warrior Little Hawk was running past just then and he took the small sobbing child from Brave One as she struggled with her packs.

By now the crush of people running from the village began to thin as the shooting grew louder. A few warriors had horses and helped the old people and children escape. One of these warriors, Yellow Hair, rode by on Old Bear's horse, clutching a small boy in front of him while the daughter of Last Bull clung behind. Other warriors swung back to fight in earnest now that most of the people had escaped from camp. A few had guns with ammunition, but most shot arrows at the soldiers.

As they left the camp circle, Calf gave the hand of the small child to Brave One and urged them on. With her precious revolver, she headed for an area west of the lodges where the warriors appeared to be making a stand against the soldiers. But before Calf had run past a few lodges, her heart leapt to her throat as she saw the old prophet, Box Elder, carrying Ox'zem, the sacred wheel lance, and stumbling toward the soldiers in his blind confusion.

A bluecoat on horseback spotted the old man and began to rush him. Before Calf could move, the warrior Braided Locks leapt from behind a snow covered lodge, his knife drawn, his two legs running to meet the four-legged charge. Calf flew into motion at once, her hand outstretched as though she could draw the blind man to her across the empty, chilling space.

"This way, grandfather! This way!" she shouted.

A shot cut short her frantic plea. Braided Locks staggered backwards clutching his face as he fell, the blood spreading a deep crimson tint across the snow crystals. Rage suddenly pushed out fear, pressing at Calf's temples, pounding in her heart, tightening her fists. She aimed her revolver at the bluecoat, slowly, deliberately, as his horse shied and plunged. She fired.

Buffalo Calf Road grabbed Box Elder's arm, pointing him in the right direction as she ran to help the groaning Braided Locks, shot in the cheek. She pulled him to his feet and with the wounded man on one arm and the blind prophet on the other, she guided them quickly over the snow toward the mesa where the others waited, entrenched behind the hastily built breastworks. They passed Two Moons, Bear Walks on a Ridge, and Wooden Leg, who had surrounded a soldier and were stabbing him to death. As Calf led the two past the grizzly deed, the sound of the warriors bartering over the bluecoat's rifle, coat, and boots followed her.

The soldiers did not pursue the beaten Cheyenne up the mesa. Instead, they set about the destruction of the village. From their distant hiding places the people watched anxiously as the moving blue dots scurried about under the naked cottonwoods and around the battered lodges, punctuating their destruction of the village with yellow flames that cut through the blanket of trees. Soon everything was ablaze as the brilliant colors painted the river's edge. The explosion of gunpowder in some of the lodges sent up occasional flares and the popping of cartridges could be heard in the distance. The smell of burning buffalo meat and the stench of charring leather swelled the air.

Throughout their destruction of the village, the soldiers came under constant fire from the Indians, who grew bolder in their anger and crept through the willows and sagebrush and over logs and rocks, picking off the white men from their concealed positions. But they could not stop the decimation of their wealth as they watched an old white-haired officer shouting the orders to burn.

Buffalo Calf Road stared numbly as the flames devoured a lifetime of work and accumulation. It was not just their homes being destroyed, their carefully painted buffalo lodges with the intricately beaded lining that represented the artistic masterpiece of a woman's life. Everything that made life bearable on the hostile high plains went with the fingers of flames: great buffalo skin robes that the coldest wind could not penetrate, warm blankets and fine bead work to trade for ponies, sturdy moccasins intricately crafted and finely decorated, practical buckskin clothing tediously prepared and sewed, and the tools of survival itself including axes, knives, and gunpowder.

The objects of their ancestral heritage vanished in the blackened smoke—men's scalp shirts, sacred shields, lances, and pipes, and women's root diggers, quilling instruments, and fleshers. Disappearing with the dawn were the musical instruments—drums, flutes, rattles, whistles—used for doctoring, for social and religious functions, and for lifting the hearts of the people. Lost forever were the priceless mementos that passed between husband and wife, friends, and parents and children, like the one-thousand dress, covered with a thousand elk teeth, which a good man provided for his wife. Not even the strongest medicine or the most earnest prayers could bring back the lifetimes that disappeared in the flames like a swallow in flight.

The hearts of Calf and her people were bad that day, as bad as they had ever been.

Here and there someone had managed to save a treasure. Still with them was Box Elder's sacred wheel lance, Ox'zem, carved at the top with the face of Sweet Medicine, great prophet of the people who was given the Sacred Arrows by Maheo, and its five wheels of various sizes lashed to a shaft with a cluster of eagle feathers hanging from the outer circle. The wheel of no beginning and no end represented the universe of Maheo. When invoked, Ox'zem's powerful medicine could conceal the Cheyenne from their enemies.

The warrior Great Eyes saved his shield, made almost one hundred winters ago and given to him by his father, Oak. Painted red with a crescent moon on it, animal parts adorned its face—four claws of a grizzly bear for strength and courage, a turtle's tail for its ability to hide and its imperviousness to death, and

25

the feathers of eagles and owls for the power of flight. Wooden Leg rescued his eagle-wing bone flute and his medicine pipe.

Buffalo Calf Road managed to bring out her mother's elkhorn flesher, worn smooth with deep cavities by generations of thumbs using it to prepare hides for tanning. Rows of scratches lined the sides where her ancestors had kept count of their age until marriage, passing it on to their daughters.

Except for these and a few other precious items, the people of Old Bear's camp would leave a rich winter to enter a poor spring. For the first time Calf thought it good that many Cheyenne were wintering on the reservations of Chief Red Cloud and Chief Spotted Tail, although she hated the idea of her people living on reservations according to white rules, taking food from them, slowly losing the old ways. At least they would bring back to the tribe some of its ancestral objects and its lost pride.

As Buffalo Calf Road sat on the cold mesa with the others helplessly watching the destruction below, her thoughts turned anxiously to Black Coyote. Had he and the other hunters escaped the notice of the blue-coats? Was he safe? Worry for the Coyote pushed out thoughts of their burning lodge and possessions. Little Seeker clung to her mother and, as if seeing Calf's thoughts, sobbed for her father.

The sun rose high overhead before all the flames sank to the ground. Suddenly Black Coyote stood before her. Little Seeker leapt into his arms as he hugged Calf, and the three of them embraced in unspoken pain and relief. When Calf looked into the Coyote's flashing eyes, she saw a deep bitter rage, and she knew he seethed over this new injustice of the white man against her people.

Along with Black Coyote, many of the warriors on the hunt had returned, drawn back by the sounds of battle and gunshot. As their numbers swelled, the warriors began to move against the soldiers still in Old Bear's fallen camp.

The Indians launched a successful flank attack from the west, pressing the soldiers hard and driving them southward from the ruined village. But as the soldiers retreated, they drove the pony herd ahead of them into the snow-covered hills along the Powder River. This last blow hit the Cheyenne hard for, without the herd, movement across the snow-covered land would be very difficult. The children, the sick, and elderly especially would suffer.

On the mesa, Calf helped wherever she could. One person had been shot dead and a number lay injured. Medicine Woman and Bridge, both healers, invoked their powers over the wounded. Whirlwind already lay dead, shot through the head. Bridge worked over an injured warrior, Red Haired Bear, who bled profusely from his side, by using the last ear of sacred corn, which had the power to stop bleeding. One of the women, Bighead, brought water she had gotten by melting snow over a hastily built fire. While Young Eagle blew his medicine flute, Bridge coaxed some red tea into Red Haired Bear and, using chants and a rattle, put him to sleep. As Bridge passed the yellow gourd rattle and sacred corn over his naked side, the red flow slowed to a thin trickle. Then he gently patted the ugly wound with sage leaves and sprinkled it with the powder of puffball weed.

Medicine Woman moved quickly, purifying the gunshot wounds with burned juniper branches plucked hurriedly on the mesa by Singing Cloud, a shy pretty girl who often watched Medicine Woman at work. The older woman chanted as she mixed the herbs from her bundle, using just the right proportions. As Singing Cloud held the precious mixture, Medicine Woman began the laying on of hands. Next she took the mixture and, raising the wooden bowl to each Sacred Person in the four directions of the universe, she prayed. The ritual completed, she spread the mixture over the wound and moved to the next patient.

Not only warriors were hurt. An old man had collapsed during the frantic scramble up the mesa and, barely breathing, had to be carried to the top. The small granddaughter of Red Eagle was hit in the arm by a flying bullet, but the wound was clean and Medicine Woman thought it would heal quickly.

When the warriors below had pressed the soldiers as far as they could into the hills below the ruined village, they returned to the mesa. Among them strode Last Bull, gesturing angrily to the other men.

"The chiefs are to blame for this!" he stormed, as

many turned away in embarrassment at the harsh words.

Calf understood what he meant, although she had never liked Last Bull, the arrogant chief of the Kit Fox warriors who wintered on Red Cloud's reservation. Calf recalled the troubling events that lay at the heart of Last Bull's complaint against the chiefs. Just days before, he and his family had caused a commotion in camp when they returned unexpectedly from the reservation with disturbing news. On his arrival, Last Bull had insisted that soldiers were coming to fight all the Indians who were off the reservation, Cheyenne and Lakota—Oglalas, Hunkpapa, Miniconjou, Brule, Blackfeet Lakota—and others. He reported that a command had gone out two moons ago ordering all Indians to come into the reservations or be considered hostile.

At the time, the unexpected news had shaken the peaceful camp, but some, like Wooden Leg, had argued that the soldiers would not attack because the Cheyenne were protected by treaty. Others had concluded an order sending them to the reservation was unlikely, given the difficulty of moving camp through the deep winter snows. Some, like Calf, who distrusted the soldiers, had urged that they prepare for the worst.

On hearing Last Bull's report, Old Bear, the only old man chief of four present in camp that winter, had summoned the civil chiefs, representing the bands, to consider the unwelcome news. After their deliberations Old Crier, messenger of the Cheyenne, had run through camp with the decision: Despite Last Bull's protests, the chiefs had concluded that they were at peace with the whites and their treaty would not allow the soldiers to attack them.

Still, an uneasiness had hung about the camp in the days after Last Bull's warning. Calf thought it foolish to dismiss the threat of attack and fretted that so many of the men were away on the hunt. Many in camp remembered stories of soldier attacks on Indian villages. Some, like Calf, had lived through one.

In the days before the attack, Last Bull had smoldered at the affront of being ignored. He was not one to forget such an insult. And now, here he stood on the mesa, blaming the chiefs for their failure to prepare.

As Calf pondered the events of the last few days, Old Bear and the chiefs began a count on the mesa to be certain everyone was present. Black Coyote again joined his wife and daughter. Coyote's sister, Chicken Woman, immediately poured out the news of Calf's bravery in the battle.

Black Coyote fixed his gaze on the remarkable woman who had consented to be his wife five winters ago. Her dark eyes, high forehead and cheek bones, and her firm jaw stood framed by her straight black hair, parted in the middle and braided. Loose strands fell about her face now, wispy and disheveled from her ordeal. Although she sat quietly beside him, the Coyote thought of her tall, slender figure, head carried high whenever she moved. Her self-control made her seem fearless, almost unmindful of her own safety. That worried him a little. Hardened by suffering, not much given to laughter, and wise beyond her twenty-three years, Calf excelled in many things. She was an outstanding shot, as good as anyone in camp, and a skilled rider, though not as good as her friend Leaf, who was wintering on the reservation. Calf was close to the women of her village, but not in the gossipy way of old men. It was a closeness of admiration and respect, which she never lost a chance to instill in Little Seeker as well.

Chief Old Bear's voice broke into Black Coyote's musings as he announced with concern that Blind One, an old woman, was missing. Everyone else was accounted for, he told them, but they would have to leave this place before the soldiers could return.

Black Coyote jumped from his seat on the cold rock and said that he would find the blind woman. Calf immediately joined him and Whetstone, Coyote's brother-in-law, followed them. The three worked their way on horseback down the snowy mesa, heading for the ruins of camp. The sight of the charred village, alive with only a few whimpering dogs, confused and anxious for their owners to return, set Black Coyote to brooding again, a stopped up rage clawing at his heart. Calf tried not to think of the happy, peaceful days on the banks of the Powder River, forcing herself to face the days of suffering that lay ahead. As they rode slowly through the smoldering ruins of camp, Whetstone ranted on and on about the crawling white spiders who had done this vicious thing.

Suddenly before them stood a beautiful sight: a lodge, completely intact and untouched. Calf jumped off her horse and ran to the opening. Inside sat old Blind One, her buffalo robe pulled tightly around her, a barrier against the unseen, hostile day. Hardly believing her eyes, Calf rushed inside and threw her arms around the old woman in relief.

"Are you alright, Grandmother?" Calf asked the frightened woman who nodded, clinging to Calf as though she would never let go.

Unbelievably, the soldiers had left Blind One alone in her home, terrified but unharmed, as they carefully worked their way around this single lodge while burning everything else in sight. Buffalo Calf Road thought for a brief moment that perhaps the bluecoats could not be all bad.

The three quickly carried what they could from the lodge, especially food and blankets, badly needed now. With the old woman seated on Coyote's horse, the four quickly moved back up the mesa to join the preparations for flight.

They would travel northeast along the Powder River to find the Oglala village of Chief Crazy Horse, Old Bear announced. The sun stayed in the sky longer these days and they could still cover some distance before dark. However, the warriors with horses must stay behind and track the soldiers in order to find the pony herd and recapture as many as they could. Without horses the people would suffer in the cold flight to Crazy Horse's village, the constant prey of mounted troops. Without horses the warriors could not hunt enough food to feed the hungry people. Without horses they would truly be the poorest of all people when reaching Crazy Horse. No, the pony herd must be found and brought back to the Cheyenne, Old Bear said as he pounded his fist in his hand.

The two groups separated, the people heading northeast along the Powder River, the warriors pointing south, and the sun moving west away from them all. Before the young men rode off, Box Elder invoked the power of concealment in the sacred wheel lance, making them invisible to their enemies as they rode to recapture the pony herd. Black Coyote lingered a bit, hugging Calf tightly and holding Little Seeker. His fingers touched Calf's braid and slid down her arm as he pulled away. A deep, loving bond between them filled the silent parting.

The sun had moved halfway down the western sky as the weary band started their march on foot, a few horses carrying the old and the wounded. Buffalo Calf Road and her daughter walked with Brave One and her charges. Having recovered from the fear of the shooting, the children seemed unwilling to accept the harshness of the situation as they ran, throwing snowballs and poking each other playfully. Little Seeker ran back and forth conferring with her friend, Runs Ahead, till she was tired and hung close to her mother's side.

As Calf lifted and set her moccasins in and out of the

snow, she felt a crushing premonition that such flights would mark her life. The memories of that other escape long ago pushed into her thoughts, forgotten till now. Calf did not want to remember that terrible day that changed her childhood forever. But try as she might, she could not forget the horror that forced her to flee from her southern Cheyenne family.

Instinctively Calf reached for the elkhorn flesher dangling from her belt and clutched it to her breast. A tear slid down her cheek at the image of her lost mother thrusting the flesher into her small hands so many winters ago.

"Run, Calf! Run!" her mother had shouted as she loaded her revolver to meet the charging *veho*. "Run! Run!" The words echoed loudly through her memories as the long buried scenes flooded Calf's thoughts.

People were screaming and racing wildly about as little Calf's legs flew reluctantly away from the camp on Sand Creek, leaving behind everything she knew and loved. Without thinking, she ran toward the open plains behind camp where she and the other children played every day. Calf's heart pounded in her dry throat and her temples throbbed with the thundering hooves and exploding rifles and horrible screams. As the child glanced back between sobs and stumbles, the soldiers were everywhere, rising out of the creek like monsters charging the camp.

From the top of a knoll little Calf's eyes searched the distance frantically for her mother or father or brother. The child was alone on the endless plain. She could see where most of her people had run along the creek to hastily built rifle pits where now they crouched, besieged. The frightening blue figures on horseback began to fan out from camp, so Calf ran again, building the distance between herself and the slaughter, the tears clouding her vision and freezing on her cheeks as they fell.

Suddenly Brave One and her sister, Little Heart, stood before her, seemingly dropped from nowhere. Buffalo Calf Road remembered collapsing in their arms, clinging desperately, just as Blind Woman had clung to her that very afternoon. Brave One and Little Heart took turns carrying the sobbing child across the bleak, frozen plain.

Without any shelter from the biting wind, without a stick of wood to build a fire, without food for their hungry bellies, the two women and the child just eleven winters old shivered together under their only blanket. When the cold became unbearable, Brave One and Little Heart pulled clumps of grass and dirt, a handful at a time, and piled it over the blanket. In this way the three had passed the freezing night buried under the earth but not dead.

For an entire moon, the three orphans walked in search of their Northern Cheyenne relatives. The first snows of winter fell and they surely would have perished but for the help of Grandmother Earth, who sent a wolf to lead the three starving refugees to a dead rabbit buried under the snow, lost like them on the winter plains. At times they plucked dried berries or dug roots to fill their empty bellies. Throughout their desolate wanderings, the pain of losing her family never left little Calf. Even the caring of her beloved Brave One, who led them to the safety of Chief Dull Knife's village, could not fill the terrible emptiness.

Now, years later, Buffalo Calf Road turned to Brave One as they walked with the children, and they saw the memory of that long-ago flight from the south in each other's eyes. By now the sun tired of hanging without support in the sky, and it slipped to earth, dragging its light behind it. That night Old Bear chose a grove of naked willows as their camp, sheltered from the wind by high bluffs that crowded the trees against the river's edge.

Some of the women had chunks of dried buffalo meat in their packs saved in the frantic flight and they divided it among the crowd. But there were too many people and too little food, so everyone huddled hungry and cold that night as the hard frost took advantage of the sun's departure and the absence of blankets and robes. No fires were built for fear that soldiers might spot them.

Buffalo Calf Road, Little Seeker, Brave One, and her orphans slept close together, their bodies building a poor wall against the cold. Sleepless in the cold darkness, Calf tried to pass the night by thinking of happy times. She imagined the Coyote's warm body pressed against her skin. The yearning for that warmth sent Calf's thoughts wandering back to her wedding day. She remembered clearly the night she had first gone to their new lodge, which had been carefully prepared by friends and relatives. Black Coyote seemed strangely timid that night, but she soon sensed that his hesitancy came from a desire to please her.

It was the custom among many Cheyenne to wait a few days after marriage before having sex. The Coyote understood and respected the purpose of this practice, which enabled a couple to grow accustomed to being together and sleeping together. And although the Coyote and Calf had known each other for several years and had courted a long time, it felt strange to be alone in a lodge. So they had joked awhile, in a strained way, about the marriage guests and their comments and the gifts. Then they sat down, fully clothed, on the great fur bed. Still they talked, pouring out their dreams and hopes, while the sounds of laughter and the wedding celebration outside slowly diminished, then drifted off with the deepening night.

Calf remembered how naturally she and Black Coyote had lain back as they spoke. Warm and comfortable on the deep fur, they spoke from their hearts long after the rest of the camp had fallen silent. On that magical night, the moon hung high in the black sky and cast a glow into their lodge. Suddenly they had nothing more to say.

Impulsively Calf had reached out her hand and touched Black Coyote's arm. In an instant he was against her, caressing and kissing her cheek. Their bodies rolled as one over the deep fur, then broke in two while their hands tugged at the clothes that

37

restricted them. Naked, they sank back into the fur, warm in the chill night, all of the strangeness gone. Calf recalled the pleasure, the closeness, and finally, the two bodies becoming one. She clung to the memory as long as she could.

But now on this bitter night it was mostly the warmth of Black Coyote's body that she remembered as she huddled with Little Seeker and the others. It was almost daybreak before Buffalo Calf Road dozed a little, her exhaustion at last conquering the cold and the memories.

When the sun rose, the cold tired Cheyenne roused themselves slowly, shaking off the numbness. The march had barely resumed when the distant pounding of hoofs reached their ears. The panic and scattering in all directions lasted only a few moments before Old Crier bellowed.

"Our warriors. They've returned. Come back!"

Old Crier's words silenced the thumping hearts of the people as the pony herd, driven on by the young men, appeared downstream. Two Moons, Black Coyote, Wooden Leg, and Little Hawk skillfully directed the lead horses to the waiting band as people whooped and cheered. Even though the warriors had recaptured only half of the herd from the sleeping soldiers, the sight of the horses restored the Cheyenne's hope that they could reach their Lakota brother, Crazy Horse.

Those most in need were able to ride now, but many still moved on foot. The hard frost of the past night vanished slowly as the sun returned for yet another journey in the sky, and the ice and snow covering the ground turned to mud and water. The Sacred Persons of the Universe watched the people stretched along the banks of the great Powder River, moving like a colony of brown ants.

Black Coyote carried Little Seeker through the slush that crept into his moccasins, wetting and stinging his feet. Buffalo Calf Road, Whetstone, and Chicken Woman trudged along with him. Ahead of them Crooked Nose walked nervously, flanked by her brothers, Yellow Hair and Wooden Leg, the tallest man in the tribe, the giant among them. Little Hawk, her suitor, kept a proper distance from the modest young woman.

Even in this trouble, Little Hawk, the joker, found it hard to be serious, and he made the old people nearby smile as he poked fun at everyone.

"Look at yourselves," he teased them, "caught by the white spiders with your blankets off! And them too stupid to keep their great coats on!" It seemed the soldiers had removed their bulky overcoats before battle for an easier descent into the ravine, leaving them in a huge pile at the top. When Little Hawk and the others had crept around the soldier's camp the night before, the men sat shivering before small fires dressed only in their uniforms. In the chaos of battle, they apparently had not been able to retrieve the coats. Buffalo Calf Road smiled at the story despite her heavy heart. Even Black Coyote laughed, while

Crooked Nose blushed at her suitor's boldness.

That night Calf's people dared to build some fires against the returning frost. A small band of men had gone hunting for game that afternoon and returned with two deer and a few rabbits. Other than some hard berries plucked as they moved along the river, it was the only food they had that day. Again they shared the meat among the hundreds as best they could, parents giving much of their share to the children. Little Finger Nail, sweet singer of the Cheyenne, lulled them to sleep with his songs as Young Eagle blew his flute softly in the night air.

Buffalo Calf Road, Black Coyote, and Little Seeker slept huddled together on a pile of dry leaves. Neither Calf nor the Coyote slept much. Several times during the night Black Coyote reached out to take her cold hand and press it in his. Together they used their bodies to shield their small daughter from the cold.

For three sleeps, the Cheyenne from Old Bear's ruined camp walked with empty bellies and heavy feet through the cold and slush. They forded the icy Powder River and the Little Powder River, moving east along Fork Creek, following their scouts.

Early on the fourth day they approached the Oglala Lakota camp of Chief Crazy Horse. An Oglala scout spotted their slow advance and signaled the village ahead. A great commotion rose from the camp.

"Something bad has happened to our friends, the Cheyenne!" Crazy Horse cried as he sent word around the camp to prepare food and robes. The women rushed about, gathering together what they could, some from everyone. Then the Oglala chief rode out with many people, leading horses loaded with meat and blankets and pulling travois for the sick and wounded.

Calf watched as Two Moons, Old Bear, and He Dog, an Oglala camped with the Cheyenne at the time of the attack, rode up to meet Crazy Horse. Far behind, the people dragged themselves along the creek, their backs stooped, their clothes and hair disheveled, their aching feet wrapped in soaked rags. The horses, weak from a grassless winter and exhausted from their over-burdened march, were mostly pulled along. To the back and along the sides warriors guarded the helpless people.

Old Bear offered a pipe of petition to Crazy Horse who accepted it, pledging his help by the gesture. As the old chief and the young chief smoked the pipe, the Oglala hurried among the Cheyenne, giving them food and blankets.

Buffalo Calf Road gratefully accepted dried buffalo meat and blankets from an old woman who moved steadily despite her years. Calf caught the look of pain and sympathy in her wrinkled face. Like all Indians on the plains, the old woman had seen such sights many times since the coming of the white people, and she understood.

With the weak and wounded loaded onto travois, the men, women, and children rode double and triple on the fresh horses. Slowly the parade wound its way up the hill to the waiting camp.

Calf's heart lifted as everywhere the Oglala called out, "Cheyenne, come here and eat! Come here and eat!"

Generously, Crazy Horse's people took the wretched refugees into their warm lodges, feeding and clothing them, offering shelter, and restoring their heavy spirits. A young, childless couple took in Calf and her family. The warmth of the cozy lodge and the hot herb tea felt soothing and energizing at the same time to Calf. For a while Calf forgot that she and her family were homeless and destitute.

That night the chiefs of both bands met in council, some to tell and others to learn of the soldiers' attack on Old Bear's village. The story enraged the Oglala. All the Lakota and Cheyenne people were at peace, protected by treaty rights. Crazy Horse had already heard Last Bull's news from runners sent by Indian agents that all tribes must come onto the reservations. That order came two moons ago, and after much debate many in Crazy Horse's camp had made the same choice that Old Bear's camp had made since the order clearly violated their treaty rights.

Now, in light of the vicious, unprovoked attack on the Cheyenne, Crazy Horse told his guests there could be no more talk of going to the reservations. No, he argued, the tribes on the great plains must band together for their common defense. The chiefs agreed among themselves and reported their decision to the waiting people. They would all go together to join the Hunkpapa Lakota under Chief Sitting Bull for a war council.

Buffalo Calf Road was greatly relieved that the chiefs had not decided to give in to the army's demand that all Indians go to the reservation. To Calf, reservations meant bondage. Being there would mark the end of life as they knew it, moving freely across the great plains. She knew, too, that reservations meant dependency on white men, who had shown by their deeds that they cared little for her people.

That night, Calf slept soundly for the first time in many days. The next morning, rested and refreshed, the Cheyenne left the place on Fork Creek with their Oglala sisters and brothers, moving northeast again, this time to find the great Sitting Bull.

CHAPTER 2

Sitting Bull's village, larger than Old Bear and Crazy Horse's combined, spread proudly across the knolls overlooking Blue Earth Creek, framed by Charcoal Buttes in the distance. The Hunkpapa Lakota greeted their visitors warmly. When Sitting Bull heard about the destruction of Old Bear's village, the Cheyenne were led to the center of camp and seated in two huge circles, men in one and women and children in the other.

43

Buffalo Calf Road sat next to Brave One and Crooked Nose, who exchanged furtive glances with Little Hawk. Little Seeker and her friend Runs Ahead, like the other children, were greatly excited by all the commotion, and Calf had to urge them to sit still. In the men's circle, Black Coyote and Whetstone smiled at Little Hawk's incessant jokes about the white spiders who would soon learn that fighting the mighty people of the plains was not a game they could win.

Meanwhile Sitting Bull sent a crier through the Hunkpapa village. Soon great kettles of meat appeared and were brought to the two circles. The Cheyenne ate till they could eat no more. Hunkpapa women, men, and children approached their visitors with gifts of all kinds. One woman laid a huge fur robe at the feet of Buffalo Calf Road as her daughter shyly handed Little Seeker a ball. In the men's circle an old man gave Black Coyote a finely carved pipe. Clothes, kettles, bowls, knives, and every other important necessity were generously showered down on the Cheyenne as Sitting Bull's people sought to replace their lost wealth. Hunkpapas walked around inquiring of everyone what they needed and hurried to fill these wants. After a while, lodges sprang up in an area set aside for the Cheyenne. They had been moved there by Hunkpapa who generously doubled up with relatives until the next hunt would provide hides for new lodges. Even horses were given to the Cheyenne who had lost much of their herd.

No Cheyenne present that day, including Buffalo

Calf Road, ever forgot the great hearts of Sitting Bull's people as long as they lived. Perhaps the Hunkpapas felt especially sorry for these brave people of the Cheyenne nation, famous for its painted villages, sparkling on the plains like a sunbeam fallen to earth, and their vast pony herds, rising like clouds on the horizon. None of the Plains Indians fought as well or as fiercely as the Cheyenne and none worked as hard to keep their buffalo paunches, used to store food, full of meat. To see them destitute touched the coldest heart.

But it was not only the kindness of Sitting Bull that made Calf and the other Cheyenne glad to be among the Hunkpapa, whom they knew not so much by contact as by reputation. Buffalo Calf Road thought of Sitting Bull as the greatest chief on the plains because he strongly opposed the reservations and advocated no contact with whites. He roamed the open country from the Bighorn Mountains to the Badlands, holding firm to the old ways. A devoutly religious person, Sitting Bull made medicine often, and all Indians had heard of his great fasts and the whipping of his own body for strength. His medicine must be strong, thought Calf, as she gazed across the village with its wealth, peace, and kindness.

After the newcomers settled into their own camp circle, Sitting Bull called a war council. Calf watched as the Cheyenne chiefs left their camp to join the others. Though women were not taken into the council, Calf secretly wished she could be there. The

45

council, after all, was making decisions that would affect her and all the women. She remembered saying this to Black Coyote once when the chiefs had made a decision she thought harmful to the people.

"Women should be included in the council," she had blurted out. "The chiefs make decisions for us, as though we have no thoughts in our hearts."

She had half expected the Coyote to be angry at this challenge of the chiefs' authority, but instead he seemed struck by this new idea and puzzled over it for a moment.

"You may be right, Calf," he said at last. "It must be hard to be a woman."

Right now Calf felt as she did that day—left out of the choices to be made about their lives. A twinge of resentment passed through her heart, but she kept her thoughts to herself.

All the assembled chiefs of the Cheyenne, Oglala, and Hunkpapa debated in council what must be done. No one disagreed that this newest outrage must be answered. The young warriors insisted that all whites be driven from the Black Hills. Although the elders spoke less hotly, they too argued strongly against the soldiers' invasion of their land and the attack on Old Bear's village. Anger at the bluecoats' violation of their treaty rights and the loss of trust that resulted spilled across all the conversations. Most importantly, everyone agreed that the tribes must stand together, united as one great family against the enemy. They spoke of the Lakota, Cheyenne, and others still wintering on the white man's reservations. Agreement emerged that those camped under the army's authority must be called back to join their people in the open hills.

So the call went out for all living on the reservation to unite and join the great encampment. Runners raced to the reservations of Spotted Tail, Red Cloud, and the other reservations, and to the tribes in distant places, the Miniconjou, Blackfeet Lakota, and others. Soon the great swarming of the tribes began. It was an exciting time for Calf and the others, seeing this great coming together and feeling their power as a people grow every day.

During the Moon of the Greening Grass, the camp moved slowly west in pursuit of the buffalo, growing as it wound across the plains like a great snake. The first tribe to join them, the Miniconjou, came with their lodges and horses. The Cheyenne had hunted and camped many times with them and even intermarried. Soon the Arrows All Gone arrived, followed shortly by the Blackfeet Lakota. All the while small bands also joined them, swelling each of the camp circles. Finally some Assiniboines, Burned Thighs, and No Clothes attached themselves to the group, these last being extremely poor, their little property pulled by dogs.

Buffalo Calf Road and Black Coyote listened intently to every bit of news and rumor that rushed through camp with the new arrivals. Some reported that many soldiers had moved down the Elk River.

Others said that soldiers led by Long Hair had started from Fort Lincoln. Still others told of Three Stars ready to move from Fort Fetterman once reinforcements arrived. They learned that news of the destruction of Old Bear's camp flowed across the country over the mysterious talking wires. It seems, the Indian agents on the reservations reported, that white people believed it was Crazy Horse they had defeated. Little Hawk, the perennial jokester, roared with laughter at this new stupidity and took every opportunity to poke fun at the bluecoat attackers who did not even know their victims.

Everywhere the snow melted, leaving behind the yellow grass that quickly turned green under the sun. Every day the ponies grew stronger for the hunt. Scouts reported large herds of buffalo grazing along the Rosebud River, so the encampment headed west again.

The Moon of the Strawberries and life at the Rosebud camp brought back an old peace to the Cheyenne. With lodges and horses again, with the security of the great mass of tribes camped together, with the bitter winter behind them, they could begin to hope for better days. Reports of soldiers ready to cause mischief seemed more unreal as each day passed.

One day under a hot, late afternoon sun, Calf and Black Coyote rode out to the place where her stallion grazed with the pony herd. Since the attack on Old Bear's camp, Calf kept her horse tied behind her lodge at night. As she slipped to the ground from her seat behind the Coyote, he grasped her hand tightly. Then he too slid from the horse. The pony herd grazed quietly under the clear blue sky.

Unwilling to let go, the Coyote drew her close. The affection pleased Calf and she kissed him on the cheek. At the same time, she was vaguely aware that someone might see them, for her people frowned on public shows of affection. But those thoughts quickly vanished in their embrace. Slowly their bodies sank into the tall grass. They teased each other playfully like young lovers. Soon Calf lay on top of the Coyote, rubbing against him in a sweep of passion as the hot sun mixed with the cool grass around their bodies. Afterwards they lay together for a long while under the dropping sun, almost dozing in contentment. When at last they rose from the cool earth, Calf slipped a rope around her horse's neck. Leading their animals, the pair walked slowly back to camp.

Everyone worked hard at camp, the men hunting, the women tanning hides and digging roots. The old men sat about fashioning pipes and tools. Young people went about their chores, casting furtive and longing glances at each other. At the muddy creek banks the children fashioned images of animals and lodges and put them in the sun to dry. The older boys practiced shooting arrows while the girls played kickball.

One afternoon Buffalo Calf Road sat by the river's edge under a willow tree, musing and pushing her sewing awl in and out of the deerskin on her lap, slowly transforming it into a dress for Little Seeker. She missed her longtime friend Leaf and wondered why she still had not come from the reservation, where she spent each winter. Thoughts of her childhood friend triggered memories of their meeting years ago.

After the Sand Creek Massacre many winters ago when Calf, Brave One, and Little Heart had finally arrived at Dull Knife's camp, frostbitten and nearly starved, the family of Great Eyes took her in. Great Eyes had a child named Leaf, who was the same age as Calf. Leaf stayed by Calf for days during her sickness, feeding her and coaxing sips of red tea into her mouth. It was Leaf who helped Calf recover from the loss of her parents and the terrible winter trek in search of Dull Knife's village. Calf thought with a smile how Leaf used to tease her about the dark-haired boy who looked at Calf so intently. She remembered how they giggled together when Black Coyote watched Calf as she went for water, or when he followed at a distance, pretending to be busy as she and Leaf rode their ponies together.

The two loved riding and did it often. Calf thought about how the beautiful, reckless Leaf could handle the wildest horses better than any man in camp and how she taught Calf to ride, though the pupil could never equal her teacher. Great Eyes showed them both how to shoot and in this Calf did surpass her friend.

In recent years Leaf stayed on the reservation during

the winter moons with her husband, Bull Hump, son of Chief Dull Knife, and her child, because Dull Knife took his band there when the snows came. Leaf told Calf often how much she hated the reservation, how she felt like a restless bird without wings, each winter waiting for the geese from the south to set her free. But Leaf could survive anything, mused Calf.

Crooked Nose joined her on the shore and Calf asked her question out loud, not expecting an answer.

"I wonder where Leaf is. Why has she still not come?"

"Maybe something has happened to her," Crooked Nose answered. "The soldiers . . ."

Calf screwed up her lips, exasperated at the ever pessimistic and worrisome Crooked Nose, not wishing to respond to so ridiculous an idea. Nothing could happen to Leaf, she thought! Leaf can take care of herself.

At that moment Black Coyote, Whetstone, and Little Hawk joined them at the water's edge. Immediately Little Hawk announced that Lame White Man and Twin Woman had arrived from the south.

Calf started, dropping her sewing. Everyone knew her question without her asking it. But before Black Coyote could answer, Little Hawk jumped in again.

"Only their children are with them—Little Red Hood and Crane Woman." He turned his face toward the river.

"It's a shame your brother could not make the trip, Calf."

51

Black Coyote frowned when he caught Calf's dejected look.

"Enough of your jokes," he huffed at the grinning Little Hawk. He turned to Calf.

"He is there—in the lodge."

Calf jumped to her feet and bolted up the river bank, willow branches swinging as she passed. Black Coyote and Whetstone sauntered after her, leaving the blushing Crooked Nose confused and uncertain whether to seize the moment alone with her suitor or dash off.

In her lodge Buffalo Calf Road greeted her brother, Comes in Sight, and his wife, Pemmican Road, with great joy. Little Seeker cut in for her turn to hug her aunt and uncle, although she had already done so several times. The Coyote smiled at the sight of his wife's joy.

"Two winters! Two winters since we have seen you both!" Calf scolded them as she hurried to offer them food and drink, all the while pouring a sea of questions on them. Suddenly the wrong one slipped out.

"Is your family well, Pemmican?"

Her sister-in-law's head dropped.

"I don't know. They still refuse to see me."

Calf showed her disappointment.

"Still, after all this time?"

Comes in Sight broke in to spare his wife the pain of speaking on the subject.

"You know they never forgave us for eloping together."

Before Pemmican Road and Comes in Sight had

married, her brother had promised her to someone else. Many gifts had changed hands in anticipation of the arranged union.

"It was your right to refuse your brother's choice," Calf said indignantly, making a point she had made many times before. "He could not force you to marry against your will."

"But the horses," her brother reminded Calf. "It was not just the promise of his sister. Many horses had changed hands." Comes in Sight sought to put the best face on his in-laws' behavior.

"Horses! What are horses?" Calf admonished her brother for his defense of the indefensible. "You both loved each other and wanted to marry."

"Not just the horses, Calf," Comes in Sight responded. "You know they blame Pemmican for her brother's death."

"He died in battle." Black Coyote repeated what they already knew. "They can't be sure it was anything more."

"But it happened so soon after we eloped, only three sleeps later." Pemmican spoke now. "People thought he let himself be shot out of shame. You know how proud he was, Calf."

"Even so," Calf said. "It's wrong not to forget after all this time. What would they have you do?" She found it hard to believe that people could do this to their own daughter.

"Have you tried to see them?" Black Coyote asked innocently.

53

Pemmican Road hesitated and her husband glanced at the floor.

"What is it?" Calf asked anxiously, sensing a problem. She put her hand on Pemmican's arm.

"We sent a messenger to my father on the reservation to urge a reconciliation, but . . ." Pemmican fell silent.

Calf looked urgently at her brother, waiting.

"Her father has vowed to kill Pemmican."

"Iron Shirt has vowed to kill his daughter?" Black Coyote repeated incredulously.

Buffalo Calf Road was angry now.

"Foolish man! He is no father to you, Pemmican. Forget him!"

"It's not him, Calf. I miss my mother. . . ."

This Calf understood despite her anger. The loss of a mother and a father is a terrible thing, as she knew only too well. Even the powerful grizzly cries when its mother leaves it alone in the world.

The plight of Pemmican Road without a family brought back thoughts of Calf's own parents, slaughtered and mutilated by the white man, along with more than half her people at Sand Creek. She remembered the day many moons after her arrival, half dead, at the camp of Dull Knife when she learned that her brother, too, had survived the massacre. He visited her often at the Northern Cheyenne camp in those days, although the visits were fewer since the elopement caused such bad hearts in the lodge of Iron Shirt.

But despite the awful news of Iron Shirt's threat,

Calf's happiness at seeing her brother and Pemmican Road again crowded out her anxiety. Surely it was the idle threat of a bitter old man. She resolved that they would stay together for the summer and be happy.

By the Moon of the Ripening Juneberries, the camp had moved west to Great Medicine Dance Creek. Reports of soldiers moving along the Elk River to the north and the Tongue River to the south still persisted. The news unsettled many, but few believed that the bluecoats would move against so huge an encampment, bulging with warriors anxious to count coup— to strike a blow against the enemy by a deed in war. Buffalo Calf Road felt uneasy about the reports. Somewhere in the depths of her heart a faint but persistent foreboding had taken hold. She believed that these strangers and their army would not stop wanting the land, and what they wanted, they took.

The Coyote was of two minds. When moving among the great numbers of warriors in their midst he felt strong and invincible. But in the darkness of their lodge at night, Black Coyote spoke to Calf of a deep fear of the bluecoats' awesome weapons. Together they watched as Little Seeker slept innocently on her fur bed and they worried in silence about the future.

Two of the four Cheyenne old men chiefs, Old Bear and Dirty Moccasins, were in camp now, consulting with the heads of other tribes: Sitting Bull, Crow King, and Black Moon of the Hunkpapas; Crazy Horse of the Oglala; Spotted Eagle of the Arrows All

Gone; and Touch the Clouds and Fast Bull of the Miniconjou. Each tribe sent its scouts out from Great Medicine Dance Creek to watch the movements of the soldiers.

So, as the berries ripened for picking, the high plains became two pairs of eyes, each looking in opposite directions. The Cheyenne appointed the Elk Warrior Society to scout the area with Little Hawk as leader. Together with Little Shield, White Bird, and Yellow Eagle, he headed south toward the Wolf Mountains. The group had not been out for more than three sleeps when the peace of the camp evaporated.

Little Hawk's scouts wolf-howled wildly as they raced back into camp. Calf started when she heard the cry, instinctively touching the handle of her six-shooter which she now wore every day in her belt. The Cheyenne poured from their lodges, the riverbanks, and the hills as Little Hawk rushed to Old Bear and Dirty Moccasins.

"Soldiers, perhaps a thousand or more, rest at the headwaters of the Rosebud. We have seen the bluecoat chief, Three Stars, among them. That is not all; many Crows and Shoshoni ride with the soldiers, maybe 200."

When Calf heard the report, her heart sank deep in her chest. She was especially pained to hear that Crows and Shoshoni scouted against her people. But she understood their animosity. Cheyenne and Lakota had fought them for generations over the rich buffalo hunting grounds.

People ran with the news to the other chiefs. Criers in every camp shouted the information as a great stir rose from the banks of Great Medicine Dance Creek. Parents quickly brought their children back from play. Women hastily packed their belongings, leaving out only necessities—things they needed to use immediately. Some collapsed their lodges, ready to flee. More guards hurried to protect the pony herds.

Young warriors sought to ride immediately against the bluecoat provokers. But the old men chiefs preached peace, reluctant to wrong themselves by making the first offense. The council decided to prepare for war, but insisted the Indian warriors must not fire the first shot.

Criers ran through the camps with the chiefs' words: "Young men, leave the soldiers alone unless they attack us."

Black Coyote raged at the decision.

"Must we wait till our lodges are burned again and our people killed and scattered?"

Small groups of agitated men and women milled about, arguing the merits of waiting or attacking first. Black Coyote and Buffalo Calf Road urged riding out to meet the soldiers away from camp to protect the young and old people. Coal Bear, keeper of the Sacred Hat, one of the Cheyenne sacred objects given by Maheo, agreed, not wanting the hat to become polluted by fighting in camp, fearing that its life-giving medicine would leave them. The cautious White Bull preached restraint, but his young son, Noisy Walking, anxious for his first coup in battle, sided with the young warriors.

Black Crane, always anxious for peace with the white people who swarmed over their land, spoke.

"Do you think you can stop the bluecoats? Always there are more and more. If you beat them on the Rosebud, more will come. If you kill those, still more will rush in. They are like drops of water in the great Elk River. Always more water comes from the melting snows of the mountains. No, you cannot stop them, no matter what you do. The only course for us is to make peace with the *veho*."

"Peace! On whose terms?" The veins in Black Coyote's neck stood out and his fists tightened as he spoke. "Shall we become like sheep watched by the herders to be slaughtered and eaten at their tables?"

"We know what the enemy asks of us!" added Buffalo Calf Road, speaking from a passion in her heart. "That we live on small islands surrounded by a great white sea. That we give up our old ways and our religion and our freedom. Yes, we would be at peace then, but that is the peace of death. The day before *that* peace comes is a good day to die."

Calf's words struck deep and everyone fell silent for a moment. Then Old Grandmother began taunting the warriors.

"Calf is right. Will you wait till we are Indians no longer but white shadows? Do not listen to the old ones." She gestured at Black Crane and White Bull.

"The old ones have finished life, but they think to keep it forever."

Little Hawk smiled.

"You, too, are old, Grandmother. Shall we listen to you?"

"Yes, I am old." Her scowl turned to a toothless grin at the words of the jokester. "Every day my feet sink deeper into the earth." And turning to the young women, she said, "I am too old to steal your men anymore." The reference to her lifelong escapades was clear to all. "But I am not afraid to die—that is the difference!" Her face became serious again. "I only want to die here, in my home country."

In the end the voices of war prevailed. By sundown preparations had been completed. Many bands of young men arranged to move against Three Stars and the soldiers. Traveling by night would reduce the risk of their movements being seen. One of the bands led by Two Moons assembled 200 men, both Cheyenne and Lakota, waiting only for the signal to move. Black Coyote and Comes in Sight mounted their horses and began to join Two Moons, their packs filled with war clothes, special medicine, and war paint.

Suddenly Calf rode up on her black stallion.

"I'll go with you," she said to her husband and brother in a firm voice. Then she quickly added, as though to forestall arguments, "You will need every gun against the thousand soldiers."

Mutterings and protests rose from the warriors standing nearby.

Two Moons, ready to give the order to advance, spotted the commotion and rode back, followed by Last Bull. High Forehead, the mother of Runs Ahead, stood nearby, watching.

Last Bull spoke first when Buffalo Calf Road declared her intention to fight again.

"Have you eaten the loco weed, woman? War is a man's work! Go back to your berries and roots."

Black Coyote started forward, angry at the harsh words, but Two Moons signaled him back.

"How has this notion come to you, Calf?" he asked.

"The soldiers are many," she answered simply, "and I can shoot well." Then, as if uncertain why herself, Calf added, "It is something I must do."

High Forehead could keep silent no longer and she pushed forward. "You have a daughter. What will become of her in this foolishness?"

Calf spoke calmly.

"She will learn that each blade of grass must struggle for its place on the land."

Whetstone jumped to Calf's defense.

"Have you all forgotten so soon Calf's bravery on the Powder River? Box Elder and Brave One and the children—perhaps even Braided Locks—would be dead but for Calf."

As if the speaking of his name had brought him, Box Elder appeared from the shadows of a cottonwood.

"Let Calf go to the Rosebud," the blind prophet raised his hand and insisted in a loud voice.

"It is done, then," Two Moons said, dismissing the

matter with a wave of his hand and turning his horse toward the front of the band.

Last Bull yanked at the reins of his horse, almost snapping the creature's neck as he rode away in a huff. Comes in Sight thought again how brave his young sister was, and the Coyote nodded his approval as Buffalo Calf Road moved her horse between her brother and her husband.

All night they rode, following Great Medicine Dance Creek east, then crossing it and heading southeast toward the headwaters of the Rosebud. Before sunrise the bands began massing by a small creek that rushed into the Rosebud.

As they watered their horses and rested, the first colors of dawn slipped across the gray sky. Calf lay in the grass under a twisted hemlock, watching the colors spread in the east. Overhead a raven already flapped and soared, raspy croaks rising from its shaggy neck. Calf watched its tortuous movements through the bluish green branches of the hemlock as a strong breeze pushed through its gnarled limbs.

Two Moons, White Bird, and four others left to scout the bluecoats while the warriors prepared for battle. They painted their faces, put on their war clothes and charms, and made their own special medicine. On their heads they placed mounted birds or animals, while some used warbonnets.

Buffalo Calf Road watched Comes in Sight adjust his great warbonnet of the hundred feathers. When fully dressed in his war finest, with his face brightly

61

painted, he took his long feathered lance and lifted it to each of the Sacred Persons in the corners of the universe, praying as he moved.

Black Coyote too had his special charms, a lizard tail for swift motion and a dragonfly for concealment. He painted his face in red lines across the cheeks and on his head he wore a sparrow hawk for protection. Black Coyote was never much given to prayer, Calf thought, though he believed in Maheo. His belief, though, was more as a bird believes in the open air— it is simply there.

The most elaborate preparations Calf watched centered around Black Sun, who spent a long time getting ready, carefully painting his body yellow. On his head he positioned the stuffed skin of a weasel. He wore no clothes except for a blanket wrapped about his loins and in his hand he carried a long coup stick to touch the enemy.

It suddenly struck Calf as odd, all this preparation of the body and reliance on things by men. Bravery lies in a good heart, she thought, and that is what earns Maheo's protection. She herself made no medicine and wore no paint. Only her six-shooter adorned her belt.

As they prepared to move, the men braided or tied the tail hairs of their horses as a war sign. The scouts, meanwhile, had traveled along the bottom of the hills for some distance, periodically going to the crests to survey the valley on the side of the rising sun. Behind them the body of horses and warriors advanced slowly toward the valley.

Suddenly, as Two Moons and the others climbed a high bluff, they met Three Star's scouts rising over the top. Shots sounded, a Lakota horse fell, and the battle began. Calf watched as the first group of Indians rode against the retreating scouts at a high point just above the big bend in the Rosebud River.

Buffalo Calf Road saw now that the soldiers stretched along the river from the bend down to Bear Creek. More soldiers quickly positioned themselves on the ridges overlooking the river. The Indians broke into several large parties attacking the scattered strongholds. A great din of horses, guns, humans, and whistles emptied the ground of animals and the sky of birds.

In the first Indian charge, a young Lakota boy, Blue Hawk, never before in battle, plunged after the warriors, full of bravado. But the confusion and dust were so thick, he rode too far and found himself cut off. Within minutes, alone, far from the others, he died at the hands of Three Star's Shoshoni scouts. When Blue Hawk's older brother, Broken Bow, discovered what had happened, he was inconsolable and took a suicide vow, pledging that he would not live to see another moon.

Back and forth the battle raged all day, the advantage shifting first to one side and then to another. Calf saw many fall on both sides, dead or wounded, and many others close to falling. At one point Black Coyote and Two Moons attempted to capture some horses, but soldiers arrived, driving them back and nearly killing them. Calf covered their retreat with her six-shooter.

Later, as soldiers retreated up Bar Creek, a bluecoat was thrown from his shying horse. White Shield and Scabby galloped between the soldier and his horse and began to fight. When White Shield threw the soldier down, the bluecoat fired his gun, hitting Scabby. White Shield quickly finished the soldier and, dragging Scabby up behind him on his horse, the two escaped to safety.

Meanwhile Black Coyote and Two Moons, still intent on driving off the soldiers' pony herd, moved toward the river. Together with Whetstone and Limpy, a young man, they shot into the air, whooping and crying, trying to stampede the herd. Suddenly enemy scouts appeared on a ridge behind them, firing wildly, while bluecoats rode across a gap in front. Two Moons gestured toward a hill nearby and shouted, "Get out one at a time!"

The Coyote, Whetstone, and Two Moons made it to the top of the hill. Limpy tried to follow, but as he started, his horse collapsed, shot dead, and Limpy fell to the ground, grazed in the side.

The Shoshoni on the ridge jumped up and began riding down to kill Limpy and count coup. Limpy rolled behind the sand rocks, safe for the moment, but worried about the bridle on his fallen horse. It was a gift from his uncle, handmade and mounted with the white people's silver dollars at the brow and cheek bands. Without thinking, he dashed from behind the rocks, favoring his bad leg as he moved. In an instant, he had thrown himself on the ground behind his dead horse, untied the chin strap, yanked off the bridle and rolled back to the temporary safety of the rocks—all while the Shoshoni moved closer and bullets flew everywhere.

Buffalo Calf Road watched from a rise. She marveled at Limpy's foolishness in exposing himself so. Calf knew of the beautiful bridle and she understood its importance to Limpy. But surely, she thought to herself, a bridle is not more important than a life.

Meanwhile, as pieces of rock fell away from the striking bullets, Two Moons turned back quickly, galloping his horse to Limpy while Black Coyote, Whetstone, and others fired at the Shoshoni. But the trapped warrior could not climb on the racing animal. So Two Moons rushed back to the hill and shouted to Limpy, "Get ready!"

As Two Moons rode in again, Limpy climbed on a sand rock and jumped on behind his rescuer, the horse shying and the bullets flying. So close were the bullets that Two Moons felt one pass over his head as they rode to the sheltered hill.

Black Sun was not so lucky. His yellow body rode back and forth before the enemy, taunting and mocking, daring the soldiers to waste their bullets against his powerful medicine.

Calf, who had charged all morning with the other warriors, now shot from the trees and rocks on the bluffs above the gap in the hills. She watched in amazement as Black Sun mocked the bluecoats, Crows, and Shoshoni with his bulletproof medicine. The shots seemed to turn away from his body as though some invisible hand stopped them in flight. How strange was a man's pride, Calf thought, to expose himself in that way.

Suddenly a Shoshoni warrior leapt from the tall grass behind Black Sun and raised his revolver. The whooping yellow body topped with the weasel saw nothing of the threat. Calf gasped at the sight from her high perch and instinctively fired at the enemy Indian, but he was too far. In an instant Black Sun fell, the red blood spreading quickly over his yellow war paint.

Wooden Leg and Noisy Walking flew to his side, chasing the Shoshoni back through the gap and carrying the bleeding man to safety.

From her position on the bluff, Calf could observe much of the battle as she fired. On the ridge across from her, a strange incident drew her attention. Some Lakota warriors fired, bringing down a Crow scout of Three Stars. Immediately, two Crow women, dressed and painted for battle, rushed to the fallen man. One leapt from her horse and crouched over the body, firing at the Lakota as quickly as she could load her revolver. The other woman, still mounted, circled the pair waving her only weapon, a long feathered coup stick, and singing her chants.

When the Lakota made a rush forward, their knives drawn ready to scalp the wounded warrior, the woman on horseback charged straight at them, brandishing her coup stick and whooping so fiercely that they turned and ran, frightened by her strong medicine. From her spot on the hill, Calf stared at the women, feeling very proud of their bravery even though they were enemies. She felt strangely drawn to the pair and wished they were not fighting on the side of the white spiders.

As Calf watched them tending the wounded man, she noticed that one of them, the one who had dismounted, looked like a man in woman's clothing. Ahh! So that's her, Calf thought, remembering the stories about a not-man, not-woman Crow warrior, born a man but turned into a woman, with a woman's heart and ways. The other woman had a wild look about her as she sat on a black horse, her forehead painted yellow and topped by a stuffed woodpecker.

Just then one of the Lakota rode back, unwilling to let a woman best him. The not-man, not-woman Crow screeched a warning and the wild one, still mounted, rode straight against the Lakota's horse. She struck the Indian with her coup stick and spat on him as the not-man, not-woman Crow shot him dead with her revolver. The wild one pulled out her knife and, using gestures of revenge for the murder of a brother, took his scalp.

Engrossed in the spectacle on the opposite bluff, Buffalo Calf Road had not noticed that her brother, along with White Shield, Low Dog, Young Red Cloud, and White Bird had taken the place of the fallen Black Sun in the gap below her. Now she saw that they rode back and forth, drawing fire to themselves in the customary way of a brave warrior, taunting the enemy all the while. Calf held her breath.

Suddenly Comes in Sight's horse bolted, struck by a bullet, and crashed headfirst to the ground. Comes in Sight landed on his feet and began to run in the motion of a sidewinder snake to avoid the flying bullets cutting the air from every direction. Low Dog and the others, safely out of the open gap, gasped at the hopeless sight. Already the Shoshoni had started down the hill to kill and scalp Comes in Sight.

In an instant Calf kicked her horse and whipped it to a run, rushing out of the trees, swooping down the rocky slope from the north and across the open gap toward her besieged brother. Bullets angrily chased her from both sides. Across the gap, the men watched in awe as Calf rode into danger.

I will die today, Calf thought, as she rode straight for her brother through the barrage of angry bullets. She turned her horse sharply around, as Leaf had taught her to do, pausing only for an instant while her brother grabbed her saddle with one hand and clutched the horse's neck with his other.

With Comes in Sight hanging on the side of her horse, his great warbonnet blowing in the wind and his rifle dangling from his arm, Buffalo Calf Road sped away, back in the direction she had come and up to the safety of the bluff. A startled Crazy Horse and many others watched in admiration from the hills as the brave woman rode away from the bullets and the gap, which was now filling with bluecoats and Shoshoni, carrying with her a man touched by death. The warriors marveled that a woman had done what none of them dared to do.

When they reached the top of the ridge, Comes in Sight fell to the grass, breathless but smiling. As Calf dismounted she noticed that the not-man, not-woman Crow and the wild one had moved to the edge of the bluff across the gap, watching intently. Before the two disappeared, Calf thought she saw the wild one cast her a nod of approval from the distance.

By midafternoon the carnage ended. Cheyenne and Lakota withdrew from the hilly battlefield with their dead and wounded, victorious in their goal of stopping the troops from advancing against their village. Having shown Three Stars their great numbers and strength, having inflicted heavy casualties on the bluecoats, and having wasted the ammunition of the army on the Rosebud, the Indians fell back up the creek from which they had come to prepare the dead and treat the wounded. Thirty-six of their warriors lay dead and sixty-three wounded. Behind them, they left many enemy dead and injured.

As the Indians turned back from Great Medicine Dance Creek, Three Stars had already decided not to pursue them but to retreat to his base on Goose Creek where he remained for much of the summer.

CHAPTER 3

News of the victory over Three Stars reached camp before the triumphant warriors did. A steady din of shouts and cheers rose to greet the exhausted fighters as they swarmed back to the village during the night and next morning. But mixed with the cries of joy were the keening for the dead and the moans of the wounded.

Black Sun lay unconscious on his travois, barely breathing, as his horse dragged him from the Rosebud to his waiting family on Great Medicine Dance Creek. A new sun had not yet colored the eastern sky when he died in his home lodge, attended by his wife and daughters.

All morning the painful keening of the women passed through the buffalo skin walls as people crept quietly past. Close friends helped in the preparation of Black Sun's body, dressing him in his finest and wrapping him tightly in his favorite robe. Box Elder prayed over the body to the Great Spirit.

When the female family members emerged at last for the burial, their arms and legs were covered with blood from the mourning ritual of gashing one's body. The widow's sister immediately began to carry out the family's goods from the lodge and throw them on the ground before the assembled crowd. Everything passed hands. Even the lodge was torn down and given away until nothing remained but Black Sun's coup stick and a single blanket for the widow and each of the daughters.

Then the procession of wailing relatives and friends, including Buffalo Calf Road and Black Coyote, slowly followed the long bundle lashed on a travois to a green hillside dotted with caves. His wife carried Black Sun's stuffed weasel headdress while the men unbraided their hair and let it fall wild. Running free nearby, the dead man's horses wore battle paint with feathers in their braided tails and manes.

Calf had followed other processions of the dead before, but this one seemed especially sad to her. She remembered Black Sun exposing himself again and again to enemy bullets with his taunts. She wondered whether any purpose was served by such bravado. And now here were his wife and daughters suffering the terrible loss, saying good-bye to Black Sun forever.

As the body entered the coolness of its rocky cave a small snake slithered out into the warmth of day. Overhead a plump chickadee watched from its hole in a rotted tree limb, chirping the end of spring with its message, "Summer is here. Summer is here."

That very morning, as Black Sun followed the trail of footprints to the final camp in the Milky Way, the six tribes prepared to move on. The buffalo were becoming too scarce to feed the thousands. Reports of rich herds of buffalo grazing along the Little Bighorn River sent the camps moving west along Great Medicine Dance Creek. The Cheyenne led the march, the Hunkpapa guarded the rear, and all the other tribes moved in between.

At a site along the Little Bighorn just south of the point where the creek emptied, Buffalo Calf Road and the other women set up their lodges. Here the Indians would remain for six sleeps, feasting and dancing to celebrate the victory as the pony herds grazed to the east and the buffalo to the west.

By sundown of the first evening, everyone assembled for the ceremony to honor those who fought with the greatest courage on the Rosebud. Black, the color of victory, painted the faces of the Cheyenne, a sign of enemy fires put out and enemy lives extinguished. A "skunk" rose in the middle of their camp circle—a great fire striking out at the darkness of the night and the darkness of their foes. Old Crier began by calling out the names of the bravest warriors at the battle. As Buffalo Calf Road's name rose through the crowd, she stepped to the center before the chiefs and faced east toward Bear Butte, the Holy Mountain. Box Elder stood behind her as Black Coyote walked forward with a buffalo robe, proudly placing it on her shoulders. With a gesture toward the universe, the priest knelt, touching the dirt and his legs, reminding all that they are one with the earth. Then, calling all generations of Cheyenne to witness, Box Elder lifted his hands, repeating the name of Buffalo Calf Road twice, followed by a new name given in honor of her heroic deeds: Brave Woman.

Calf's relatives immediately began giving away the customary gifts of all kinds to the poor and to others in honor of her. Comes in Sight gave a mountain lion robe, Pemmican Road offered dresses, Whetstone distributed beaver skins, and Chicken Woman gave beaded moccasins. Calf's aunt and uncle, Ridge Walker and Vanishing Heart, gave pipes and blankets. Her cousin, Swallow, offered a buffalo robe. Finally, Black Coyote gave away a horse and Little Seeker brought her favorite toy, a small ball.

The unexpected honor deeply moved Buffalo Calf Road. It was not customary among her people to honor women in this way, although Calf knew many stories of bravery in battle by Indian women.

After all the warriors had been so honored, the dancing began as the drumming and singing spread across the hills. People roamed from camp to camp, telling and hearing of all the courageous deeds done at the Rosebud. Among the Cheyenne the most popular story was of Buffalo Calf Road's selfless act in risking her life to save her brother from certain death. And although a few, like High Forehead, harbored a grudge against her for going to fight, the women especially rejoiced at having one of their own honored in such a way. Calf's bravery so impressed her people that they named the battle after her, calling it "The Battle Where the Girl Saved Her Brother."

For four nights the celebration continued, and with each passing day the Indians grew in their conviction that white people could not hurt them now. They lived together in one great camp, thousands strong. They had driven back the troops of Three Stars. Most important, herds of buffalo gave them food, clothing, and shelter. The work of survival went on as the hunters killed buffalo while the women worked hard, curing the meat and preparing the skins. Calf and Black Coyote settled into the comfortable routine of life again.

One day, as the afternoon sun blazed high overhead, Buffalo Calf Road and the other women bent over the animal hides staked to the ground. While her mother tediously tore at the meat clinging to the skin with her flesher, Little Seeker chattered on about the Rosebud battle, asking again for this or that detail. She enjoyed the notoriety among her little friends of having the only mother at the fight.

"Why were you the only woman there, Mother?" she wondered. "The mother of Runs Ahead and the other children were not there."

Calf looked up, caught by the question.

"I was not the only one, Little Seeker. I saw two other women there."

"Two other women! Were they white women, Mother?" Little Seeker asked excitedly.

"No," answered Calf, thinking to herself of the invisible white women who never seemed to be present with their men. "They were Crow scouts for Three Stars."

"Indian women helping the enemy!" Little Seeker showed her disappointment. "But why?"

"They have never forgiven our friends the Lakota for driving them from the land of their ancestors. So they fight with the white men to get even." Calf chipped vigorously at the flesh in short, hard motions.

It was all too complicated for Little Seeker, so she pursued another line.

"But you were the only brave woman at the battle."

"No, Little Seeker, the Crow women were very brave. They saved a wounded man's life and chased away the Lakota who tried to scalp him."

"Other brave women like you?" The child seemed disappointed.

"There are many courageous women, Little Seeker—there always have been. You must not think it unusual. Remember the story of Brave One and Little Heart, who saved my life. And your aunt, Pemmican. She was strong and full of courage when she refused her brother's harsh demand that she marry a man she did not love. Leaf is brave too. She does not fear the wildest horse even when the men walk stooped from trying to ride it."

The stories intrigued Little Seeker. "Tell me more, mother. Who else is brave?"

Calf finished fleshing the hide and leaving it to dry in the sun, she slid across to another, already dry. Switching to a finer scraper, she planed and thinned the hide as Little Seeker watched and waited.

"Comes Together, White Frog's wife . . ."

"I know her," the child interrupted excitedly.

"It happened years ago, when the Pawnee attacked a

75

Cheyenne camp. They did that often and took away many women. One day they caught Comes Together, but she tricked them by pretending to go willingly. Then, in an instant, she pulled her wood-chopping hatchet from her belt and split open the head of the Pawnee warrior."

Little Seeker grimaced.

"She refused to be taken like a *veho* sheep," her mother continued, "and when the battle ended, everyone praised her as a brave woman. They sang and paraded her through the camp like a great warrior. White Frog was so filled with pride for her that he gave away horses and robes in celebration."

Buffalo Calf Road turned the hide as she spoke and began to scrape off the hair. Little Seeker had her going now.

"And there was the great Cheyenne warrior, Yellow Haired Woman, and the three young women at the Sappa who died because they jumped up, fighting to draw the white man's bullets to themselves, allowing others to escape. And Mochsi who lost her man at Sand Creek and later a new husband too. She fought with the gun of her grandfather and was captured and put in irons at Fort Reno. And your grandmother . . ."

Calf stopped. Little Seeker had heard that story many times. Calf looked gravely at the child.

"Remember, Little Seeker. Do not be like the sheep needing a herder's protection. Be like the eagle, which is free and strong and cares for itself and its loved ones."

76

Little Seeker nodded the unknowing assent of the young, but already she was distracted.

"It's Little Hawk!" She jumped up and ran to a small group of children crowded around the warrior.

Calf smiled at the sight of the little ones tugging at his arms, begging him to wrestle with them. The children loved Little Hawk and his antics. They especially enjoyed hiding and watching as he played his jokes on the women, shooting arrows at their sloshing water paunches and grinning broadly at his giggling audience crouched in the bushes. Even the men caught a good share of the fun when Little Hawk hid their arrows and ran into camp howling a false alarm. His small confidants in the conspiracy stifled their squeals of delight as the warriors frantically searched for their arrows.

What a wonder he had not married earlier, Calf thought. In a few winters he would be thirty. Now he seemed to have cast his eye on Crooked Nose, with all her seriousness and shyness, and after a year or so of courting they would marry.

The peace of the afternoon's work and play ended abruptly. Old Crier was running through camp announcing that Box Elder had sent him. Calf left her hides and moved closer to listen.

"Box Elder has had a vision. He saw soldiers marching, great strands of blue ribbons stretched across the plains. Tie your horses to your lodges. Be ready!"

Buffalo Calf Road felt numb. Is it possible they will

come again, she wondered anxiously. The inevitable crowds had begun to gather and she caught Black Coyote hurrying up the river, followed by Whetstone and Little Finger Nail. They seemed to be arguing as Calf walked to meet them.

"You heard?" Black Coyote asked Calf.

"Yes," she answered simply.

"It's only a dream," Little Finger Nail insisted.

"The old priest's dream!" the Coyote reminded him.

"But he only said he saw soldiers marching, not that they were coming here," the young man ventured.

"Where would they be going?" Black Coyote's temper flared. "We are the ones they call hostile Indians. We are the ones refusing their order to go to the reservations. We are massed, many thousands strong, to resist them. Who would they march against? The hollow Indians on the reservations?"

"Why must they fight anyone? Maybe they march on a peaceful mission." Little Finger Nail persisted in his refusal to believe the worst.

"Peaceful?" Whetstone grunted in disbelief.

"They are humans like us. No one wants war forever. Our scouts saw them withdraw from the Rosebud." The Nail was determined to convince them, but Black Coyote threw up his hands in despair.

"Humans? They are vicious and without honor. They lie and cheat us out of our land. They make false promises and break the treaties sealed with our peace pipes. They do not even fight for themselves but for a faraway chief in the place of the rising sun. It is said

78

they are paid to fight. How can a warrior who is paid to fight have honor?"

His words were true, but her husband's rage at the whites worried Calf for its intensity. Little Finger Nail fell silent, not sure what to think, though he knew what he wanted to believe.

Box Elder's warning had caused a small stir in the camp, but it was hard to be afraid under the protection of so many warriors. After six sleeps in their camp on the Little Bighorn, scouts advised that the buffalo herds were moving north along the river. So the tribes followed in pursuit, the long string of people shifting along the bank with the river's current.

Buffalo Calf Road felt a little disappointed to be moving again, although movement in the summer was usually frequent in the best of times. She began the hard work of taking down their tall lodge and packing the huge buffalo skin cover. It was the heavy work that always fell to the women.

At a point a little north of the spot where Great Medicine Dance Creek emptied into the Little Bighorn, they crossed over to the west bank where the six great camp circles settled again, stretched on the bank as far as the eye could see. The women worked in pairs, lifting the heavy lodge poles into place and hanging huge pieced buffalo skins around them. After clearing the ground within the lodge, unpacking their possessions and gathering wood, the women lit their fires for the meal.

That night, under the cottonwoods with their leaves

strung like green hearts pointed to the ground, a social dance was held. In the middle of the Cheyenne camp circle, the women and girls cleared the ground as the young men arrived with a long pole on which to hang the buffalo skin from the Sacred Hat Lodge. Soon the sparks of a great cottonwood fire flew toward the stars, disappearing in flight. Young Eagle blew his love flute while the drums and songs mixed in the joy of the night.

Buffalo Calf Road and Black Coyote strolled to the dance, their hands barely touching as they walked lest they make a public display of their affection. Whetstone, Chicken Woman, Comes in Sight, and Pemmican Road followed. The married couples stood at the edge of the circle watching the festivities for the young people and remembering the pressures of the days when they were unattached.

The young women clustered together, wearing their best dresses and beaded moccasins and talking earnestly as though they had no thought for the young men who waited to be asked for a dance. Buffalo Calf Road smiled to herself as she watched the separation of the sexes, thinking how soon the two groups would dissolve together like the white people's coffee and sugar.

She caught Little Finger Nail glancing at the lovely Singing Cloud and Little Hawk joking away the time until Crooked Nose could get enough courage to ask him to dance. Then, as if on some invisible pre-arranged cue, the young women broke away from each other and moved toward the young men. Only the shy Crooked Nose hung back. Little Hawk, suddenly alone, busily began throwing logs on the bonfire.

Calf edged toward the fretting Crooked Nose. "I like a huge fire," she said simply, giving the young woman a chance to talk if she wanted.

Crooked Nose smiled nervously, looking quite pretty in her deerskin dress.

"I think I won't stay long, Calf."

"Not stay? But why? Little Hawk will be disappointed," Calf offered.

Crooked Nose glanced at the ground.

"There are so many young women . . ."

"What are they to Little Hawk?" Calf asked.

"He's such a great warrior and I . . ." Crooked Nose looked down again.

Calf was surprised that Crooked Nose should be so unsure of what everyone else took as certain.

"Do you care for him?" And knowing the answer already, Calf went on. "Then you must not wait for another to set eyes on him."

The urgency of that point took hold of Crooked Nose. Glancing quickly in the direction of Little Hawk, she nodded at Calf in appreciation and, taking a deep breath, she walked hesitantly toward the handsome warrior pretending to care for the fire. A smile quickly spread across Little Hawk's face as Crooked Nose approached. In an instant they were whirling around the great fire, hand in hand.

Most of the young people were dancing now, while the older Cheyenne sat about watching and talking and remembering their lost youth, half with regret and half with gratitude. Calf looked around at the assembled groups. Old Grandmother smoked her pipe on the edge of the camp circle as her young grandson, Spotted Deer, attentively hovered over her. The fourteen-year-old boy strained to peer across the great fire in the direction of Yellow Bead, who squatted with her aunt on a buffalo robe.

On one side of the fire, Bear Rope and his wife sat with their daughter, Comes in Sight Woman, and her husband. Calf thought how the two women had endured a hard life with the rough, stern Bear Rope. She knew that little affection passed from mother and daughter to the older man.

On the other side of the fire, Calf saw that Twin Woman and Lame White Man watched Crane Woman, their daughter, dancing happily with one of the young men as orange reflections from the flames played across her body. Broad Faced One, already twenty-six but still unmarried, stayed close to her parents, seemingly determined to remain single.

Black Crane, the peacemaker, Coal Bear, Old Crier, Dirty Moccasins, and Old Bear sat around their ancient circle telling stories of the past, as old men always do. Looking at the old men, it suddenly struck Calf that only Box Elder had not appeared at the festivities. For a moment she noted his absence as an ominous sign, but just then Wooden Leg commented that peace and happiness must be covering the whole world tonight. Nowhere would any man plan to lift his hand against another, he said. Calf hoped he was right as she watched him leave to dance with his friends at the Lakota camp.

Before the moon had traveled far across the sky, many of the older people began returning to their lodges, leaving the young people to dance under the watchful eyes of their chaperones until the first sign of dawn. Buffalo Calf Road and Black Coyote walked under the stars stretching across the universe, almost close enough to touch. They arrived at their lodge where Little Seeker lay peacefully asleep. Even the cottonwoods did not speak in the cool stillness of the night broken only by the throbbing of drums.

As Calf closed the lodge flap against the night air, Black Coyote put his arm around her, drawing her close and breathing in the pleasant scent of sage rubbed on her body. Their eyes met in the blackness of the lodge as Calf pressed her lips against his cheek and his mouth while the pounding of the distant drums became the pounding of their hearts.

A hot summer sun rose over the peaceful camp the next morning. Finding it hard to rise this day, the tired people stirred slowly. At first only a few of the women moved to do their chores, then some young boys went off to tend the great pony herds grazing close to the camp.

Calf rose early and could tell that it would be a hot day. As she gathered her paunches to fetch water, she glanced at Black Coyote still asleep on their fur bed. He seemed peaceful in his sleep this morning and he stayed in bed later than usual.

Calf felt glad to see him so restful today. Lately he seemed agitated, talking often and bitterly about the white spiders crawling over the land. At night he often tossed fitfully in bed in a state somewhere between sleep and wakefulness, seldom fully in one or the other. Though it seemed silly to her, given his strength and courage, Calf worried about the Coyote. When he rose, Black Coyote looked happy and held her close before leaving the lodge.

By midmorning, much later than usual, many of the young men were plunging into the cool waters of the Little Bighorn. Those who had bathed earlier stretched out under the cottonwoods along the bank, dozing among the cool leaves, sheltered from the blazing sun.

Suddenly the late-morning laziness broke under a burst of rifle shots rushing from the direction of the Hunkpapa camp farther down the river. A great confusion broke out everywhere, with children crying for their parents and mothers running about wildly, looking for their children. Women threw together small packs for flight. Many people ran immediately from camp, heading north away from the shooting. The boys tending the horses began driving the herds into camp as the warriors quickly put on their war paint and dress and hastily made what medicine they could.

A Lakota crier rode swiftly through the camps shouting.

"Soldiers have attacked the Hunkpapa! More blue-coats are coming. Get ready! Get ready!"

In the confusion many people fled across the river away from the fighting at the Hunkpapa camp, only to find that soldiers approached from that direction as well. A frantic rush back across the river began. Some Cheyenne, Wooden Leg among them, had already ridden to the Hunkpapa camp to help. Now it became clear that the Cheyenne at the head of the huge camp would be attacked as well.

When the first alarm sounded, Buffalo Calf Road was at work painting the lining of her new lodge with scenes of the buffalo chase and hunt, trying to repli-cate their lodge destroyed during the Powder River attack. She had taken to wearing her six-shooter in her belt all the time now and she immediately grabbed more ammunition from the pouch on the wall. As she dashed from the lodge shouting Little Seeker's name, Black Coyote rode up and without dismounting swooped down on the child, like a giant hawk, and sat her on the horse in front of him, her body tight in his arms.

"Hurry," Calf urged as she ran for her horse, tied to a cottonwood behind her lodge.

As Calf uttered the word, Black Coyote nodded and pressed his horse to the ravines north of the camp where most people were taking refuge. There he left Little Seeker with his sister and the other women caring for the children.

While saddling her horse, Calf saw Lame White Man, the Southern Cheyenne chief, rush past wrapped only in a blanket, his moccasins, belt, and gun dangling from his hands. Quickly he led his daughter, young son, and wife from their lodge toward some horses roaming about camp. He must have been caught in the sweat lodge when the guns sounded, Calf guessed, as her thoughts raced with her body. The warriors had begun riding toward the river where the soldiers had been spotted across the Little Bighorn.

Before Calf finished fastening her saddle, Black Coyote had already turned back toward the abandoned lodges. As Calf mounted her stallion, the Coyote rode furiously back to her side, his horse trampling the grass and sage and shying at the hidden prickly pear cactus that tore at its legs. Together Calf and Coyote rushed to the river, low now from the summer dryness. Pressing their horses, the pair crossed the Little Bighorn River, muddied by the many legs racing across its waters.

Already the bluecoats, greatly outnumbered, had begun to inch back from the river and up a gently sloping ridge toward the east. Crazy Horse led a charge of Lakota and Cheyennes, circling north, then east around the troops. Behind Greasy Grass Ridge to the south, Gall, the great Hunkpapa warrior, led more Lakota up Medicine Tail Coulee, closing the circle around the persistent enemy. Farther down the river, Sitting Bull's Hunkpapas pressed the soldiers who had attacked their village, forcing them back across the river and cutting them off from the troops that advanced against the Cheyenne.

Buffalo Calf Road and Black Coyote stayed with the warriors pushing up from the river, many of them dismounting and crawling up the ravine. From their hiding places in the gullies, Indians shot their arrows in a tall arch, striking the bluecoats and their horses. Calf stayed on her horse, firing at the soldiers as Black Coyote crept along the ravine close to the troops.

The horrible noise of battle surrounded Calf and she thought the sounds would overwhelm her. Above the blasts of rifle and gunfire rose the pounding hooves and tortured whining of the frightened and wounded horses. All around them the whooping war cries, the shouted commands, the calls for help, and the screams of the wounded filled the battlefield. In the distance the women and old people sang their stout heart songs of courage for the warriors. Only the earth and sky stood silent around the mass of humanity turned on itself.

As Calf watched from her black horse, a Cheyenne warrior charged after an Indian wearing a warbonnet who fought with the soldiers. The enemy Indian suddenly turned and charged the Cheyenne. In an instant the two, facing each other, raised their rifles and fired at the same time. Calf gasped as both fell dead and the full measure of the tragedy—Indian killing Indian—sank into her heart.

"Why?" she screamed into the deafening air. But it

threw the word back at her without an answer.

Just then a young Cheyenne, full of the boldness of youth, charged too close to the soldiers and lost his horse. He will surely be killed, Calf thought. So she pressed forward and with a swooping motion pulled the boy onto her stallion, riding toward the river where the women had caught some of the soldiers' horses. Getting another mount, the young man nodded in gratitude as Calf left him.

Lame White Man was just returning from the Hunkpapa camp where he had ridden to call back the Cheyenne fighting there. Followed by Wooden Leg and others, he rode close to the soldiers who were being pushed farther and farther back up the ridge as they left a trail of their dead and wounded comrades behind. The brave older man rode back and forth in the open, close to the retreating bluecoats, drawing their fire to himself and rallying the warriors. Calf caught the sight and thought with dismay of Black Sun.

"Come," shouted Lame White Man, gesturing with his arm. "We can kill them all now."

Comes in Sight, together with Yellow Nose and Contrary Belly, charged close to the soldiers too. At one point Calf's brother lunged toward a soldier at the rear of the retreating unit. Comes in Sight knocked the man from his horse with his great lance and in the confusion dismounted long enough to seize the blue-coat's rifle and count coup on him. Considered an act of great bravery by the Cheyenne, Comes in Sight did this without killing the soldier.

But only moments later other Indians leapt on the man, stabbing him to death and cutting off his arms and legs. Calf turned her face from this gruesome sight in disgust.

Meanwhile, Yellow Nose had snatched the flag of the cavalry from a soldier and proudly carried the swallow-tailed banner around the battlefield for all to see, as the soldier's frightened horse stampeded up the ridge.

Outnumbered, the soldiers fought fiercely for their lives as Calf and the others pursued them. Exposed as they retreated up the sloping hill, they hid behind sagebrush or fallen horses, firing at the swarm of Indians pressing on them. But one by one they fell, leaving behind a crooked trail of bodies. All this came at a high cost to the Indians, many of whom paid with their lives for the enemy retreat.

At one point, Calf spotted a Lakota warrior staggering on the field alone. Slowly stumbling away from the soldiers, he tottered dizzily toward the spot where Wooden Leg crouched in a ravine, firing from his position. Calf watched in horror as the Lakota fell and rose, fell again and rose again. When Wooden Leg saw that the man's whole jaw had been shot away, the sight made him sick and he vomited on the scarred earth.

Numbed by all the killing around her, Buffalo Calf Road fought now almost without feeling. She was close enough to see some of the soldiers' faces, twisted in fear at the sight of the whooping painted bodies stretching before them like a great impenetrable forest.

In the midst of the soldiers stood a tall, yellow-haired man, his jaw set tightly under a long moustache, shouting commands. On his head stood a broad-brimmed white hat, dirty now and soaked with sweat. His buckskin breeches were tucked into tall leather boots and cinched at the waist by a brace of pistols, hunting knives, and bullets. The familiar blue flannel shirt with its double row of shiny metal buttons hung open at the neck, the sleeves rolled up as if to free the imprisoned arms. The weary, dirty, haggard man looked so unlike the cool, neat, arrogant officers Calf was used to despising. Yet something looked familiar about this man, his strange yellow hair and moustache. Calf wondered if this was the hated Long Hair who had slaughtered her people on the Washita eight winters ago. His hair was not long now, and yet . . . He was infamous among her people, who often described the soldier chief with the yellow hair and big moustache. If this is Long Hair, Calf thought, he and his soldiers destroyed the village of Black Kettle, killing the old chief and many men, women, and children. If this is Long Hair, she thought, he made a promise five moons after the vicious attack when he smoked the peace pipe with the chiefs. Never again would he fight the Cheyenne, he had said, giving his word.

His word! The thought that there might be yet another broken promise enraged Buffalo Calf Road.

Always the deceit and treachery of the white spider, spinning its web larger and larger, seeming to build a home for itself, but trapping the innocent instead!

Calf kicked her heels into her stallion, forcing him to gallop swiftly toward the yellow-haired officer. The startled bluecoats gaped at the sight of the woman warrior suddenly in their midst. Calf had no taste to kill the doomed officer, only to show her contempt. Before the surprised Long Hair could react, Calf had raced past and struck him on the shoulder with her quirt stick, disappearing again into the swirling mass of bodies.

As Calf circled back to the ravine leading into the Little Bighorn River, she spotted a Lakota woman, Moving Robe, the sister of One Hawk, who had rushed in grief onto the battlefield after hearing of her brother's death. Her eyes fierce and flashing, Moving Robe rode slowly around the battlefield, carrying One Hawk's coup stick in memory of him. Calf edged close to the woman in a protective gesture as the men backed away in respect for Moving Robe's brave act.

The remaining soldiers were now clustered near the top of the ridge, crouched behind their dead horses like trapped dogs. Lakota criers began to circulate among the warriors giving instructions for the final blow.

"Keep your eyes on the suicide warriors! They will charge the bluecoats and distract them. Then all of you rush to the ridge and shoot before the soldiers reload."

Several Lakota, including Broken Bow, who lost his brother at the Rosebud, and five Cheyenne, Noisy Walking, Cut Belly, Limber Hand, Fist, and Roman Nose, were among the young warriors. All of them had taken the vow of suicide, some because they had lost relatives to the whites, all because they chose the immortality of honor attached to death in battle.

The Lakota and Cheyenne watched as the suicide boys rode into view. After stampeding the remaining soldiers' horses, the warriors plunged into the midst of the bluecoats grouped on the ridge and began to fight hard, hand to hand, like wolves charging a cornered dog. All the suicide boys fell before it was over, their bodies twisted with the fallen soldiers.

Buffalo Calf Road's stomach clenched at the sight of the suicide boys. She had watched the young men grow over the years. Now they were wasting themselves for something called honor. The soldiers, after all, were trapped and doomed. Calf had learned much about the ways of men since joining them in battle. Somehow what had seemed grand when told around the campfires seemed wrong here on the battlefield. Calf understood the bravery of fighting and dying in defense of one's people and way of life. But dying for honor, that was something else.

By now the Indians were swarming like bees over the enemy, stabbing and shooting and clubbing them to death. Black Coyote was in the swarm but Calf held back and watched the twisting mass writhing in pain like a huge beast with hundreds of lunging and kicking arms and legs. The pain of watching the madness sickened her.

Buffalo Calf Road turned her horse back toward the river. Slowly, her back erect in her saddle and her eyes fixed on the lodges in the distance, Calf walked her horse through the dead and mutilated bodies littering the crushed grass along the slope.

The sun had crossed the middle of the sky and already Calf saw that the women had begun moving over the battlefield searching for the dead and wounded, keening in mourning as they went. Young boys stalked the dead and near-dead soldiers, counting coup by stabbing or shooting arrows into their bodies. Some women used their hatchets and sheath knives to beat and mutilate the bodies of this pregnant enemy that kept multiplying in their midst, attacking their villages and killing their people. Many cried and wailed as they moved, stripping the bodies and chopping off limbs and heads, avenging their dead and maimed relatives. Some soldiers had already been scalped and mutilated by the warriors. Everywhere the great wailing of death and the singing of victory rose to the Sacred Persons watching from the corners of the universe.

In the confusion, Crooked Nose frantically searched among the dead for her brothers, Wooden Leg and Yellow Hair, and for her beloved Little Hawk, convinced as always of the worst. She fought back tears as she ran from one body to the next until she came upon a dog howling in agony as it lay by its dead master, its paws clinging to the body of a young soldier sleeping his endless sleep. Crooked Nose fell to her knees in pity at the sight, burying her face in her lap and covering her ears with her hands. She hid from the sight until Little Hawk found her. Gently he lifted her from the tear-soaked ground and, holding Crooked Nose tightly, guided her back across the river to camp.

Two Southern Cheyenne women searching among the dead at the top of the doomed ridge recognized the body of the yellow-haired officer with the moustache. Both had escaped from the Washita massacre and remembered bitterly Long Hair's promise the following spring that he would never again fight the Cheyenne.

Yes, the two women agreed, this was the dreaded Long Hair who smoked the peace pipe with their chiefs under the Sacred Arrows. This was the one called Custer by his people. After that fateful meeting, the old men chiefs had sprinkled ashes from the peace pipe onto his tall boots, vowing that if he broke his word Long Hair himself would become dust. So, they said, he had broken his promise after all, and now the Great Spirit had brought about his death.

"He should have listened more carefully to our chiefs in the south," one of the women remarked. Then she grabbed the sewing awl hanging from her belt and pushed its sharp point into each of his ears, deep into his head.

"Now his ears are opened and his hearing is

improved," she declared as the other woman nodded assent.

Buffalo Calf Road sat alone in her lodge as one by one the Cheyenne gathered their dead and wounded. Through the buffalo skin walls came the women's keening for the dead. Strangely, the sound calmed her.

The family of young Hump Nose, a close friend of Wooden Leg, tearfully carried the dead youth back to camp. The body of Lame White Man was discovered covered with dust and partly scalped. Last Bull, his brother-in-law, rode to the hill where the dead man's wife, Twin Woman, and her children waited. He told her the sad news. A Lakota warrior had killed Lame White Man by mistake in the confusion of battle, thinking him one of the enemy scouts.

Twin Woman bit her lips at this irony—killed by his own people! And he need not have gone to fight at all. He was not a young man and it was the young who fought in battle, each generation relieving the last of the duty. But nothing could stop him from going and his parting words to his wife had been, "I must follow my boys into battle."

Quietly the grieving Twin Woman and her daughter, Crane Woman, prepared the travois to carry his body. His family dressed the dead man in a fringed buckskin outfit taken from an enemy soldier. Like the other families of the dead, they prepared the body for burial in a hillside cave.

The wounded, too, were brought back on travois,

one by one across the river. Bighead had arrived first at the side of her wounded nephew, Noisy Walking, shot three times and stabbed in the side. He had seen only eighteen winters and now he lay badly wounded as his father, White Bull, rushed to his aid. The older man knew how to make good medicine and he set to work treating the wounds after his son was carried back to camp. His mother built a willow dome shelter for Noisy Walking and spread thick buffalo robes on the ground for him to lie on. Then the anxious family waited.

Through it all Buffalo Calf Road stayed alone in her lodge, numbed by the killing and death.

But in the midst of the burials and doctoring, the fighting continued farther downstream near the Hunkpapa camp, as it had since the morning attack on the village. Almost one-third of the soldiers in that unit now lay dead while the rest, pushed back across the river, had entrenched themselves on a ridge, pinned down by the Indians.

Calf knew that Black Coyote had gone to join the Indians downstream. He would not stop as long as a single soldier remained. Little Seeker stayed with her aunt, Chicken Woman, who had kept her safe in the ravines north of camp.

Would the fighting never end, Calf thought in despair? As she sat alone, the old premonitions crept through her stomach up into her throat. Outside her lodge, the consequences of war went on.

One of the men killed in the fight downstream was

an Arikara Indian, Bloody Knife, scouting for the soldiers. He had been raised as a Lakota but later left his Lakota father and sister to return with his mother to her people. For two winters he had scouted for Long Hair and now he lay dead in a field below the Hunkpapa camp. When the women went among the bodies on the battlefield, the daughters of Bloody Knife's sister moved with them. Finding the unknown dead Indian who had scouted for the soldiers, they cut off his head. Propping the head on a pole, they paraded the trophy through camp, until finally they came to their home lodge.

"Look, Mother," the girls called. "This Indian will never help a white man again."

When the woman emerged from her lodge, the sight of her estranged brother's head on the pole carried by her daughters leapt at her and she collapsed in a heap at their feet.

Elsewhere the trophies of war were not so deadly. Many warriors now sported the captured weapons of the troops, although many pieces proved useless without ammunition. One warrior returned with a repeating rifle and a small box of cartridges. And other useful items were found: bridle bits, saddles, belts, jackets, and leather boots, which could be cut up to make other things.

Some goods were puzzling. Wooden Leg found a folding leather packet in the pocket of a dead soldier with three stripes on the left arm of his jacket. Inside the packet lay a pile of green paper with pictures and odd writing he could not understand. Bemused, Wooden Leg tore up the green paper and gave the small packet to a friend.

Another Cheyenne found a white metal object on a bluecoat. The round thing had glass on one side covering some odd markings on which two small, pointed, metal sticks seemed to move ever so slowly. The young man took the strange thing, peered at it up close and thought he heard a sound. When he put it to his ear, he bolted in alarm.

"It is alive. It speaks," he exclaimed.

Others rushed forward to listen.

"Tick, tick, tick, tick, tick," the metal piece spoke.

The group puzzled at length about the strange object and its possible use. It must be the soldier's special medicine, they concluded, until one of the reservation Indians explained that the white man used the object to follow the movement of the sun during each day. This made no more sense to them than the other speculations.

Another metal object that seemed alive surfaced. Although round and covered with glass like the other piece, it did not speak. Instead a single arrow danced and rested, always pointing north. Perhaps the metal piece could tell the movements of the troops. Keep it, everyone decided.

Others wondered about an odd sight on the battlefield. One of the soldiers had gold among his teeth. No one could figure out how the metal got there, much less why it was there.

By now Black Coyote had returned from the battle still raging downstream.

"There is no way to get at the remaining soldiers," he reported to Buffalo Calf Road. "But we have them pinned down."

"It's good you're back," Calf said simply as she put her hand on his shoulder. She could feel the tension knotting his muscles, so she began to rub the spot with the palm of her hands.

Suddenly, above the noises of mourning, recovery, and victory, a commotion rose in the center of the Cheyenne camp circle. Black Coyote left their lodge to see what was happening. He spotted Last Bull glowering over two young cousins, Wolf Tooth and Big Foot.

Since Box Elder's prophecy that soldiers would attack, the two boys had hid in the brush down by the river every night. Hoping to win the war honors for themselves, they planned to sneak through the warrior society guards and ford the river. They, and not the Kit Foxes or the Elk warriors, met the enemy first.

Having discovered the boyish escapade, most people thought the innocence of the youths humorous, but Last Bull was furious. "You dare to put yourselves above the warriors!" He tongue-lashed the boys with his menacing face. "What can boys do that men cannot?"

"We only thought to make our people proud of us," Big Foot responded, his voice quivering.

Black Coyote moved closer.

99

Last Bull shouted, "Proud of you? You who cannot hunt a rabbit yet!"

His contempt for the young boys embarrassed some who milled around. Buffalo Calf Road came out of her lodge, annoyed at the loud and angry voice of the man she disliked.

"The council of chiefs appointed those men to guard the camp. The rest of you were told not to start trouble with the soldiers," Last Bull roared on.

The boys hung their heads, silently hoping this embarrassment would quickly end. But Last Bull would not let go. Instead he grabbed his quirt stick and began whipping the boys. The stunned onlookers turned away in shame. No Cheyenne would strike a young person, certainly not in public, and not without the gravest provocation.

Instinctively Calf moved forward, but before she went a step or two, Black Coyote had already pushed in and grabbed the quirt stick, stopping it in midair.

"The enemy is out here," he said angrily, pointing toward the Hunkpapa camp. "Go fight them!"

Last Bull glared at the Coyote as he tried to pull his quirt stick free. But Black Coyote held firm and the two boys slunk away to their lodges.

Just then a great excitement rose from the Arrows All Gone camp situated just below the Cheyenne circle. What is it now, Calf wondered, exhausted in body and spirit.

A large crowd of Lakota crushed around a band of Indians who had just arrived. The Lakota were not of

100

one mind regarding the band. Some suspected they had been with the soldiers and shouted, "Kill them! Kill them!"

Others were not so sure and responded, "Wait. Find out who they are. Wait."

Above the din an angry voice bellowed, speaking not Lakota but Cheyenne.

"I have never helped any soldier. I am all Indian—no part of me is white! I am Cheyenne. Would I strike my own people?"

Wooden Leg and Yellow Horse ran down from the Cheyenne camp, followed by Calf, the Coyote, and others. They recognized the voice of Little Wolf, the most respected of all the four old men chiefs of the Cheyenne, thundering from the crowd. Calf was over-joyed to see that Little Wolf was among them again.

Wooden Leg pushed through the Lakota who would not believe the words of Little Wolf. He warmly greeted the chief while the crowd continued to shout. Other Cheyenne began to arrive, Little Hawk, Whet-stone, White Bull, and others. Sick at heart because of his wounded son, Noisy Walking, White Bull lashed out at Little Wolf.

"Now you come—after the battle is over!"

"You stayed too long on the reservation," Black Coyote accused.

The Lakota continued to press for an explanation, so Wooden Leg repeated the questions to Little Wolf. "Have you been with the soldiers, they want to know?"

The old man's temper flared.

"No," he answered sharply. "Do you think me crazy? Look!" With a wave of his hand he indicated the families behind him, their horses loaded with household goods and dragging their lodges. "Is this a way to march with soldiers? Tell them who I am. Tell them I am all Indian."

"What happened? Why do you come now, at this moment?" Wooden Leg persisted as the Lakota pressed their doubts.

"We come to join you for the summer hunt. Yesterday we spotted the soldiers moving toward the divide leading to the Little Bighorn, so we hid in the hills and watched. Early this morning some soldiers spotted our men and shot at them. We kept hidden and watched as these soldiers reported back to the troops. From the hilltops we heard gunfire and saw Indians running from camp. We remained hidden and did not know what was happening. When we saw Indians moving in camp again we came forward—only to be greeted as enemies!" Little Wolf added indignantly.

After Wooden Leg repeated the account to the Lakota and assured them of Little Wolf's identity as one of the Cheyenne old men chiefs, they let the man and his band pass.

In the Cheyenne camp, some murmuring against Little Wolf continued. He stayed on the reservation too long, some grumbled. Had he not heard of the attack on Old Bear's camp three moons ago? Or the fight with Three Stars on the Rosebud? Why had he kept the Sacred Bundle, given by Sweet Medicine, away from his beleaguered people so long? The sullen Bear Rope was angriest of all and went about camp speaking against the old man.

Buffalo Calf Road grew annoyed at the complaining.

"This is no way to greet the keeper of the Sacred Bundle," she said to more than one person.

But most people, like Calf, were glad to have the Sweet Medicine Chief back with the bundle destined to preserve the tribe. They were glad, too, to have the popular women of that family back, including Feather on Head and Quiet One, who were the wives of Little Wolf, and Pretty Walker, his daughter, a tall, independent, straight-walking girl, as fearless as her father. Even Little Wolf's two sons, Woodenthigh and Pawnee, were well liked. Little Hawk especially grinned in pleasure at the return of his good friend, Woodenthigh. The grumbling soon stopped when Feather on Head and Quiet One passed out gifts of sugar and coffee brought back from the reservation.

All that afternoon, warriors moved back and forth down the river where the Hunkpapas still pressed the soldiers dug in on the ridge. A supply wagon and reinforcements had met the bluecoats when they retreated to the hill, so they had plenty of ammunition. And although the Indians failed in their attempts to storm the position in an afternoon charge, they pinned the bluecoats in tight and the old men predicted they would soon be desperate for water.

None of the Indians in any of the camp circles celebrated that night, though hundreds of enemy soldiers lay dead and naked on the ground like so many worms after a rainstorm. The pain of death lay too heavy on both sides and too many mourned for their lost ones or watched anxiously over the wounded. Young men still fought down river past the Hunkpapa camp while old men circulated through the camps singing stout heart songs to keep up their spirits.

Many Cheyenne and Lakota women gashed their arms and legs out of grief for the dead in their families. Others sat all night in the darkness next to cold stone graves on the hillside, keening their death chants. Here and there a big fire lashed out at the darkness as a grieving family burned their lodge. Many people prayed for the Everywhere Spirit to deliver them once and for all from the white plague that dogged them wherever they went.

In the early hours of darkness, Noisy Walking's eyes still looked out on the world as his crumpled body lay on the thick buffalo robes. His friends came quietly to wish him well, and Buffalo Calf Road came with food for the family, unwilling to take care of their own needs.

White Bull hovered over his son, imploring the Sacred Persons and making his medicine that had been so successful with others in the past. Outside the willow dome shelter, Noisy Walking's mother, who had once given him life, sat helpless to do so again. The youth's hand trembled with every move and a

104

great thirst consumed him. In a voice so weak it could barely be heard, he begged his father for water.

The Medicine Man grieved to refuse his suffering son. Believing that water would harm the youth, he answered gently, "No. Water will kill you. You must not drink now."

But before he could see another sunrise, Noisy Walking began his lonely journey to the Milky Way, and his inconsolable parents wept over his lifeless body.

CHAPTER 4

The sun rose on the sleepless Cheyenne for a second day. For two nights the camp had stayed awake, the first in laughter and joy and courtship, the second in tears and sorrow and parting.

Little Finger Nail sat alone on the ridge where the last soldier had fallen above the Cheyenne camp. To look at the stones on the ground and the sun in the sky one would never guess, he thought, that anything had changed. But then his eyes shifted and a twisted corpse crept into view and then another and another. No, he brooded, the earth and the sky never change, only the lives of people. The Nail remained motionless for a long time, thinking, trying to comprehend the enormity of the slaughter that came so quickly out of nowhere, like a summer thunderstorm crashing on a quiet scene.

Finally, Little Finger Nail picked up the ledger book in his lap, a gift from Whetstone, who found it in a pack on a dead soldier's horse. With pencil in hand he began to sketch the warriors and soldiers, but he drew them full of life, erect and proud on their horses, because he could not bear to think of them dead. Little Finger Nail worked intensely, the pictures flowing from his fingers as other times the songs flowed from his lips. As he drew, the Nail hardly noticed the stench that was beginning to creep over the land.

When at last two young boys appeared on the ridge searching the battlefield for any spoils missed by the others, Little Finger Nail closed the ledger book. He rose, walked back down the hill, across the Little Bighorn and straight for his lodge where he sat alone for the rest of the morning.

Not far away the thirsting soldiers, surrounded on a hill just past the Hunkpapa camp, tried to fetch water from the river as the old men predicted they would. In twos and threes they came, crawling down a ravine cut into the hillside. When they reached the open plain leading to the river, they ran fast, dipping a bucket into the precious water, turning back even as they dipped. But a volley of arrows and bullets met them and one by one they pitched forward, falling into the river or onto the ground.

During the afternoon word came from Indians scouting the countryside that yet another column of soldiers marched up the Little Bighorn valley. Buffalo Calf Road groaned at the news, and an argument began in the camps. The young men wanted to stay and fight; the older people cautioned against it. A council of chiefs was called and once again Calf and the others waited.

Calf wearied of the same arguments—run, fight; fight, run—so she stood silent, watching Little Seeker and Runs Ahead playing. She tried to think of the future, what it would be like, but no image would come to her. The emptiness frightened her, for herself and Little Seeker.

As Calf stood alone, the young man who had found the ticking round piece came by, shaking the white metal and peering into the glass.

"It is dead," he said simply, more to himself than anyone. Then, as if to reinforce the point, he turned to Calf and, sticking the small machine against his ear again said, "It does not talk today." Turning it over several times, he studied the strange object in puzzlement.

"Dead!" he repeated. "It is not good medicine for me." And listening for one last time, he threw the metal piece to the ground and walked away.

Soon Old Crier announced the chiefs' decision.

"Too many young men have died. Sitting Bull says we have killed enough whites too, that we should let the rest live. Our chiefs agree. We leave at once."

Black Coyote was furious.

"Again they tell us to run away! It is a mistake."

Calf agreed. "They will never let us alone now. We have killed too many of them."

Whetstone and Comes in Sight nodded in agreement.

"We should stand here and make an end of them," Comes in Sight said. "We cannot stay together forever. When the Lakota leave us . . ."

Echoing the sentiment, Black Coyote stormed, "Never again will we be as strong as we are now with so many warriors in one place."

"It is the only way they will honor the treaties," Calf added. "When we are weak and defenseless, they devour us like so many cattle. If we prove to the *veho* that we cannot be beaten, that they cannot kill us all, they will be forced to leave us in peace." Then, on second thought, she added wistfully, "I wish it were not so."

"But it is so, Calf," Chicken Woman said. "We are the only free Indians left on the plains. All the others have been herded onto reservations—land the whites do not want—and these reservations shrink each year."

They fell silent. How odd it seemed to Calf that in this moment of their greatest triumph against the bluecoat persecutors they should feel such foreboding.

By afternoon, the great procession of the tribes began moving in the direction of the Bighorn Mountains. Little Seeker rode behind her mother, dozing as she clung to Calf. A long cloud of dust rose as thousands of Indians with their enormous pony herds moved like a great army of brown tumbleweeds covering a vast plain. Behind them the Indians set fire to the grass, covering their movements with a spreading black wall of smoke. Behind them the battered remnants of the trapped bluecoats watched the retreat with relief. And farther behind still, Hunkpapa scouts watched the new column of soldiers coming up the Little Bighorn.

Most of that night the tired people kept moving, resting for a while before daylight in the open without lodges. At the first sign of sunrise, the weary march began again and late in the day they camped at the mouth of Greasy Grass Creek. For sixteen sleeps Calf and her people continued, like a great slow frog, leaping ahead, stopping, then leaping again.

Then the hard decision came. Game was not plentiful and there were many hungry mouths to feed. The six tribes would have to split in search of food. So the great body separated into its parts, none of them quite whole now without the others.

Calf had dreaded this moment for some time. It hurt to leave new friends and new strength. And while the number of Cheyenne had greatly swelled since the winter camp, Calf and the others felt exposed and vulnerable after the break up. But there was nothing to do but go on.

The Cheyenne pulled themselves to the mouth of the Powder River where it emptied into the Elk River and set up camp. Occasionally a reminder of their enemy puffed past on the Elk River in the form of a noisy fireboat belching smoke, which the young warriors delighted in shooting at. Otherwise life settled into a quiet routine.

Toward the end of the Moon of the Reddening Cherries, the last of the four old men chiefs, Dull Knife, joined them. Some grumbling greeted him as it had Little Wolf, but Dull Knife explained that the reservations were now ringed by troops who kept the Indians from leaving. They would have come sooner, Dull Knife said, but they had trouble getting away. He reported that the news of the great Indian victory at the battle of the Little Bighorn had raced across the country on the talking wires and whites smoldered in anger and humiliation at the defeat of their general, called Custer. The pleasure of hearing what a stir their victory had caused was so great that few pushed their complaint that Dull Knife should have come sooner.

Buffalo Calf Road had been digging yucca roots for soap on a hill when she spotted the band approaching camp from the east. In an instant she recognized a sleek white stallion and leaving her roots she raced down the hill.

"It's Leaf," she called to Crooked Nose and Chicken Woman, stooped over their digging.

The young woman sat tall in her saddle, listening intently to the exchange between the men. Unlike most of the other women, she wore her long black hair loose over her shoulders, the wind catching the dark wisps and brushing them across her cheeks. When she saw Calf, Leaf jumped from her horse and the two friends embraced warmly.

"You've been away so long!" Calf said, half scolding, though she knew Leaf had nothing to do with the absence.

"Everyone talks about you, Calf," Leaf said excitedly.

Calf looked surprised.

"About the battles! How you saved your brother at the Rosebud and how you fought so bravely at the Little Bighorn! I'm so proud of you, Calf," Leaf ran on.

Calf brushed off the compliment.

"Are you well? Is everyone well? Bull Hump and your child? Your father, your cousin Red Bird?"

"Yes, yes," Leaf laughed. "Everyone is well—better now that we are here." With a turn of her head and a sweeping gesture of her arms, she tried to take it all in—the wide river, the rolling, endless hills, the big sky. "And you? You are the ones who have suffered." She stopped for an instant, and added scornfully, "While we sat at our beads."

Calf let the remark pass.

"Little Seeker and Coyote are both well. And my brother and Pemmican Road . . ."

Leaf's big eyes darkened.

"Pemmican? Are they still here then?" She looked troubled.

"Yes, why?"

"Look." Leaf nodded in the direction of the new arrivals, many still mounted.

"Iron Shirt!" Calf gasped.

"He still rages at her. I'm afraid he will do something if he sees her. Do you know of the threat?"

"Yes," Calf answered. "Pemmican told me."

"It may be just talk." Leaf tried to reassure her, but then thought better of it. "But a man like that, still sick with grief at the death of his son . . ."

"You're right," said Calf. "I must warn her."

"Go." Leaf agreed. "We'll talk later." Pressing Calf's hand, she watched her friend hurry away.

A rather large group had come out with Dull Knife. Besides the brooding Iron Shirt, his wife, and remaining son, one of the council chiefs, Wild Hog, brought his family. A great hulk of a man with a broad face to match, Wild Hog brought with him his Lakota wife, his son, and his daughter, a graceful quiet girl on the verge of womanhood. So close, so caring for each other were these four, that they all bore the name Hog—Wild Hog, Hog's wife, Hog's daughter, and Little Hog.

Also riding out with Dull Knife were Iron Teeth and her husband, Red Pipe. Hearing of the great victory of their people over the soldiers at the Little Bighorn and at the Rosebud, they felt quite invincible now. Iron Teeth and Red Pipe had decided to leave the reservation for the sake of their small children who must not grow up ignorant of the old good life hunting buffalo on the plains. So the couple came, as many were encouraged to come now, bringing their oldest son, Gathering His Medicine, another son, and three daughters, one just born and the others still young.

Then, of course, the family of Dull Knife himself came—the Beautiful People, they were called by the bluecoat troops—his two wives, Short One and Pawnee Woman, his three sons, Bull Hump, Little Hump, and a young boy, and his three daughters, called the Princesses. Neither Short One nor Pawnee Woman were Dull Knife's first wife. His first wife had killed herself in grief when Dull Knife brought the beautiful Pawnee captive to his lodge as his wife. The women of the tribe held it against Dull Knife for a long time, till he married yet another, Short One, whose kind and gentle ways healed the wounds.

Bull Hump, the eldest and husband of Leaf, was a prominent Dog Soldier. His younger brother idolized Bull Hump and was named for him because the boy always hung by his side. One of the Princesses was also married to a fine young warrior.

Dull Knife, his aged face pock marked from the white man's sickness called smallpox, had a good disposition and loved the land and the people. As early as twenty winters ago he had understood how the coming of whites would change their future. He had tried everything to bring peace and preservation to his beloved Cheyenne.

One other old man arrived that day, Great Eyes, an Elk chief who came from a long line of great warriors and wise shieldmakers. After the attack on Old Bear's

113

camp, Great Eyes had returned to the reservation with his feathered shield to join his daughter, Leaf, and his favorite nephew, young Red Bird, who had seen but ten winters and now rode with his great uncle everywhere he went.

As for Iron Shirt and his family, no one really knew why they came. For a long time they had been among those who stayed on the reservation year round. The brooding father of Pemmican Road, with his wife and son always at his side, stayed by himself and talked to no one. So everyone wondered.

In her lodge, Pemmican Road sat quietly as Calf told her the news, fingering a small bone ring hanging from a leather necklace around her neck.

"He gave me this when I was a child," she said.

"What will you do?" Calf asked.

"What can I do? Run away from my family as we run from the white man?"

Calf looked down. She had no answers.

"No," Pemmican continued. "I will not run away." Then, pausing a while, she added, "Perhaps he has softened toward me . . . ," her voice trailing off.

Calf would not support the empty hope.

"Leaf says he is still sick with grief. He is not the man you knew, Pemmican." And turning to go, she entreated her sister-in-law, "Please be careful."

But Pemmican was determined to make things well again with her family. Immediately she prepared the finest gifts she had—a great buffalo robe, a fine pair of beaded moccasins, and the best horse she and her

114

husband owned, a beautiful pinto. Then Pemmican Road chose as her emissary Little Hawk, who could bring a smile to the sternest face.

A midsummer sun, throwing its heat through the openings in the cottonwood trees, burned on the lodge where the sad young woman waited alone. Pemmican had told no one of her gifts, not even Calf, and Comes in Sight hunted far to the west that day with Black Coyote, Whetstone, and others.

As Pemmican Road watched anxiously through the open flap, a fat raven dropped to the ground in front of the lodge, pecking at the tiny droppings of an earlier meal. A small swallow landed nearby and inched its way toward the tiny feast, jerking as it moved. But the raven would have none of sharing the find and it flapped at the bird, squawking in anger and driving the unwelcome guest into the air.

When Little Hawk returned, not long after he had left, leading the pinto and clutching the great robe and moccasins, Pemmican's heart sank.

"I'm sorry," Little Hawk said, dejected. "He would not listen."

That night, after the camp fell asleep and only the breeze on the high plains stirred, Pemmican slipped from her lodge and crept to the edge of the village where Iron Shirt slept. She wanted to cry out, to run in and embrace her mother, but she choked back a sob and, pulling the leather necklace over her head, she hung it on the flap of her parent's lodge. A tired dog whined a little in protest as Pemmican stumbled past in the darkness, sobbing.

The next morning the red-eyed woman stayed in her lodge, talking to no one except Calf who stopped by to see if she was well. The lonely day passed for Pemmican, somehow, and another night came on her.

It was very late—even the hoot owl had fallen silent—when Pemmican heard a scratching on her lodge, faint at first, then more urgent. She bolted up in her bed and stared through the darkness toward the dim moonlit opening in her lodge, meant to welcome the breeze on this hot night. Suddenly the opening went dark. Pemmican gasped. A figure stood hesitating in the doorway. Then a familiar voice spoke her name.

"Pemmican?"

"Mother!" The young woman leapt to her feet, and the two embraced. The sorrow of many winters poured down their faces as they clung to each other.

When Pemmican lit a small fire in the center of the lodge for light, she saw her mother's face for the first time in a long time, as though she was seeing the face of a stranger she once knew. Deep furrows cut into the older woman's brow and the once joyful eyes sat deep in their sockets. Pemmican caught a twitching of the left eyelid and a nervous fingering of a small object. It was the leather necklace with the small bone ring.

Her mother handed Pemmican the keepsake.

"Did he send you?" Pemmican asked.

The older woman's eyes grew wild for an instant as she shook her head.

116

"No. No. He does not know I am here." Then she added imploringly, "He must not find out."

Pemmican was disappointed. Then, as she watched her mother's face, she became worried.

"Does he . . . does he treat you badly?"

The downcast eyes and the silence answered Pemmican. But when the woman saw her daughter's anxiety, she spoke quickly.

"He is sick, Pemmican. Do not blame him. Ever since your brother died . . ."

A pang of guilt shot through Pemmican.

"He is a good man," the older woman said.

"A good man!" Pemmican cut in scornfully. "Why do you stay with him?"

"He is my husband," the answer came. "Where would I go?"

The answer seemed so obvious to Pemmican.

"With me, Mother," she said, dropping to her knees and clutching the woman's hands. "You can place your lodge next to ours. We will care for you."

For the first time Pemmican saw the fear in her mother's eyes as her grief turned to desperation.

"I must go, Pemmican, before . . ."

The thought of another separation made Pemmican desperate.

"Please, Mother, stay. It is your right to leave him. Please!"

The older woman pulled away.

"He must not see you, Pemmican." Then, looking sternly at her child, she insisted, "Go home! Go south

117

where you belong—now!"

In an instant she was gone, leaving the young woman angry and worried and bitter, not knowing what to do next. In the lonely silence of her lodge, Pemmican lay wide eyed as a tortured sleeper after a nightmare. But in a very little while the nightmare crashed into her consciousness again.

A rifle blast shot through the camp and Pemmican knew at once, without thinking, what it was. Her piercing screams answered the shot as she bolted up, desperately covering her ears.

By the time she ran from her lodge, Calf had rushed to her side.

"Pemmican! Pemmican! What is it?"

But the young woman seemed not to hear and stumbled wildly through the camp, her long hair and her loose night clothes flying as she ran. Calf could barely see as she chased Pemmican through the trees and the lodges. Dogs began to bark and people started to peer into the darkness, anxious at the commotion.

When Pemmican got to her parent's lodge she stopped abruptly. A body lay on the ground and a dark figure bent over the heap. Pemmican dropped to her knees beside the crumpled figure on the ground. Her brother, Rising Sun, was shaking the body, begging it to speak. Calf gasped in alarm at the sight of the three. Then she froze as she spotted the dim outline of a fourth figure standing in the doorway of the lodge, a rifle pointed at Pemmican.

"No!" Calf screamed and threw herself in front of

Pemmican, who suddenly noticed her presence.

Pemmican rose slowly, mechanically, and pushing past her sister-in-law, she walked straight to Iron Shirt.

"It is me you want to kill. Me! Not her! Here I am. You can kill me now. Kill me! Kill me!" Pemmican screamed.

A gathering crowd watched in horror as the young woman stood in front of the rifle, taunting the old man. Iron Shirt's eyes burned in the darkness, his hatred draining into his fingers. His hands began to shake, then his rifle. He steadied his grip and aimed again. But again he hesitated, as Pemmican continued to scream.

"Kill me! Kill me!"

Finally the shaking hands dropped to his sides, the rifle with them, and the old man stood limp and silent, staring at the ground. Pemmican turned back to her mother lying on the ground. Already Medicine Woman crouched over her, hurling instructions at Singing Cloud who rushed off to get juniper and sage. Turning to Pemmican Road, Medicine Women said reassuringly, "The wound is not too bad. We will make her well."

The next morning Dull Knife came to Iron Shirt's lodge. He addressed the old man sternly.

"You have violated the first commandment of Sweet Medicine. You spilled the blood of another Cheyenne. It is the wish of the chiefs that you leave. We will not have the peace of the camp destroyed."

When Iron Shirt did not respond, the old man chief left. He looked in on the wounded woman who lay in Medicine Woman's lodge.

"I have told him he must leave, but you are welcome to stay," he said.

"No," the tired woman answered. "He did not kill Pemmican. I will go with him."

"As you wish," Dull Knife said, turning to leave.

Outside the lodge he addressed Rising Sun.

"Your mother will go with him. Prepare a travois."

Meanwhile, forced back to her lodge after the incident by Rising Sun's bitterness against her, Pemmican waited for news. Calf had not left her side all night. Little Seeker, ignorant of the night's trouble, darted in and out with her little friend, Runs Ahead. The noise of the children chattering and giggling sounded far away to Pemmican Road, engrossed in her thoughts.

At last Singing Cloud came.

"Your mother is much better this morning. It was a clean wound." Hesitating she went on. "The chiefs have exiled Iron Shirt."

Pemmican leaned forward. She had not considered that possibility.

Not wanting to raise false hopes, Singing Cloud added quickly, "Your mother will go with him."

Pemmican's face dropped. Calf put her hand on the woman's shoulder.

"I'm sorry. It was her decision," Singing Cloud said. "She is grateful you were not hurt." Then, gently, knowing the cutting edge of the words, she finished.

"She asks that you not try to see her again."

Pemmican fell silent and sat motionless long after Singing Cloud had gone. And though Calf tried to console her, Pemmican Road remained strangely quiet and unresponsive.

Two sleeps passed before Comes in Sight and the others returned from the hunt. After the third sleep, Calf rose to find her brother and sister-in-law packing. Their lodge lay dismantled on the ground as Comes in Sight led the horses forward.

"But why?" Calf asked her brother.

"Pemmican grieves so. Perhaps in the south she will forget."

Calf understood, though she felt the sharpness of her own loss. When she embraced Pemmican, Calf saw how changed the young woman looked, her face drawn and empty, her movements slow and awkward.

"Please come back soon," Calf entreated her.

With Black Coyote and Little Seeker at her side, she watched the two ride slowly away, thinking how long it would be before they could rest again. Calf worried too that the pair might meet soldiers on the long journey to Southern Cheyenne country.

For the rest of the summer, the men hunted while the women tanned hides and dried meat for the long winter. Several times they moved camp, following the dwindling herds of antelope and buffalo that seemed to grow scarcer with each passing moon. A few times the scouts spotted soldiers moving about and eventually word came that the Lakota camp of American

Horse had been attacked. But the bluecoats did not bother the Cheyenne again that summer.

Buffalo Calf Road and Black Coyote once again settled into the routine of camp. Although Calf missed her brother and Pemmican Road, she had Leaf back again.

The two friends found time to ride together as they had years before. And whenever possible, they did chores together, gathering wood and roots, sewing, tanning hides. They talked of the old days and the present, but almost instinctively they avoided speaking of the future, as though a cloud made it impossible to see.

Soon word came that Three Stars was in the area again, enlisting scouts from all the tribes with the promise of many horses. When Black Coyote found out that his uncle, Lone Bear, had joined the troops of Three Stars, he withdrew into a sullen isolation for days.

But mostly these were good times for Calf and her people. Black Hairy Dog, keeper of the Sacred Arrows, came from the reservation with his holy bundle. Thus the two most sacred objects of the Cheyenne, the Arrows and the Buffalo Hat, sat in their lodges in the center of the camp, facing Bear Butte, the sacred mountain to the east, and blessing the people. In the village was the Turner as well, a piece of rawhide trimmed with buffalo tails, powerful enough to turn away anything from sickness to bullets, and the Sacred Wheel Lance, powerful enough to make the people invisible. The Sweet Medicine Bundle, filled with sweet grasses and a root that was the body of Sweet Medicine himself, completed the assemblage of holy objects of the community. With all these things together again in the village, many thought nothing could harm them.

Besides, everyone was too busy now getting ready for the bitter onslaught of winter. That attack was certain to come, while an attack from the soldiers might not. Early fall found the men still hunting and the women and children gathering berries of all kinds—sarvisberries, sand cherries, plums, chokecherries, currants, and bull berries. The women pounded the berries till the seeds and pits pulverized into a wet mush. Next they pressed gobs of the moist pulp into flat small cakes and laid them on skins to dry in the sun. Sometimes they pounded meat into the mixture for drying, as when they made their favorite pemmican of fresh chokecherries and buffalo meat. Preparing for winter was difficult, but survival on the bitter plains depended on it.

As winter drew near, the Cheyenne set up camp on the west side of a swift stream far up the Powder River in the foothills of the Bighorn Mountains. The chiefs selected the site for its strategic value: Nestled in groves of cottonwoods, box elders, and willows, a fortress of towering red rock surrounded the village. Only three points of entry broke the sandstone wall. To the north a narrow trail cut through the steep hills down into the valley; to the northeast a deep, dry ravine wound through the sheer stone cliffs emptying into camp; to the southeast another narrow opening pierced the rock wall. An easy site to defend, everybody agreed, so here they would spend the winter.

The Moon When the Water Freezes at the Edges passed into the Moon of the Fallen Leaves. Meanwhile, Cheyenne and Lakota scouts kept watch on Three Stars's movements. As the moon shrank to a thin crescent, scouts spotted huge columns of bluecoats pouring out of Fort Fetterman, over 2,000 strong, with the largest train of supply wagons and pack mules they had ever seen. The Cheyenne and Lakota noted with bitterness that some of their own warriors, mostly from the reservations, as well as hundreds of other Indians, now marched with the soldiers.

It was a hard thing for Calf and the others to bear, this betrayal. Calf thought a lot about why Cheyenne would join the enemy fighting their own people. Was it the gifts the bluecoats showered on the turncoat Indians? The horses, the beautiful saddles, the food? Somehow that explanation did not seem adequate to her. More likely, Calf thought, despair of the heart did it. Many Indians succumbed to a sense of hopelessness in the face of the white power. They no longer believed it possible to live according to the old ways. So many joined what they felt they could not oppose. But turning against their own people was something Calf could never understand, and a bitter anger rose in her against such cowardice.

For Black Coyote, the news of so many Indians joining their enemies wounded his spirit badly. At times he seemed almost paralyzed by the treachery and sat about camp in a sullen depression. At other times, he moved about constantly in an agitated, overly active frenzy. When Calf tried to talk to the Coyote about his state of mind, he insisted he felt fine. But she knew he was not fine.

Meanwhile, at abandoned Fort Reno to the north, Three Stars waited out a savage blizzard for four sleeps as Cheyenne and Lakota scouts watched anxiously from the hills, huddled against the cold. Then, while Three Stars rested at Fort Reno, an Indian rode swiftly to join the soldiers. The Lakota watching in the distance recognized him as Sitting Bear from the camp of Crazy Horse and they wondered what new betrayal this could be.

The moon had begun to swell again when Three Stars led his troops away from Fort Reno, heading north. The Lakota and the Cheyenne conferred. The bluecoats were headed in the direction of Crazy Horse's village—Sitting Bear must have betrayed its location. The Lakota scouts left immediately to warn their people while the Cheyenne scouts turned west to report what had been seen.

The news of Three Stars's great army of soldiers and turncoat Indians alarmed Calf and the other Cheyenne, who had felt peaceful and secure in their snug village until now. But they were relieved, too, that the immediate danger had passed for them, though they feared for their Lakota sisters and brothers.

Again Black Coyote reacted badly to the news. Buffalo Calf Road worried about his quietness. Instead of the belligerence that talk of the bluecoats usually aroused in him, he hung listlessly about their lodge and hardly spoke at all. She sensed his feelings of futility and foreboding and understood them well. But he seemed strange to her, almost as though the news had drained his body of all its energy. He hardly seemed to notice Little Seeker who ran in and out chattering in her childish ways, and when Whetstone stopped by, Black Coyote barely nodded.

Through the next few days, the Coyote remained withdrawn in his depression. Calf anxiously did his chores for him, tending their ponies in the herd. One morning, however, after returning from the stream with water, Calf felt a heavy burden lift from her chest as she spotted Black Coyote feeding his horse behind the lodge. He greeted her warmly, as though nothing had happened. Calf wondered at it all.

Early that same morning before the camp was fully roused, Last Bull and the Kit Foxes had ridden noisily into camp, returning from a raiding expedition. A band of Shoshoni, long hated by the Cheyenne, had unluckily fallen across their path and the Kit Foxes boasted thirty Shoshoni scalps and other body parts.

"Tonight we hold a scalp dance to celebrate," Last Bull shouted as he swaggered through the village.

Calf did not hide her disgust at the sight.

126

"Look at the fool. Still he plays at his war games."

"War games?" Whetstone asked innocently.

"What is the point of that slaughter? Tell me!" Calf snapped. "Indian killing Indian for no purpose but to swell the pride and vanity of men! I tell you we are destroying ourselves. Every time we make an enemy of another Indian, we hasten our own destruction. Instead of banding together against the real enemy, the white spider, we send him the help of Indians we turn into our enemies."

Black Coyote stared at her. "You do not understand the ways of men," he rebuked her gently.

"I understand!" she answered abruptly. "I do not approve!"

By midmorning there was more to think about than the slaughter of the innocents. Box Elder had spent the better part of the morning in prayer and the Sacred Persons had answered him with another vision. Gazing toward the sun he would never see again, a frightening sight greeted the blind prophet. Pouring out of the sun were not its warm and healing rays, but great crowds of bluecoats and enemy Indian scouts. Closer and closer they came till they reached the Cheyenne village and began killing its people.

Box Elder bolted up from his kneeling position and cried out for his son, Medicine Top.

"Quickly!" he told the young man. "Tell Old Crier to warn our people. The soldiers will attack our village. The women must go now to the top of the cliffs; they must bring supplies and build breastworks. There they must stay with the children—only then will they be saved!"

Immediately the frightened people reacted to Box Elder's warning, scattering to saddle their horses and pack their belongings. Buffalo Calf Road groaned at the news and mechanically set to packing once again. But their frantic preparations barely began when Last Bull and some of his Kit Foxes stormed furiously through camp.

"I will have my victory dance!" he shouted angrily.

When some continued to saddle their horses, Last Bull slashed the saddle cinches, cutting the horses in the process.

"I say you will stay. No one will cheat me of my victory. I claim my warrior's right."

As Last Bull's menacing tone became more violent, Black Crane, the old peacemaker of the tribe, hurried forward.

"Since when does Cheyenne fight Cheyenne?" the old man chastised them. But seeing the look on Last Bull's angry face, Black Crane knew the man would not relinquish his right to a victory celebration. Fearful lest Cheyenne blood be spilled by Cheyenne, he urged the people not to resist.

"Stay calm," he said. "We can leave in the morning after the celebration."

A grumbling rose from the crowd, but it quieted quickly when Last Bull kicked his horse forward toward the people. His fury made him look wild and out of control but his men stood firm in support of

128

their leader. Crow Split Nose, a chief of the Elks, stepped forward now, and the old rivalry showed itself again.

"Box Elder is right. We should leave."

"Are we to run every time that old man has a dream?" Last Bull asked scornfully.

"It is not just the dream," Split Nose answered. "The scouts have seen other signs. Soldiers may be near."

Last Bull had not forgotten his own warning to the people of Old Bear's camp and he still smarted from the dismissal of his advice by the Elks.

"You dare warn *me* of soldiers! I will listen to your warning as you listened to mine!" Last Bull raged. Then, mocking the Elk chief, he asked, "Are you afraid?"

"I do not care for myself," Split Nose answered angrily. "Our families will suffer again. I want them safe."

"The women and children!" Last Bull sneered. "We are here to protect them. Or do you think you cannot defend them?"

Split Nose started forward but immediately Black Crane blocked his way.

"We must stop this," the old peacemaker insisted, "before someone gets hurt."

Turning to the people, Last Bull shouted, "Go back to your lodges! Prepare for the celebration."

A low murmur rippled through the crowd, but it died as all ripples do and the gathering slowly melted away, till only a single figure stood exposed. It was

129

Buffalo Calf Road. Staring straight at Last Bull, she spoke.

"I will take my child and go to the rocks."

"The rootdigger again!" Last Bull snarled, glaring at Calf. He wanted to rush up to her and beat her for the insolent woman she was. But he thought better of it when he saw the revolver in her belt glistening in the cold sunlight. So he tried to demean her instead.

"And they call you Brave Woman!" Last Bull laughed. "Will the Brave Woman run and hide with the children?"

Her voice calm and firm, Calf said again, "I will take my child and go to the rocks." Then, turning her back on the Kit Fox chief, she walked away toward her lodge as he ground his teeth at the affront.

Before Calf had finished packing, Black Coyote returned from the pony herd.

When he heard what happened, the Coyote said, "We must make the others leave too."

"We cannot force them," Calf responded. "They have made their choice—they are afraid of Last Bull."

"Cowards!" Black Coyote exclaimed.

Calf touched his arm.

"Get Brave One and the children."

He nodded and went outside where already the women hauled sticks and logs to throw on the skunk for the victory dance.

Leaf, hearing of the heated exchange with Last Bull, stopped by Calf's lodge as her friend packed a few things.

"Last Bull is a fool!" Leaf said angrily. "You are right to go."

"Please come with us, Leaf," Calf entreated.

"I would have to leave my family, Calf. Dull Knife has decided that Black Crane is right. They fear Cheyenne spilling Cheyenne blood more than they fear the soldiers."

Calf shook her head and took Leaf's hand.

"Be careful."

The warmth of the fall afternoons had long since moved south as Calf's small party picked its way on horseback over the snow-covered ground through the ravine leading out of the village. Black Coyote led the way followed by Chicken Woman, Whetstone, Vanishing Heart, his wife Ridge Walker, and their daughter Brave One and her charges, Calf, and Little Seeker. Little Finger Nail would have come too, but he was in love with Singing Cloud and feared for her when her old father refused to leave. Slowly they climbed the steep rocky slope to the rimrocks high above the village where they prepared to spend the night.

The dry air grew colder as the sun dropped in the sky and the small band huddled together in their buffalo robes around a small fire. Tonight Calf and the others would sleep without lodges and keep warm as best they could. From the valley below the music and singing rose up the cliffs, and they knew the dancing had begun. In the clearing in the center of the village, the flames of the great skunk danced too, and as the

131

darkness deepened, only its glare and the sound of music reached the silent Indians on the rimrocks.

No one slept much that night, neither the celebrators below nor the watchers above. Before dawn most of the villagers had retired to their lodges, but many still feasted and danced.

Buffalo Calf Road was wide awake long before the first light spread across the sky from the east. When a little faint color moved at last across the darkness, Calf was at the edge of the rimrocks. With a buffalo robe wrapped tightly around her shoulders against the biting frost, she strained to see in all directions. For a while she could see nothing.

Then, as the sunlight rose in the sky and the hills and ravines came into view, Calf gasped aloud. North of the village, faint in the half light, Calf spotted the troops. The noise of Last Bull's victory still traveled through the bitter air as the bluecoat officer, Bad Hand, led his men against the people of Dull Knife and Little Wolf, Old Bear and Dirty Moccasins. From the north they swept toward the village, following their Indian scouts—Pawnee, Shoshoni, Arapaho, Lakota, and even Cheyenne—who had been bought by the promise of horses and favors and land.

Down the narrow trail north of the village rode the great column of bluecoats and their Indian scouts in a line so long the Cheyenne on the rimrocks above could not see the end. Buffalo Calf Road's heart plummeted as her eyes searched the distance for an end.

132

"We must go to them," she said anxiously, turning to Black Coyote.

"The fools!" Black Coyote muttered, but he moved toward his horse and quickly began his war preparations.

Calf glanced at Little Seeker and then at Chicken Woman, and the two women understood each other.

"I will care for her. Go." Chicken Woman nodded as she began hastily building breastworks.

Below, the enemy already had reached the opening into the valley and ridden through a grove of cottonwoods. Little Wolf was alone with the pony herd when the attack burst into view. Before he could move, Little Wolf's horse fell dead under him. When he rose to flee, a bullet struck and he too was left for dead.

Just as the first charge began, a small figure jumped out of the thick underbrush and raised a rifle. In an instant a bluecoat pointed his rifle at the shadowy resister and the two shots rang as one. The Cheyenne boy, youngest son of Dull Knife, fell dead as the enemy poured through the narrow entrance, spilling in every direction.

Panic seized the camp. Those who had gone to sleep earlier woke to the nightmare and fled into the bitter cold, not fully dressed. The revelers ran away from the great warm fire and into the cutting morning chill. Up the rocks and through the ravine they flew as the valley filled with bluecoats and enemy Indians.

On hearing the attack, Box Elder got his Sacred Wheel Lance and immediately a group of warriors surrounded him. Together they moved quickly to the Sacred Hat Lodge where Coal Bear and his wife had already taken the bundle of Sacred Arrows and tied it to her back. Medicine Bear seized the Turner, and while the warriors led the three away, he covered the rear, waving Turner from side to side to keep the soldiers' bullets away. With the power of Turner and Box Elder's Ox'zem, they made it safely to the dry creek bed.

Others were not so fortunate. Crow Split Nose, the Elk chief, was among the first to fall dead at the north end of the camp. White Frog was also shot, and Comes Together, his brave wife who had fought off the Pawnee years before, dragged him away from the bullets.

The lodge of Little Seeker's friend, Runs Ahead, stood at the end of the village in the path of the attack. Her father leapt out of the lodge to fight, and Runs Ahead and her mother frantically threw on what clothes they could. The two ran from their home into a storm of bullets and before their feet moved twenty paces, Runs Ahead's mother, High Forehead, collapsed in a heap on the snow. The child fell to her knees, screaming and tugging at the bleeding corpse till her father came. Seeing it was no use, he lifted the child onto his horse and carried her to the rocks behind the village.

Not far from the spot where High Forehead fell, Iron Teeth and Red Pipe herded their children away from the gunfire. Carrying her baby in one arm and urging the other children on, Iron Teeth moved quickly through the snow as her husband and eldest son, Gathering His Medicine, stayed behind to fight off the soldiers. Anxious for them, Iron Teeth glanced back as she ran with the children. Her legs froze in the snow when she saw Red Pipe staggering, clutching his chest. With the baby in her arms, Iron Teeth started back as he fell. She saw her son rush to Red Pipe's side, then turn to her, shouting.

"No! Go back! It is too late."

Iron Teeth's younger boy grabbed her arm as Gathering His Medicine rushed to his mother's side. Together they held her as she strained forward.

"No, Mother," Medicine choked on his sobs. "He is dead. Save the little ones." Taking the baby from her arms, he pulled her toward the rocks behind the village.

Everyone was frantic. Little Finger Nail rushed to the lodge of his beloved Singing Cloud. He found the young girl stooped, trying to pull her terrified old father from his sick bed. Together they lifted him from the pallet and Little Finger Nail carried the frail body into the snow.

Hog's daughter and wife ran back and forth helping the old people and the children escape. Leaf rode her white stallion toward the north end of the village, shooting her revolver at the intruders. Pretty Walker, daughter of Little Wolf, moved quickly through the camp, helping where she could, fearless of the bullets that moved closer and closer. Even Crooked Nose had stayed behind to help a sick woman escape.

By now Buffalo Calf Road had reached the village with Black Coyote, Whetstone, and Vanishing Heart. Confusion, terror, and violence met them, a familiar scene by now. As Calf rode into camp she spotted a Shoshoni about to club a fallen Cheyenne. In an instant she raised her revolver and fired. The Shoshoni pitched headfirst onto the Cheyenne, who pushed the body away and sat up, still stunned.

"Last Bull!" Calf mumbled as the arrogant warrior stared at the woman who saved his life.

A small child stood nearby in the snow, half naked and crying. Quickly Calf swept the child onto her horse and turned back toward the cliffs. But she had not gone far before the screams of a woman pierced the din of war. It was one of the Princesses, crouched over a lifeless body in the snow. Calf jumped from her horse, and holding the reins tightly, she rushed to the woman. The eldest daughter of Dull Knife cradled the dead body of her husband in her arms. Gently Calf put her arm around the Princess.

"Come," she whispered. "The soldiers are everywhere."

The Princess looked at Calf in shock, her grief-stricken eyes uncomprehending.

"Come," Calf pleaded again. She firmly pulled the woman to her feet as the dead body slid to the ground. After climbing on her horse where the child still sat, she pulled the Princess on behind her and the three fled up the ravine to the cliffs.

Not far from the spot where Dull Knife's son-in-law fell, Pretty Walker had just helped an old couple onto a stray horse and was looking for an escape herself. Suddenly she noticed an old woman in a clearing, caught in the open, confused and unable to run. Before she could react, a bluecoat rode up to the woman and jumped from his horse. Pretty Walker clutched her throat as her breath stopped. But the man quickly picked up the old woman and sat her on his horse, which he sent racing to safety with a hard slap on its rear.

Pretty Walker watched in amazement and gratitude. But as the bluecoat turned back on foot, a Cheyenne warrior charged by, shooting the young man in the leg. Before the warrior could turn to charge again, Pretty Walker rushed to the soldier, who was unable to stand, and threw herself on him. The bewildered Cheyenne lowered his rifle and rode off when the young woman motioned him away.

Quickly Pretty Walker clutched the soldier under his arms and dragged him away from the bullets to the thick underbrush at the edge of camp. The young man looked deep into her eyes. For an instance nothing made any sense, and neither could understand why they fought each other. They sensed that on a better day they might have been friends, even lovers. When Pretty Walker saw that he was safe, she bolted from the underbrush and ran for the ravine.

Box Elder, who had reached the safety of the dry riverbed, was left by the warriors with the others, huddled against the cold and the soldiers. He was not there long before he called to his son.

"Is there a knoll nearby?" he asked anxiously.

Medicine Top looked around and told his father there was.

"Take me. Quickly," the old prophet said.

Medicine Top led him up the knoll. Before they reached the top, Box Elder stopped and told his son to stay behind. Then the solitary figure slowly felt his way to the top where he sat for a bit, filling his pipe and lifting his powerful voice in song. In the valley below the eerie singing rose above the noise of violence and pain. When he had finished filling his pipe, Box Elder knelt on the ground and prayed. Then the old man offered the pipe to Maheo and the Sacred Persons, lifting it to each of the four directions of the universe. Suddenly the tobacco in the pipe burst into flames as though the sun itself had lit it. The others watched in amazement.

By now, the attention of the soldiers was drawn to the strange old man and they began to fire at him from a nearby ridge. Behind the rocks the women began to sing stout heart songs for courage. Just then Long Jaw, a Cheyenne warrior, jumped up on a hill nearby and began running toward Box Elder, his bright red cape flapping wildly in the wind as he ran, his dog barking at his heels. Up and down he jumped, now in sight, now out of sight, taunting the soldiers and drawing the bluecoat bullets to himself. More soldiers rode near, shooting, drawn by the strange pair on the knoll. But

138

their bullets seemed unable to stop the wild young man in the dancing red cape and the calm old man with the flaming stone pipe.

Buffalo Calf Road had raced back into the valley again. Her eyes caught for a brief instant the strange drama on the knoll. She marveled at the blind prophet, inspiring his people even at this moment of terrible despair. A great warmth for the old man swept through Calf as she moved quickly to help others escape.

Meanwhile, nine Cheyenne were trapped in a long gully, pinned down by enemy scouts. Leaf, who still rode her stallion and fought alongside the warriors, saw that her husband lay in the gully with the others. Frantically she looked about for horses. If they ran from the ditch surely they would be killed, but with horses there might be a chance, she thought.

Her eyes searched the area. Everywhere there was fighting, mostly hand to hand now. Only one riderless horse caught her eye. It reared and shied at the terrible din. Immediately Leaf raced to the horse and, grabbing its reins, calmed the animal as only she could do, then led it toward the gully.

The scouts were momentarily distracted by the strange pair on the knoll above, untouched by the rain of bullets. Seizing the instant, Leaf slid on the far side of her horse and, leading the other by its reins, rode swiftly to the near end of the gully where her husband, Bull Hump, along with White Shield and Yellow Eagle, crouched together. The three leapt from the gully onto the horses, White Shield and Yellow Eagle on one, Bull Hump on the other with Leaf. Before the enemy Indian scouts could take careful aim, the four vanished into the tumult. The scouts immediately charged the gully, killing Tall Bull, Walking Whirlwind, Burns Red in the Sun, Walking Calf, Hawk's Visit, and Four Spirits.

Leaf and the three men she saved were the last Cheyenne to leave the valley alive. Over a thousand bluecoat and enemy Indians filled the valley now and there was no escape.

On the cliffs above, Calf and Black Coyote assisted with the wounded and the grieving. The Coyote hardly spoke as he helped carry the injured to safety. Little Seeker clung to her mother, doing as she was told. Calf's eyes met Leaf's as they hurried about, but neither spoke her pain.

Grief and despair hung heavier over the morning than the bitter cold. Old Grandmother thought with apprehension of the future her young grandson, Spotted Deer, would face. As he tended the old woman, Spotted Deer's eyes frantically searched the rimrocks and rested only when he saw his beloved Yellow Bead safe with her aunt behind some breastworks. Even Little Hawk did not joke now but helped prepare a dead body for hasty burial in the rocks, his face knotted in anger and grief.

Little Runs Ahead sat in her father's lap, clutching the grief-stricken man and sobbing for her lost mother. Twin Woman, still sorrowing at the death of her husband at the Little Bighorn, sat holding her small son and clinging to her daughter, Crane Woman. Bear Rope raged in anger at his wife, simply because she stood near at hand and the white man could not be reached. Comes in Sight Woman, his daughter, tried to calm her father and shield her mother, but the sullen man raved as though they were to blame.

At the edge of the rimrocks, Iron Teeth, who had come from the reservation that very summer so that her family could live again the old life, peered down into the ravine leading from the valley. Unable to believe her husband dead, she watched anxiously for Red Pipe. He will come, he must come, she told herself again and again.

The old chief Dull Knife stood silent with his grieving family. He had lost three—his young son, his nephew, his son-in-law—all dead at the hands of the murdering whites and their Indians. When the eldest Princess began gashing her arms and legs in mourning for her dead husband, only Leaf tried to stop her.

"Please," Leaf pleaded softly. "Do not do this now. You must flee with us."

But the young woman kept cutting at her arms and legs as the blood flowed over her clothes and onto the ground.

"Let her be," Pawnee Woman said to Leaf. "It is our way."

"Our way!" Leaf answered a touch defiantly. "Is the incurable wound of the heart not enough for women. Must they wound the body as well?"

As the survivors huddled on the high cliff, numb

141

from the cold and grief, the enemy below looted and destroyed the possessions of the Cheyenne. Over a thousand buffalo robes, desperately needed by the freezing people now, were confiscated. Metal goods—kettles, pans, tools—crumbled under the axe. Flames ate the rest: the lodges, clothing, saddles, and a whole winter's store of meat and other foods.

Once again Calf and the other Cheyenne watched helplessly as the soldiers put the torch to their worldly possessions. The valley filled with flames till great black clouds of smoke rose to the cliffs above, choking the desperate survivors. Unlike the destruction of Old Bear's camp, when many Cheyenne slept safe with their wealth on the reservation, now there would be none to replace the lost beauty, comfort, and safety of the Cheyenne's material glory.

No, the bad hearts at the destruction of Old Bear's camp were nothing compared to this. More than forty Cheyenne—women, men, children—lay dead after this massacre, and many more lay wounded, some critically. On this day, when the cold grew more and more bitter and the snow began to fall, most of their protection against the bitter high-plains winter was gone.

Calf sat for a moment with Black Coyote and Little Seeker. Taking the Coyote's hand, she spoke.

"We must not let the white spider sting us onto the reservation. Promise me. I will not have my child born in one of those prisons."

The words jolted Black Coyote and he gazed into

her defiant eyes. After a moment he lifted his tired hand and stroked her black hair.

"You are with child then?" he asked gently.

She nodded.

"I promise," he said.

CHAPTER 5

After burning the Cheyenne village, Bad Hand took his troops and began to leave, taking away confiscated goods and hundreds of horses captured from the Cheyenne's pony herd. As they withdrew, the blood-stopping wails of the Shoshoni scouts suddenly rose to the Cheyenne on the high cliffs. Everyone understood the grief-stricken cries of mourning and though nobody looked at Last Bull, they guessed that the Shoshoni had found his sack containing scalps, the right hands of twelve Shoshoni babies and the head and arm of a Shoshoni woman.

For a long while Calf and the others sat quietly, listening to the wild, mournful keening of the Shoshoni who pounded their revenge on the captured sacred drum of the Cheyenne. Suddenly the wails stopped and all was quiet except for the fading whistle of the Cheyenne sacred flute, played now by a Pawnee.

Nothing remained for the Cheyenne but to flee in search of help for their freezing, hungry people. They would try to find Crazy Horse's village, though Calf wondered uneasily whether Crazy Horse too had been attacked.

While warriors searched the charred village for survivors, Calf and the others prepared for flight. Bridge and Medicine Woman, assisted by Singing Cloud, did what they could for the wounded while others made travois to carry them away. Among the many wounded was Little Wolf, left for dead near the pony herd.

Few had on adequate clothing—some had even fled into the cold without moccasins when the attack began. So they covered their bodies against the freezing air and snow as best they could, tearing strips from their dresses and shirts to wrap around their feet and ears and hands. The only warm robes were those brought to the cliffs the day before by Buffalo Calf Road, Black Coyote, and their small group, plus a few others saved in flight. These were shared among the youngest children and the sick.

As for food there was some dry meat, again brought the day before by Calf and her party, but it was only enough to feed a few of the thousand who hungered now.

At last the shivering band set out across the mountains. There were still horses saved from capture, so many were able to ride. But as the tattered procession moved slowly with its wounded and dying, the air, already bitter cold, turned to invisible ice. Looking at the ominous sky, Calf thought uneasily that the great white grizzly of winter would soon be on them.

By darkness, a violent snowstorm hit and the mountain cold felt more brutal than anyone could remember. Unable to see, they stopped for the night in a narrow pass, hoping to escape the worst of the cutting wind and snow. But steadily the cold became unbearable.

Black Coyote and Calf held Little Seeker between them, but the child seemed to be turning to ice as they wrapped their bodies over her. All around them the moans of the wounded and freezing became one with the howling wind.

Suddenly the Coyote jumped up, his jaw tight and his eyes wild. Pulling his hunting knife from his belt, he began stabbing his horse, a creature dear to him for years. Calf watched in horror, thinking the Coyote had gone mad.

When the wretched animal fell dead, Black Coyote quickly slashed open its belly, cutting hard and deep. Calf instantly understood, and lifting her daughter from the ground she plunged the freezing child's body into the steaming entrails of the dead horse.

Immediately others began to do the same and before the horrible night passed hundreds of horses lay dead, giving their flesh for food and warmth to the half-naked, starving people.

Near Calf and Black Coyote, Little Hawk hovered about his beloved Crooked Nose and her family in the absence of her brothers who were hunting when the attack occurred. Close by, Little Finger Nail sat with his beloved Singing Cloud and her old father, who was wrapped on a travois. No one spoke, but as the cold grew worse and worse, as the pain became unbearable all around him, the Nail thought of the Sacred Persons watching from above and wondered.

For many the dead horses were not enough. Eleven babies froze to death that first night in the bitter Bighorn Mountains, all of them in their parents' arms. Others froze to death, too, and countless more suffered frostbite. Never had there been a day and night such as this for the Northern Cheyenne, thought Buffalo Calf Road. And throughout, the purpose of the terror and pain revealed itself to no one.

For two days the snowstorm continued. With so many horses killed, most moved through the deep snow on foot now. Calf still had her horse, though she offered it to Old Grandmother to ride. Several people, Scabby among them, died during the flight of wounds received in the attack. During the second night, three more babies froze to death.

The death of the infants brought tears to Calf's eyes, the drops freezing on her cheeks before she could wipe them away. Never would they taste life, she thought. But then the bitterness of reality stood all around her, and Calf's cold heart imagined that there might be no life left for the Cheyenne to enjoy. The thought jarred her and her hand moved to her belly where an unborn Cheyenne waited for a taste of that life.

At last, weak from hunger and numb from the cold,

the grieving march came down from the mountains to the Tongue River valley. Several days had passed. The bitter cold eased a little and they followed the stream north.

Then, just below the mouth of Hanging Woman Creek, Cheyenne scouts spotted a small band of Indians ahead. A wave of fear rolled over Calf and her people lest they be bluecoat scouts. The band inched forward slowly, then, in a burst of recognition, trotted quickly ahead.

Calf sighed with relief. It was Wooden Leg and nine other Cheyenne warriors, all of them gone from the camp on the Powder River days before the attack. The raiding party was still searching for Crows when they spotted the wretched people moving along the river—their own people, left secure and wealthy in the mountains only days before, now poor and helpless on the trail.

Eleven endless days and nights after the massacre the Cheyenne found the Oglala camp of Crazy Horse on Beaver Creek, where once again their Lakota sisters and brothers received them well, sharing what they had. For a full moon the Cheyenne and Oglala stayed together, moving up the Tongue River in search of buffalo meat and skins for lodges. Being together again eased the pain for Calf and the others and a bit of hope found its way into some hearts.

But toward the end of the Moon of the Big Freeze, a strange event occurred that surprised Calf and her people. A peace delegation from the army arrived at the camp of Crazy Horse. Two Miniconjou, Foolish Bear and Important Man, brought the terms of surrender from the army. All weapons and horses must be given up by the Lakota and Cheyenne, the order insisted. For its part, the army promised to forget its grievances against the Indians and drop all claims to punishment for the killing of Custer's troops.

Black Coyote turned to Calf and laughed bitterly at the terms.

"They will not punish us for killing the men who attacked our peaceful village? And for this we must give up our horses and guns!"

But some were not so offended. The sight of the Cheyenne, destitute and grieving again, had greatly impressed the Oglala. Now many argued for peace with the whites. Others, however, recalled the countless broken promises of the army and the living death on the reservations.

Again the internal divisions among her people made Buffalo Calf Road uneasy. She argued strongly that they must not think of surrender.

"Do you believe for a moment the bluecoats will treat us with respect? They never have in the past," Calf said emphatically to those wavering about what to do.

Unable to agree among themselves, a small delegation of Oglala chiefs was sent to parley with the army chief, Bearcoat. But the excursion ended in tragedy. Before the peace party could reach the soldier fort, a group of Crow army scouts approached. Ignoring the

Lakota truce flag, they fell upon the Oglala chiefs, pulling them from their horses and killing all five.

News of the outrage reached Crazy Horse's village. Calf could sense a panic of the heart seizing her people. A council immediately met and the men hatched a secret strategy, unknown to the women. A party of fifty Cheyenne and Oglala would attack the troops of Bearcoat in order to draw them into a carefully laid ambush up the Tongue River near camp.

By the end of the Moon of the Big Freeze, Bearcoat had taken the bait and started up river. For days the Indian decoys struck and withdrew, struck and withdrew, drawing the soldiers closer to the trap. On the sixth day of the Moon of the Frost in the Lodges, a violent snowstorm hit. By the following afternoon an unforeseen event unfolded that would alter the Indian plan.

Since the women and children had not been told of the coming ambush, they moved freely about, making their own preparations for the impending separation of the two tribes. Game was not plentiful and it was increasingly difficult to find food for so many. Some Cheyenne had already begun to move up the Tongue River while the Oglala made plans to move east up Hanging Woman Creek. A strange uneasiness took hold of Calf during these preparations, a sense of things falling apart.

Calf's friend, Crooked Nose, had spent the morning helping the widow of Lame White Man and her family pack. Twin Woman still mourned the death of her husband on the Little Bighorn and Crooked Nose had taken to helping her since the tragedy. By afternoon, her preparations complete, Twin Woman urged that they begin the journey up the Tongue River following those who had already begun to move. Fearing another attack on their village, Twin Woman became more anxious each day to move her remaining family to a safer place.

Calf tried to reassure the older woman and calm her fears. But Twin Woman saw no point in waiting, and Calf could not think of strong arguments to keep her. The splintering of the tribe had begun, some gone, some staying for a while. Calf knew everyone would have to move on, but this breaking apart in pieces troubled her.

A few others wanted to leave as well, including old Sweet Taste Woman, the widow of a black man captured by the Cheyenne when he was a boy many winters ago, and her daughter, Finger Woman, with her two children, a boy and a girl. Helping the old woman was a young boy named Black Horse.

As the group stood ready to leave, Buffalo Calf Road said good-bye to Crooked Nose, who had been prevailed upon to go with Twin Woman to help. The young woman expected her family to catch up in a day or two. But clearly Crooked Nose was nervous about leaving, especially without saying good-bye to the man she would soon marry, Little Hawk, who was away scouting with the warriors. She held Calf's hand longer than necessary for a parting.

"I'll see you in a few days," Calf said, forcing a thin smile.

"Tell Little Hawk I'll wait for him to follow," Crooked Nose implored, as though he would need any urging.

"Don't worry," Calf nodded, trying not to show her own concern.

The afternoon sun stood high in the sky when the small band of women and children set out with their belongings, accompanied by a warrior, Big Horse, who would be scouting in their direction. A great peak called Wolf Mountain towered above them, watching their every move. As the women headed north, Big Horse left them for short periods to scout the area ahead. At one point he discovered a camp full of soldiers and hurried back to warn the women.

But it was too late. Bluecoat Indian scouts had already found them and taken the four women and five young people prisoners. Big Horse arrived in time to see the party being led away by the scouts. Unable to save them alone, he sped back to Crazy Horse's village to sound the alarm.

Little Hawk, who had just returned to camp, took the news of the capture of his beloved Crooked Nose badly. He shouted for the warriors to leave with him immediately, but the chiefs urged caution since the matter was being turned over to the warrior societies. Little Hawk would have none of it. Along with Crooked Nose's brothers Wooden Leg and Yellow Hair, as well as Black Coyote, Whetstone, and a few

151

others, he raced out of camp. Even Little Finger Nail, artist of the Cheyenne people, embittered since the massacre by Bad Hand's men, rode with them. The warrior societies, meanwhile, arranged for a war party to move out and attack the soldiers at dawn.

Calf did not sleep that night. In the small lodge given to her by a kind Lakota woman, she sat watching Little Seeker tossing in her troubled sleep. A gloom hung thicker than the darkness all around the lodge. Gentle fearful Crooked Nose would not leave her thoughts.

An anger gnawed at Calf's stomach, swollen with the new life within. This time her anger turned not just to the bluecoats but to the men of her own camp. They had not told the women of their plan, of their maneuvers to draw the soldiers near the camp for an ambush. Had Sweet Taste Woman, Crooked Nose, and Twin Woman known of the danger, they would never had set out. The thought of it deepened her fury.

Calf knew why the men kept such secret at times like this. Enemy scouts would be forewarned if all movement in the camp did not proceed as normal. If the women had been told, they would have protected themselves and their children—they would have abandoned camp and the bluecoat scouts would sense the danger. Calf understood all this, but still a silent rage ate at her as she brooded over the war games of men. The women had a right to know.

Snow fell again that night as the temperature plunged and the war party slowly made its way toward

152

the soldiers. The larger party had caught up with Little Hawk's band. When they reached the bluecoat camp, Little Hawk and the others watched from their cold positions on a high rocky ridge.

Black Coyote crouched with the others in the dark among the icy rocks. He felt guilty about the hostages and he knew what Calf would be thinking as she, too, waited in the night shadows. It was the only time he could remember not sharing the truth with her.

At last a creeping gray dawn moved in, carrying thick storm clouds from the west. In the river valley below the bluecoats already stirred, scraping away the night's heavy snowfall from small patches of ground to build cooking fires. The warm domestic smell of coffee and fried salt pork rose to the ledges above, heavy with their burden of angry men. In a rage Little Hawk leapt to his feet and his voice rang across the valley.

"Eat well, bluecoats! It is your last meal."

Immediately, the warriors rose from behind their rocks and dropped a volley of arrows and bullets on the troops below. The Cheyenne and Oglala outnumbered the soldiers two to one and they would surely have driven the soldiers away. But Bearcoat had with him the large, dreaded two-bang gun that spit great round bullets larger than a fist. There was no ducking the exploding balls that tore people to bits when they hit.

Still the warriors held their ground, a position of advantage on the craggy stone ledges overlooking the troops below. Some concentrated on breaking the bluecoat line to the right while others tried to circle the soldiers to squeeze them in a great trap. But the soldiers intercepted the thrust to the right while another detail dug in across the river, preventing the trap from closing.

As the warriors maneuvered left and right, Bearcoat stood next to the great two-bang gun, shouting commands as he pointed here and there with a branch in his hand. The great balls crashed and echoed through the valley as the standoff continued and snow began to fall again. Finally, aware that the Indians could remain indefinitely entrenched in their stone fortress, Bearcoat ordered his infantry to charge the ridges above and rout the hostiles.

Burdened by heavy coats and boots and artillery, the foot soldiers began their slow tortuous charge through the deep snow. The rugged terrain soon forced the bluecoats to break into groups as they struggled with the cold, snow, and rocks.

Above them, a Cheyenne warrior named Big Crow taunted the soldiers, drawing the bullets to himself as he sang and danced. Great is my medicine, thought Big Crow, as his feathered warbonnet jumped with his movements and his red war shirt and blanket flapped wildly on his back. Now and then he stopped his war dance to fire his carbine, captured from a bluecoat on the Little Bighorn.

As the soldiers drew close to the ridge they concentrated their fire on Big Crow and before long the defiant warrior's medicine failed him and he crashed to the ground, fatally wounded. By now the snowfall had become a blizzard and it was nearly impossible to fight the unseen enemy.

Two Moons addressed the warriors.

"We must leave now. There is nothing more we can do."

"No!" shouted Little Hawk. "The women and children are still prisoners. We cannot leave them."

Two Moons understood Little Hawk's special grief, but he answered, "We cannot fight the two-bang gun. We must use the cover of the great white grizzly to lead our people away from the soldiers."

"I will not leave my sister!" Wooden Leg responded.

Whetstone dared to utter the words in all their minds. "And are you sure she lives? The white spider and Crow would not spare the lives of our women and children. Have you forgotten the massacre by Bad Hand's soldiers?"

The words threw Little Hawk into a deeper fear for his beloved Crooked Nose.

"I will go down there!" Little Hawk insisted.

"No, my brother," Two Moons said. "Your death will not bring them back. Your grief for Crooked Nose makes you speak foolish words. You know that together we could not break the enemy line. What can one person do?"

Black Coyote stood silently listening. Now he put his hand firmly on the shoulder of Little Hawk and spoke above the howling wind.

"If they have not killed her by now, they will let her live. We can come back in a day or two when they do not expect us and try again."

Little Hawk's desperate eyes peered at the Coyote.

"I promise to come back with you," Black Coyote assured him.

"And I," added Whetstone, as the others nodded assent.

Slowly the Indians left the stone ridges, carrying the stricken Big Crow and helping the wounded as best they could through the blowing snow. Before they had gone far, Big Crow gasped his last request to Little Finger Nail and the others who carried him on foot.

"I am dying," he whispered. "Leave me here among the rocks and hurry to our people. They need you. I have no more need of help. Tell my family I have done my share."

Sadly Little Finger Nail and the warriors wrapped Big Crow in a buffalo robe and laid him against the sandstone rocks sheltered from the wind.

"Go now," he begged them in a soft whisper.

The Nail turned quickly away, stumbling down the rocks as the tears froze bitter against his cheeks.

Back at the camp Calf and the others heard the news and the order to leave. She and Black Coyote barely spoke as they moved about their lodge making ready to flee. Calf's anger at Black Coyote and the men had not yet subsided.

Finally, in sorrow, the Coyote put his arm on Calf's shoulder and whispered, "I'm sorry."

"It's done," she said, softening a bit. "Now we must get Crooked Nose and the others back."

The Cheyenne and Oglala quickly packed their belongings and under cover of the snow fled up the Tongue River away from the bluecoats. By evening the air warmed and the snow turned to rain as Bearcoat led his men after the Indians. But the soldiers were exhausted, and Cheyenne and Lakota scouts watched as the army finally abandoned the chase and turned back.

For ten days the bluecoats marched north away from the Indians. Little Hawk, Black Coyote, and others followed them, but it was impossible to get near the heavily armed troops. When the warriors first caught sight of the captured women and children under guard, Little Hawk lurched forward and would have ridden into the enemy column if the Coyote had not stopped him.

For days they dogged the troops, waiting for the chance that never came. When at last the soldier fort on the Elk River swallowed up the troops and their captives, a door closed in the eyes of the lighthearted Little Hawk that would never again open to the world.

As the others got ready to move out, Little Hawk motioned them away.

"I will stay awhile," he said to Black Coyote.

So they left Little Hawk, sitting straight on his horse, staring at the fort in the distance, as though his eyes could pierce the barricade and rest on his beloved Crooked Nose.

Several days later the warriors returned to their people far up the Tongue River. Buffalo Calf Road stood watching as the weary Coyote rode up to their lodge. A twinge of anger still passed through her heart at Black Coyote and the other men, but her concern now was for Crooked Nose. Before she could ask the question, Black Coyote shook his head sadly.

Calf misunderstood his gesture.

"Crooked Nose is dead?"

"No," he answered quickly. "They are all alive, but the soldiers have taken them to the fort on the Elk River. I am afraid we will never see them again."

Calf dropped her gaze to the ground without speaking.

"There was nothing we could do," he added apologetically.

"And Little Hawk . . . ?"

"He would not return with us. He sits watching the fort."

In the days that followed the women sought each other out, sharing their common grief. One morning Calf and Leaf drew water together from the ice-covered river. The bright colors of dawn still tinted the eastern sky when a lone rider entered the village. It was Little Hawk, his gaunt face impassive.

Calf started forward, but Leaf caught her arm, and he passed without noticing them.

Separated from the main camp of the Oglala now, Calf and her people moved to the Bighorn valley, where they spent the rest of their troubled winter on

Rotten Grass Creek. Of the two holy objects of the Cheyenne nation, only the Sacred Hat remained, tended as always by Coal Bear and occupying the place of honor in the center of the camp. After the attack on their village early that winter, Black Hairy Dog had fled with the Sacred Arrows to join their Cheyenne relatives in the south.

It was not good, the two sacred bundles being separated, and Calf and her people felt the absence. That loss heightened the emptiness in the lodges of the dead and captured Cheyenne. Even the absence of Little Hawk's jokes and tricks oppressed the camp, and the children no longer sought him out or dogged his footsteps when he wandered gloomily through the cottonwoods heavy with snow.

But the moons still passed, one by one, till the Moon of the Light Snows brought the hope of spring and a fresh start. Despite their troubles, the Northern Cheyenne still camped together as a people, with few left on the reservation. Still they persisted in the old ways, following the shrinking buffalo herds. With the bitter snows behind them, the men hunted often now.

The grass was not yet green when Black Coyote and his hunting party prevailed on Little Hawk to join them. The sad-faced warrior had stayed to himself most of the winter, shunning the company of his friends. Even when Calf brought him food, he hardly spoke, though he mechanically thanked her. But the quiet warmth of the spring sun touched his heart a bit,

159

and though he still spoke little, he joined his friends as they rode from camp to hunt the buffalo, with no premonition of the events already in motion that would crush his life a second time.

Two days after Black Coyote, Little Hawk, and the others left, Buffalo Calf Road stood outside her poor small lodge repairing the hide walls after the winter's fury. It was the worst winter she could remember, aside from the winter she had lost her parents. Everywhere in camp there was suffering. Few had enough clothing or cooking utensils. There were not enough blankets and robes to keep out the cold. With their winter stores destroyed by Bad Hand, few had enough to eat and most looked emaciated. Many still suffered the effects of frostbite in their flight from the massacre.

These days Calf thought often of the unborn child in her womb. It was uncomfortable to move much under the kicking mass, and a feeling of regret over the pregnancy dogged her thoughts since the massacre of her people by Bad Hand. Calf wrestled often with the depressing thought of bringing a child into such a world.

Suddenly two riders galloped into camp. Calf strained to see. A gasp rose in her throat and the bone sewing needle fell from her hand. On one of the horses sat Sweet Taste Woman.

Calf ran to meet the old woman as a crowd pushed around her horse. Everyone was talking at once, asking if she was well, asking if she had been mistreated by the soldiers, asking for news of the other captives.

Calf inched forward through the crowd and grasping the old woman's knotted hand, she asked anxiously, "Where is Crooked Nose?"

The tall, thin old woman slid from her horse.

"She is at the soldier fort with the others."

"Is she well?" Calf pressed.

Sweet Taste Woman shook her head and shrugged.

"She is sad, always sad. She sits alone all day and at night she sobs."

Calf's brow tightened.

"Do the soldiers mistreat her then?"

"No, no," the old woman answered. "They fed us well and kept us warm. They promised no one would hurt us."

"I don't understand," Calf said.

"Everyone was homesick at first. But we got used to it. Only Crooked Nose did not. She believes she will never see her people again." Leaning forward, the old woman added, "And she does not believe Little Hawk still loves her. When he did not try to save her . . ."

"But he did try," Calf interrupted. "He and the others."

Sweet Taste Woman shrugged again. "How could she know that?"

Just then Little Wolf, the respected old man chief, pushed forward. For the first time Calf noticed a white man still mounted on a second horse, a dark stocky man with a moustache and long hair that hung from a

161

large hat. On his legs he wore big leather covers such as the white cattle herders had, so the Indians called him Big Leggins. Behind him Calf saw that a string of pack mules stood snorting from the run.

After Little Wolf and the white man exchanged greetings, Sweet Taste Woman told the chief that Bearcoat had sent them. Little Wolf motioned the pair to come and meet with the chiefs.

Once again the council met as Calf and her people milled about waiting. If only Little Hawk was there, Calf fretted. It was so like Crooked Nose to believe the worst, she thought. At last Old Crier brought them word from the council.

"All the captives are well—the soldier guards keep them safe. The white chief Bearcoat sends gifts for the Cheyenne. He promises that all who surrender will be treated kindly. Then the hostages will be returned safely. The council will decide what to do."

Surrender! Calf's heart sank at the word. So the argument begins again, she thought with exasperation.

Already the chiefs of the warrior societies had gathered in a huge lodge, arguing both sides of the question. Outside, Calf and many others stood listening to the loud discussion. The Elks and the Kit Foxes could not agree. Into the night they argued, long after the evening chill had prodded the anxious listeners home to their warm lodges.

A second day of talk still saw no agreement among the warriors, so the civil chiefs intervened again. In the council lodge Two Moons spoke as Calf and the others again listened outside.

"My friends. Every day more whites come from the place of the rising sun. Their wheel wagons roll across the open plains like an endless river. We cannot stop them. We cannot run from them. Under what rock can we hide when the land crawls with spiders? How much longer can we hunt the buffalo? Already the herds grow smaller. Our friends from the south tell us of the greedy white buffalo hunters with their great guns who kill a large herd in a single day and leave their meat and bones to rot in the sight of Maheo. Soon the food of our people will vanish. Already we are reduced to beggars, depending on the kindness of our Lakota brothers and sisters. No, peace must come or our people too will disappear from the earth. I will go to Bearcoat as he asks. Those who wish to join me are welcome; others may do as they choose."

Calf's heart sank at the words. Her hand moved instinctively to her swollen stomach in a protective gesture. She wished the Coyote was with her.

Then Calf heard Chief Little Wolf address the group.

"Friends. There is wisdom in the words of Two Moons. But you know we have made peace with the white people before—many times before. And always they reward us with the gun. If we surrender, we must surrender from strength. Before we decide anything we must parley with Bearcoat and find out his best terms. Then we will know what to do."

Most nodded in agreement, though some still refused to hear any talk of surrender. At last it was decided. Two Moons agreed to lead a party to talk to Bearcoat and secure the release of the hostages. In all, a delegation of nineteen chiefs rode with a few warriors, accompanied by Big Leggins.

As Buffalo Calf Road watched the warriors and chiefs ride out of camp, an ominous wet mist hung over the lodges. If only Little Hawk had not gone hunting, she thought. If only he were riding with the warriors going to Bearcoat's fort. If only Crooked Nose could talk to Little Hawk. If only . . .

On the way the party rested at the mouth of Hanging Woman Creek in sight of Wolf Mountain where they had fought Bearcoat that very winter. As the others made camp, Little Finger Nail and Wooden Leg searched among the hillside rocks for the body of Big Crow. At last they found him in a thin grove of small pines, propped against the sandstone rocks where they left him in the storm. His buffalo robe had blown open; Little Finger Nail wrapped it gently over the body again as Wooden Leg began covering him with stones. When only a mound of rocks stood on the spot, the two quietly turned and climbed down to join the others.

When at last the warriors and the peacemakers reached sight of the soldier fort, Big Leggins motioned them to wait as he rode ahead and disappeared among the clustered buildings. Soon he emerged again with a man dressed in a great fur coat

164

and riding a white horse. Behind them a line of mounted soldiers followed at a distance.

Two Moons and three others rode forward to meet Bearcoat. After the greeting, Bearcoat removed his hat and gestured with it toward the fort, signaling the chiefs to follow. The rest of the warriors, including Wooden Leg and Little Finger Nail, waited outside the fort.

When the Cheyenne had been fed, they sat with Bearcoat in council and heard the terms of surrender: They must give up their arms and their horses. In return, these horses would be sold and the money used to purchase cattle and other domestic stock for the Cheyenne to raise. If they remained peaceful and followed government directives, they would be treated justly. Straight-eyed and tough, Bearcoat smiled broadly under his moustache after he spoke the terms. But the chiefs sat stiff and impassive until at last Two Moons spoke.

"We will carry your terms to our people."

Bearcoat looked surprised. Two Moons continued.

"Now you will allow our people to return with us."

"I'm sorry," Bearcoat answered. "The women and children must remain here until your people surrender." Catching the glare in Two Moons eyes, he added quickly, "You may speak with them before you leave." Then, as if in afterthought, "One of your chiefs must stay behind as well." Again eying the glare, he made a casual gesture with his arm, "As a sign of your goodwill, of course."

This was not expected. The chiefs glanced at each other and at the armed soldiers around the room. Someone had to volunteer. No one could demand this of a chief. A murmuring rose among the nineteen. At last White Bull rose.

"I will stay."

"Good!" Bearcoat said, jumping to his feet and pumping White Bull's hand. "You will be my scout and not my prisoner."

Motioning one of the soldiers forward, he signaled the young man to take White Bull away. Then, leaning toward Two Moons, Bearcoat pressed them again.

"I need scouts. We must have an end to this nasty war. If you and your warriors come in, it will be to honored places in my regiment. Your families will be cared for like the families of my own men."

Then came the ultimate appeal of one military man to another.

"You will still be warriors. You will still fight Indians as your ancestors have always done." And knitting his brow over his hard eyes, Bearcoat added, "It is only the white man you will no longer fight. Do not think that I don't understand the honor of men such as yourselves. Only in war is there honor for men." He spoke the words slowly, and though they did not answer him, he knew he had them now.

The late afternoon sun had already lost its battle with the cold air when the chiefs walked from the council building toward the large tent holding the Cheyenne hostages. Joy and sorrow at once overcame

166

the captives. While the women bemoaned their fate and that of their race, the children approached the chiefs who stood impassive, fearful of showing any emotion. One of the Cheyenne chiefs picked up a small child tenderly but kept his face motionless the whole time. When the chiefs inquired after their health, the women assured them the soldiers treated them well.

In the excitement Crooked Nose hung back, her eyes frantically searching among the newcomers crowding into the tent. When Little Hawk did not appear among them she fixed her gaze on the door. As Twin Woman ran on with the details of the capture and the moons that followed, Crooked Nose inched back against the wall, her dark eyes sunken and glassy.

Then the chiefs addressed each captive, taking messages to be delivered to family and friends. When they turned to Crooked Nose, she did not speak but shook her head. She had no message.

Before the men left, Twin Woman pressed them.

"When will they let us go? Why can we not return with you to our people?"

"Bearcoat will not permit it," answered Two Moons. "He will not free you till our people surrender to him."

Twin Woman gasped. "Surrender?" Her eyes sank to the ground in unison with her heart.

Crooked Nose heard the words, too, and she seemed to shrink into the wall.

Finger Woman stepped forward anxiously. "Our people will never surrender."

"Courage, sisters. We will do what we can."

Two Moons raised his hand in farewell and slowly the chiefs filed out of the tent into the creeping darkness. Once outside the fort, Two Moons assured the waiting warriors that the women and children were well. Wooden Leg was greatly relieved for his sister.

Before daybreak, the chiefs and warriors gathered their things and prepared to head for the mouth of the Little Powder River where Calf and the Cheyenne waited anxiously for news. In the big tent in the fort, everyone still slept, everyone but Crooked Nose. Soon dawn would appear and with it yet another day like the last and the one before the last.

Crooked Nose did not think of Little Hawk now. Because he did not come with the others, because he sent no word, because he had not come all these moons, she shut him from her mind, believing he no longer cared for her. It was the future she thought of now—the days that stretched before her in the great tent, the useless days with nothing to fill the time. Her people's surrender was the best that could happen now, and that was the worst.

Crooked Nose thought of her friend Calf as she stared into the emptiness—strong brave Calf, who always knew what to do better than the men with their proud false faces. How different she and Calf were and how much she wanted to be like Calf. She knew Calf would never surrender, that she would never see Calf again. And her own family? They, too, would not surrender, and she would never see them again. A sinking hollowness filled her body, but tonight the sobs did not come.

Crooked Nose felt strangely quiet in her despair. What would Calf do if she were here? Crooked Nose knew the answer before she thought of the question. Slowly her hand groped in the darkness, creeping across the floor next to her pallet. Then her fingers dug into the packed earth till they touched the white people's cold metal. Methodically she pushed away the dirt on all sides.

Without rising, she lifted the small pistol from the ground. As her soiled fingers closed about the handle and trigger, the image of her dear brother, Wooden Leg, giving her the pistol a long time ago, flashed through her mind. A tiny smile broke the straight line between her lips. And although she tried hard not to remember, she thought of Little Hawk holding her tightly as they danced around the great fire.

Outside the faintest light of first dawn hovered over the sleeping fort. In the heavy silence, the gunshot sounded like a cannon shattering the darkness.

Calf had already begun to stir in her bed when a cold scream pierced through her brain, like a great winter icicle. She bolted to a sitting position, gasping.

"What is it?" whispered the vigilant Coyote, home at last from the hunt.

Calf clutched her forehead, breathing heavy and fast.

"What is it?" he asked again, searching the dim morning light.

"Crooked Nose . . ." Calf gasped. "Something has happened to Crooked Nose."

That day, as Calf and the others still waited for news from the peace delegation to Bearcoat, a group of Indians arrived from Spotted Tail's reservation. With them came the great Brule chief himself, Spotted Tail. They carried yet another set of terms for surrender, this time from Three Stars, now based at Fort Robinson.

When Spotted Tail saw the wretched condition of the Cheyenne, he renewed his appeal that they surrender. He told them the reservation Indians were well fed and well treated. No one had been punished for fighting the soldiers in the past. All they had to do was turn themselves in to Three Stars and surrender their weapons and horses.

"For what?" Spotted Tail was asked by a belligerent Black Coyote.

"For a reservation of your own in the north," was the reply.

"Did Three Stars promise this?" someone in the crowd asked.

"He promised to use his influence with the Great White Father in Washington who is his friend," Spotted Tail continued.

After bringing him to the council lodge, the chiefs spoke to their Brule brother for a long time. When finished, Spotted Tail gave them gifts from Three Stars. After he left, the chiefs agreed to make no decision until the delegation to Bearcoat returned.

Calf grew more uneasy with each passing day. She sensed a mood of defeat in the camp. She understood that Three Stars and Bearcoat each wanted the credit for bringing the Indians to the reservation. Each would pressure the Cheyenne until they surrendered.

Since Black Coyote had returned from the hunt and learned of the peace delegation to Bearcoat, he was moody and depressed. Little Hawk had frantically ridden after the chiefs when he learned of their departure for the soldier fort on the Elk River. But days had passed since the chiefs left and Calf suspected Little Hawk would meet them returning from the fort, too late to see Crooked Nose. Worst of all, the moon drew near for her child to be delivered, and Calf worried about the timing.

When at last the delegation returned from Bearcoat, the tension and grief mounted. A somber, tight-lipped Little Hawk rode into camp first, with a bundled corpse strapped on his horse. Too late to join the delegation into the fort, he had met the chiefs returning from their mission, carrying his beloved Crooked Nose. Now he rode with her, bringing her back to her people. The news of Crooked Nose's suicide stunned Calf and the whole camp and their despair deepened. Still Bearcoat held the other hostages, including a new one, White Bull.

Word that none would be set free unless the Cheyenne surrendered deeply grieved their families and friends. And the terms of surrender were no better than those of Three Stars. Weapons and horses must

171

be surrendered, but without these the old life of the hunt was dead.

Buffalo Calf Road went directly back to her lodge after seeing the lifeless body of her friend and hearing the news. Sitting on her bed, Calf wept bitterly—first for Crooked Nose, but then for herself and those who still lived. Calf tried to calm herself, but the tears flowed uncontrollably. It was not like her, she knew, to act in this way. Yet the past few months had drained her—not just because of what had happened, she thought. It was the unborn child who weighed on her spirit, as it weighed on her body.

As Calf sat sobbing on her bed, Black Coyote came in and approached hesitantly. He put his hand gently on her shoulder without speaking a word. The Coyote's touch had a strangely calming effect. The sobs eased and the Coyote held her tightly. As Calf stopped crying, the two lay back on the buffalo robe bed, still holding each other. As they clung together, their small lodge shut out the bickering and arguing, and they drew strength from each other for a few quiet moments.

Meanwhile the old men chiefs held council to decide whether to surrender. When they could not agree, the decision went out that each Cheyenne must choose what course to take. For Buffalo Calf Road and Black Coyote there was no choice. But most people talked and argued among themselves for two days.

Those in favor of surrender cited their destitute condition. That was bad, but worse, they said, was the

172

knowledge that the army would never leave them in peace, would never allow them to recover their lost wealth. To be hounded in all four seasons of time—this awaited all who refused to surrender. A sense of tired hopelessness pervaded the camp.

Still some pleaded hope and courage in the old ways. They pointed to the false security and dependency of reservation life. They berated those who spoke of scouting for the army: Surrendering was bad enough, but to help the enemy kill friends revealed a bad heart. Better to be hungry and free than to be well fed and imprisoned, argued Calf, the Coyote, and others. Look at the great Sitting Bull and Crazy Horse, they said. Both had long argued against surrender. Sitting Bull had gone to the Grandmother's country far to the north rather than surrender.

But the points on both sides were all old points, and in the end Calf knew it was not the arguments that decided anything but the hidden feelings of those who argued.

Calf sensed from the beginning that the sentiment for surrender would prevail. What shocked her was how few finally refused to go in. Including herself, Black Coyote, and Little Seeker, thirty-four people would stay out, and ten of these were children. Strangest of all, Calf found herself in a small band of resisters of which the highest-ranking chief was Last Bull, who was out of favor now and blamed for the many deaths in the winter attack of Bad Hand.

It struck Calf as ironic that she found herself struggling to preserve the old way of life with the person who represented in her mind the worst of that old way. To her the nomadic hunt meant endurance, freedom, and kinship with nature, but to Last Bull hunting and raiding meant power, status, and conquest of nature. Calf killed, when she had to, in order to survive, and she mourned each death. But Last Bull killed from a false need to prove his manhood, and he took great pleasure from it.

Most of those going to the reservation decided to surrender to Three Stars at Fort Robinson, which was next to Red Cloud Agency, the Lakota part of the Great Sioux Reservation under an agent appointed by the Great White Father in Washington. Many were familiar with the reasonably good conditions at the agency and wanted to join their Lakota friends there. And of course, Three Stars had promised to intercede for them with the Great White Father so they might have a reservation of their own. A small group, including Two Moons and the families of White Bull and the other hostages, headed for Bearcoat's fort on the Elk River.

Some would have stayed out but could not: Little Finger Nail, again following his beloved Singing Cloud, whose old father insisted on going in; Old Grandmother, wanting desperately to end her days on the open plains but unable to care for herself; and Leaf, forced by family ties back to a life she despised.

When the time came, Calf pressed Leaf's hand in farewell, but neither could speak and they fought back the tears. As the crooked line of travelers pulled out, one by one, a terrible gloom filled Calf's breast. Motherless little Runs Ahead, always still now, passed with her father. The sullen Bear Rope, followed by his sad-faced wife, his daughter, and son-in-law, spoke to no one as he rode.

Next came Red Bird and his uncle, Great Eyes, still carrying his ancient shield, saved somehow from Bad Hand's plundering. Spotted Dear rode close next to Old Grandmother and looked often at Yellow Bird, nearby with her aunt. He seemed not to notice that she glanced often at Dull Knife's party, where Little Hump sat on his mount near his older brother.

Feather on Head and Quiet One, wives of Little Wolf, quickly and efficiently gathered their things. But Pretty Walker looked as unhappy as Leaf about going, Calf thought. The injustice of woman's position, dependent on the decisions of men, angered her.

Little Hawk, downcast and indifferent, still mourning the loss of Crooked Nose, rode out with Little Wolf's son, Woodenthigh. Even Whetstone, pulled by his friendship with Black Coyote, but seeing that everyone was going in, left. His leaving hurt the Coyote, Calf knew.

The widow Iron Teeth, surrounded by her children, rode a horse pulling a travois piled with meager belongings. Iron Teeth's plight especially troubled Calf. The woman had come full circle, riding back to the reservation she had left to recapture the old life, but now as a widow. Calf felt bitter at the sight.

175

However, of all the emotions welling in her this morning, none hurt more than the sight of Brave One herding her little ones to her horse. Calf ran to her dear friend and tearfully embraced her. When the last of the party rode from the nearly deserted camp, it seemed to Calf she was losing her family for a second time. A terrible loneliness settled over her.

The small band was isolated now—friends and relatives gone, the sacred objects of the tribe gone, all gone where the old men chiefs had chosen to go. Nothing remained but the big sky hanging over them and the empty plains surrounding them. The little group clung together like the last humans in the world, mocked by the presence of one yet unborn.

Only five families moved with the band. The rest were young warriors, unmarried. Already the Moon of the Greening Grass was on them, but the last of winter's cold still lingered over the high plains as they moved in search of the game. Only five lodges stood in the small camp now, for most of the young men slept in the open or made lean-tos. Of the unmarried men, only Wooden Leg slept in a lodge, having been invited by Last Bull, who still felt grateful toward the young man for helping his family escape the attack on Old Bear's camp.

Calf knew from the beginning that it would be hard to survive with so few. Game was scarce and the men left often to hunt. Camp had to move frequently, always with watchful eyes for soldiers or raiding Crows and Shoshoni. There were no scouts now to

176

warn them of danger. It was hard work the whole time, with little rest and less to show for their labors.

Not many sleeps passed before the time came for Calf's child to be delivered. When Calf woke Black Coyote to get help, he led Little Seeker by the hand and rushed from their lodge. The starless black night made it hard to see as he groped his way to the lodge of Many Colored Braids. His wife, Long Feather, knew some medicine and she would help Calf. She came quickly, but the child did not.

It was a hard delivery. Calf sensed a reluctance in the infant to enter the world. She understood. When at last Long Feather dragged the baby from its warm home, a loud cry of objection cut the silence as the cold air wrapped itself about the child.

"Is it well?" Calf asked weakly, as Long Feather searched the baby's body.

"Yes, yes," the woman assured her. "It's a boy."

This last bit of news did not matter to Calf. She shrugged. To bring any child into the world now was all that mattered, and Calf was not happy. She lay on her bed exhausted, physically and mentally.

When the Coyote came to see the baby, Calf forced a smile. In the dim firelight she caught the Coyote's furrowed brow and tight lips as he gazed at the child. He was worried too, Calf knew, though he tried not to show it.

After a while Long Feather gently motioned for him to leave. She would stay with Calf and the baby tonight; the Coyote could join Little Seeker in her

177

lodge. Black Coyote looked at the baby again, sleeping now, and taking Calf's hand, he kissed her on the forehead and left.

As Long Feather moved softly about the lodge, Calf's heavy eyelids cut off the firelight and left everything dark. After awhile a tiny point of light appeared in the distance. Calf strained to see it and when she could not, she inched forward, moving toward it. Darkness surrounded her and she felt uneasy. The light was all there was, so she started to walk faster, trying to reach its source. But it never seemed to move away or to get closer.

Calf reached out her hands, grabbing for the light. In her groping Calf struck something beside her. She stopped. Feeling in the darkness around her, she panicked. Above her and beside her a wall of crumbling earth arched her path. She could move back into the blackness or forward toward the light, but otherwise she was imprisoned in a small earthen tunnel.

Calf started to run, to call out. But only the lonely echo of her own voice came back, and the dot of light got no closer. Terrified and gasping for breath, she raced for a long time through the narrow tunnel as hunks of earth fell on her. Suddenly the point of light began getting smaller. Faster and faster she raced until the tunnel went black.

A baby cried out. Long Feather was reaching for the infant when Calf opened her eyes, moist from the sweat drenching her forehead. Her heart pounded and her mouth burned with dryness. She looked and looked before she fully realized where she was.

It was almost morning and Calf did not sleep again that night, though her body ached with tiredness. Soldiers had been spotted by the hunters the day before and Calf knew they would have to move at daybreak.

Shortly after dawn the other women arrived to help dismantle Calf's lodge. Black Coyote prepared a travois for her and the baby. After they had eaten, the small band again inched its way to nowhere, more slowly now because of the mother and infant.

By the time the Moon of the Strawberries arrived, green grass for the horses was plentiful. The Cheyenne were not so fortunate. Many sleeps passed without enough food to eat. Everyone was thinner now and the children sometimes cried from hunger. Without game, there was not only a lack of food but also of skins to renew their dress, lodges, beds, and other necessities. They had to be very careful when they moved. Cabins of white people seemed to be springing up everywhere, like cactus flowers after a spring rain.

As conditions got worse, Black Coyote grew more belligerent toward whites. He would have stolen their cattle and driven them from the land, but Wooden Leg and the other warriors cautioned against it. It would alert the soldiers and bring the army against them. The Coyote backed down when he thought of the children, but he hated the white spiders with a simmering rage that steamed and bubbled under the surface.

Black Coyote slept little these days and his sharp

eyes grew darker as he hunted without success. When Calf went hungry there was not enough milk for the baby, and Little Seeker hung listlessly about all day. The Coyote was frantic. Had they come this far to starve to death? They lived now on what berries and roots the women could gather, but their stomachs still grumbled.

One morning before dawn Black Coyote rose from his sleepless bed. Calf watched anxiously as he dressed quickly in the darkness and disappeared through the door. The hungry camp still slept when the lone rider galloped away.

The sun already stood part way up the sky when the Coyote stopped his hard ride and slowed his horse to a walk. To his right the tall sandstone cliffs glistened red against a turquoise sky. He dismounted and, leading his horse, slowly picked his way through the prickly pear cactus. As he cleared a rise, a cabin built of neatly hewn logs suddenly popped into view far in the distance. It stood with a twisted ribbon of smoke reaching to the sky, tucked in a small valley between the sandstone bluffs and rolling brown hills. In all directions a small herd of cattle roamed the open range, nibbling at the sparse patches of green sticking out of the sandy earth.

Quickly the Coyote's eyes searched the valley till they rested on a steer far away from the house, feeding among some junipers near the rise where he stood. His mind rapidly assessed the situation: no one around, animal not too large to get back, spot hidden from view. His hand instinctively touched the gun in his belt, but he thought better of it. Tying his horse to a shrub, he crawled down the rise to the juniper clump. The animal lazily turned to look at the intruder, then went on chomping its grass.

Swiftly Black Coyote raised his knife in the air and plunged it into the animal's neck. Again and again he stabbed the beast till its anguished grunts and whines stopped and it fell on the dry earth in a pool of its own blood. Moving mechanically now, the Coyote turned the warm carcass on its back and slit its underbelly. He worked quickly, hidden behind the juniper trees, skinning the animal. When the hide finally let go of its last hold on the body, Black Coyote spread the large piece on the ground. Hunk by hunk he cut the choice parts of the meat and piled them on the skin till it could hold no more. Then he wrapped the hide around the pieces and tied the four corners into two knots. After he had dragged the precious bundle over the rise, he loaded it on the back of his horse, tying it securely. Then he crawled back to the remains of the steer, and clawing at the earth with his hands, he buried the rest. The sun blazed high in the sky when he began his journey back.

It took longer to return to camp than to ride out. With the heavy burden of food he could not push his horse as much. Still, it was daylight when he rode into camp, and the children, sensing something, ran to meet him. A ripple of elation spread over the tiny camp circle when they saw the bundle, especially

181

since several of the men had already returned empty handed.

Wooden Leg came forward to praise the hunter, then realized the nature of the catch. He looked at Black Coyote and shook his head.

"Don't worry," the Coyote assured him. "The carcass is buried. Even the vultures will not find it. They will never know." Then, almost as if he wished they could know, he added, his voice rising, "They have driven away our game and taken our land. They must know we will never leave them in peace."

Just then Calf emerged from their lodge and he went to meet her. That night, despite some uneasiness over the incident, everyone in camp feasted and laughed for the first time in many sleeps.

Yellow Hair dared to dream again.

"Soon our friends will leave the reservation and join us. Then things will be as they were."

Some nodded assent, but Calf knew it would never be like that again. The feast was just a reprieve. In the days that followed only the old hunger returned. There was some sickness in the camp too, especially among the children, and it became harder to move about.

Finally Chief Last Bull called the men together. He was convinced that the other Indians would not rejoin them. Without them there were not enough scouts to find the buffalo herds. Without them it was impossible to protect the camp from attack. Others were convinced that without the sacred objects, Maheo and the Sacred Persons would not look favorably on them.

182

Most were homesick for family and friends and found the separation from their people as painful as the hunger. A few still argued for patience. Yellow Hair, Growing Dog, and Medicine Wolf tried to convince the others to hold out till their people left the reservation.

Black Coyote sat listening to the men. The talk of surrender angered him, but he was torn. When he thought of the children, of baby and Little Seeker and the others, his heart ached. The children could not hold out. They became more sickly as the days passed. Still, how could he ever go to a reservation? Rage at the thought of it made him dizzy. And his promise to Calf . . . Black Coyote said nothing. He did not know what to say.

Finally a half-hearted decision was made. White Bird and Yellow Eagle would go together to the reservation and secretly find out the conditions there.

Eight sleeps later they returned. There was no sign that anyone would leave the reservation just now. Everything seemed fine there. Food and blankets were plenty. Nobody had been punished for past offenses against whites. Certainly it was better than starving to death.

When Black Coyote heard the news, he walked back to their lodge where Calf sat nursing the baby. He told her what White Bird had said, searching her dark sunken eyes as he spoke, not knowing what to expect.

"I will keep my promise to you," he added gently when he finished.

Calf reached for his hand and touched it softly, so softly her hand seemed to have vanished.

"No," she said wearily. "We cannot let the children die. We cannot."

She sat silent a long time. Then she spoke again.

"We stayed to preserve the old ways, to be free. We're not free when we must steal from white people to live. We're not free when our children starve. There are no old ways apart from our people. The Cheyenne are a great family. But our family is lost to us."

Calf looked at the ground. She seemed so strange to him.

"If it were only you and I . . ." she said. "You know I would die before I surrender. But the children . . . I cannot kill the children."

She frightened him. Calf was not herself. He had never known her to be so defeated. It was the baby. Since the baby was born . . .

The next morning the hungry band piled what little they had onto horses and travois as they prepared to leave. Yellow Hair, Growing Dog, and Medicine Wolf decided to try staying out a little longer. They still hoped others would come. As the tattered line pulled out, the Coyote lingered awhile with the three. Leaving was the hardest thing he had ever done.

For three sleeps they traveled. Almost no food remained now and the children moaned with hunger. On the fourth day they saw a house in the distance. Little Horse could bear the cries of the children no longer.

"I will ask them for food. For the children . . ." he said.

Black Coyote ground his teeth. Beg food from whites? But he too heard the children cry and he said nothing.

When they approached the cabin, Wooden Leg offered to go with Little Horse. Calf watched, her brow knit, as the two dismounted and climbed over a rail fence circling the house.

After they knocked, two white men appeared at the door. The men looked badly frightened so Wooden Leg made peace signs to them. Using gestures, Little Horse asked for food. The men seemed to understand and they returned quickly with some beef meat and coffee and sugar. The Indians were glad and they motioned their appreciation to the nervous white men. But the cabin dwellers did not understand what Wooden Leg meant when he said his band's hearts were good toward them.

That night the hot sweet coffee worked its magic in the empty stomachs of the Cheyenne, and Calf and the others slept more soundly than they had in a long time.

Toward the end of the fifth day of travel, the smoke from hundreds of Indian lodges appeared on the horizon across the White Water River. The camp stood next to the water, nestled in the thick groves of cottonwoods. Great white clouds hung low in the sky as the bright sun peered through the fluff at the newcomers.

185

Calf strained to see and a rush of nostalgia swept over her. For a moment it seemed she was home. Then she saw the soldier fort next to the camp.

CHAPTER 6

U p and down the twisting river, great camps of Oglala, Arapaho, and Cheyenne stood. There were many soldiers as well, in their own camp. When the anxious little band approached the river, the soldier chiefs came forward to meet them and shook hands with Last Bull and some of the men. Black Coyote hung back, his face tight and sullen.

Some of the Indians recognized White Hat among the soldier chiefs. They knew him to be fair and kind and they trusted him, though they also knew he was not a big soldier chief. More than any other bluecoat, White Hat understood sign talk, so he spoke to the Cheyenne now. He greeted them, told them they were welcome, and assured them food was plentiful as his eyes passed over the thin shabby people. Then came the order they feared.

"Everyone must turn in their horses now. And you men must give up your guns."

Instantly Calf's hand flew to the pistol in her belt. She leaned forward on her horse and let the folds of her cape fall over the weapon as her fingers pushed it deep behind the belt. At the same time a muttering arose among the men. Last Bull motioned them to be quiet. Then he dismounted and, taking his rifle from his saddle, handed it to a soldier standing with White Hat. The others reluctantly began to do the same.

Suddenly Black Coyote jerked back on the reins of his horse and the animal lurched up on its hind legs.

"No," he shouted. "I will not give up my gun."

Three mounted Indians dressed in soldier uniforms broke from the bluecoat line, riding straight for Black Coyote. Swiftly the Coyote aimed his gun at them and cocked the hammer. Last Bull rushed to Coyote's side, pushing the others out of his way as he moved. Then he knocked the cocked gun aside and bellowed.

"Are you crazy?" Then more quietly, "Look at them. Who will you fight? All of them? Fire a shot and they will kill us all."

Black Coyote's eyes flashed and burned, but again the rage was pushed inside, deep in his bowels where it would stay imprisoned, guarded but growing.

"Give me the gun," Last Bull urged. And knowing how to get it, he added, "Quickly, before you get the children killed."

The Coyote let him take the gun and Last Bull handed it to a soldier. Then Black Coyote slid from his horse, but instead of handing the reins to the soldier, he let them fall and turning his back, defiantly walked away.

Calf sat still watching the scene, not moving an eyelid. But something snapped inside her, like a branch bent to the ground by a heavy snow that stays a while, then springs back.

"What have we done?" she thought.

When Wooden Leg turned in his rifle, the soldier looked at it a long time. Then he walked over to White Hat and they whispered about the weapon. Wooden Leg held his breath. He had taken the rifle from a soldier in the big fight on the Little Bighorn. No one else in the small band had such a gun. White Hat examined it carefully, and other soldier chiefs approached to look. Finally White Hat walked up to Wooden Leg.

"Where did you get this gun?"

Wooden Leg pretended not to understand the question at first, but White Hat persisted in sign talk so clear he could not play ignorant for long. Wooden Leg told the truth.

"It was during the great battle on the Little Bighorn. I seized it from a soldier near the river early in the fight."

Many had taken such guns from Long Hair's men and it puzzled Wooden Leg that these bluecoats seemed so surprised. He concluded that other Indians must not have turned in their rifles. White Hat spoke again to the other soldier chiefs, then turned to Wooden Leg and made more signs.

"You are a brave man. No soldier will harm you. Do not be afraid." Then he shook Wooden Leg's hand firmly.

When at last the band was allowed to move, the sun hung low in the sky. But the campfires of the

188

Cheyenne burned high that night and everyone celebrated the return of the brave ones. There was more food than they could eat, for all their friends brought some. The children smiled again as they ate and chattered with their friends.

Leaf, Brave One, Pretty Walker, Old Grandmother, Comes Together, Chicken Woman, and all her other friends came to greet Calf and bring gifts for the new baby. It was good, but it was not the same. Calf kept looking at the soldier fort outlined in the darkness against the moonlit sky. All the while she felt the pain of loss inside, like the ache she had felt that winter long ago when she lost her parents.

The next morning wagons came from the agency buildings with supplies for the band. Food, clothing, and blankets rested in piles as two men were chosen to distribute the goods to everyone. Calf could not believe this generosity from whites. Bluecoats walked about, but no one seemed frightened of them.

"Generosity!" Black Coyote scoffed later. "They have our horses and our guns. This is payment!"

Later that morning the Coyote, reunited with Whetstone, began moving through the camps. Whetstone seemed quiet and uneasy. When the Coyote pressed him, Whetstone revealed what he knew. For some time the soldier chiefs had been asking the Cheyenne if they would go south to join the Southern Cheyenne in Indian Territory. The bluecoats argued they could join their relatives there and be as one tribe again, as in the old days. But the Indians knew that was not the real reason. It was no secret that the settlers pouring across the northern plains wanted the Indians out. Whetstone had also heard that the talking wires told of the great white chief's decision to send as many Indians south as possible, including other Indians being sent there from many parts of the country.

Black Coyote turned red when he heard.

"You didn't tell us when we came yesterday?" Black Coyote accused. "Why?"

"It would have spoiled your homecoming." Whetstone replied sheepishly. "What could you have done? Besides, it's just talk. It may never happen."

When Calf heard, she froze. Then the old anger rose in her.

"So again we are betrayed with false promises. A reservation of our own in the home country! How do they feel?" she asked, gesturing at the camp and thinking bitterly that only the Cheyenne had no reservation of their own.

For a long time Calf and Black Coyote went about talking to others, trying to get at the truth. It became clear that not more than a handful of the Cheyenne people favored going south to Indian Territory. Almost everyone wanted desperately to stay in the north country. The reasons were always the same. This was home: the awesome, rugged, challenging high plains with its many rivers and streams. They and their ancestors were of the land; they knew and loved it and were part of it in life and death. The sacred mountain, Bear Butte, stood in the north, giving its power to all

190

who came for renewal. Besides, many Cheyenne had traveled south to visit friends and relatives there. They found the sticky, moist, hot weather unbearable and stifling, and they seldom stayed long. They had also heard their southern relatives tell of the absence of game in Indian Territory and the total dependence on government food and supplies.

"A death, not a life," Calf concluded in her circle of friends. "What do the chiefs say?"

"They can say nothing," came the answer from Little Finger Nail. "They are not consulted."

"Not consulted?" Black Coyote repeated incredulously.

"No," the Nail answered bitterly. "The bluecoats only speak to Standing Elk."

"Standing Elk?" Calf interrupted.

"Standing Elk!" Leaf repeated, her voice rising. "He's urging everyone to agree and go south. Standing Elk, who would not hear of surrender two moons ago. And it's clear why. The soldier chiefs pour gifts over him. He scouts for them now."

"Forty-four chiefs of the Cheyenne," Wooden Leg added indignantly, "and one pretends to speak for all! It destroys the authority of our people to have an Indian picked by soldiers speak for us—and a bought Indian at that."

Little Finger Nail, grown tough and cynical now, shrugged his shoulders. "What authority? Without guns no one has authority in the white people's world. And this is the white people's world."

191

"We have our Sacred Hat, and the Sweet Medicine bundle. They are most important. They will save us," Wooden Leg said with confidence.

The Nail looked straight at Wooden Leg, his eyes penetrating deep. "Did the Sacred Hat save us when Bad Hand massacred our people? It was there. The Sacred Arrows were there too—all the sacred objects were there. Did the Sacred Hat save the Cheyenne babies in the flight from Bad Hand? It was there. Did the Sacred Hat save our people from poverty and hunger and surrender? It was there."

"Do not blame the sacred objects," Wooden Leg protested.

Little Finger Nail threw up his arms.

"When times are good, the sacred things are responsible, and they are praised. When times are bad, they are not responsible. No, the sacred objects are never responsible—they are things, capable of nothing." He paused and thought a moment. "Or maybe they are responsible, or Maheo is. But if they are, then they act by whim, without sense or meaning, and they play with us, like the wind plays with the helpless tree, pushing its branches here and there."

He fell silent. Calf stared at the young man. Leaf, Wooden Leg, Black Coyote, and the others sat in mute shock at the words. She had never heard anyone speak so darkly of the holy things, but his words roused something in her, and Calf thought for a fleeting moment that she felt the same way but could never have uttered the words, even to herself.

The next day Standing Elk strode among the people. "Everyone get ready. Tomorrow the soldiers take us from here."

Buffalo Calf Road and the other Cheyenne were enraged. They milled about all day, frantic to find a way out. The old chiefs met, the council met, the warrior societies met. But after all, there was nothing they could do.

Some guns, including Calf's, had been hidden from the army. Yet next to the guns of the soldiers, who today suddenly sprang up everywhere, they were pebbles against a mountain. Even if they all had guns, without horses nothing could happen. A tripling of the guard around the army ponies did not go unnoticed by the Indians. Even the great Crazy Horse, pushed to come onto the reservation by the sufferings of his own people, could not help the Cheyenne now.

The old men chiefs of the Cheyenne tried to appeal to White Hat. They sensed that he did not approve of the decision, but he was not a big soldier chief. When they went to Three Stars and Bad Hand, the two assured them that if they did not like it in the south they could return north at any time.

So, only three short sleeps after the starving band came in, Calf and the others found themselves packed on horses and wagons, headed on a great journey to a strange place far away. It was almost the end of the Moon of the Strawberries when nearly a thousand unwilling Cheyenne left the place called Fort Robinson by whites.

A very tall, restless, energetic soldier chief with many men guarded them on the long journey. Calf thought him strange looking. Dark, bushy, wiry hair stood high on his head over a face covered with a thick moustache and very long whiskers. He never stayed still, always organizing, directing, stopping, or beginning something. Calf heard the soldiers call him Lawton, but the Indians called him Tall White Man.

This hairy man behaved kindly to the Cheyenne. He did not push the march, so they moved slowly and camped often, sleeping in soldier tents at night. The Cheyenne had been given their horses back. Food was plentiful since a herd of cattle and wagons of food followed them. Yet the Cheyenne chiefs asked Tall White Man if they could hunt for wild meat that Indians liked better. He listened and agreed.

Thirty warriors at a time were allowed to hunt with rifles and were given five bullets each by the soldiers. The gesture made their hearts good toward Tall White Man. Buffalo and antelope still roamed some of the high lands, especially at the headwaters of rivers where few white people had yet come.

Calf watched the Coyote closely, worried about the effect of the forced journey on him. But oddly, there were days on the march when Black Coyote seemed revived, not happy, but revived. On his own horse again, riding in the hills empty of cabins, hunting in the old way, the Coyote brought meat to Calf. He seemed almost to forget being a prisoner at those moments. He seemed, too, to forget that the cool high lands would fly north and the hot flat lands would replace them.

Calf often rode beside Leaf and they both marveled at the kindness and friendliness of the soldiers. Were these different bluecoats than those who had attacked Old Bear's camp or the camps on the Little Bighorn and Powder River? Or were they the same men, just following different orders? Leaf and Calf wished they knew.

Buffalo Calf Road thought a lot about white people these days. Who were they? What did they believe? She wondered most about the invisible white women. Where were they when these things happened? Did they approve of what their men did to Indians? Did these women ever try to stop them? Did white men in council ignore women as Indian men did? No white woman had ever hurt her or her people, at least not that she knew.

Calf thought she would like to meet a white sister and talk to her. Then she thought it odd that the word sister—*nahkahim*—had popped into her mind when she thought of white women. The word brother never came to mind when she thought of white men.

Along the way a soldier pointed to a house in the distance and told the Indians that the wife of Long Hair, called General Custer by the soldiers, had once lived in that house. Again Calf wondered.

After sixty-nine sleeps they camped beside a soldier fort. Calf soon learned they were near the reservation that was their destination. The agent from the reservation came to the Cheyenne with an interpreter. The two men went to each tent and wrote the names of the men, merely counting the women and children as so many heads. Then the agent told the Cheyenne that they must turn in all the guns before coming onto the reservation. This meant the guns given them by Tall White Man's soldiers, for no one knew of the guns still hidden by the Indians.

Little Wolf went immediately to Tall White Man. He asked that they be allowed to keep the guns for hunting and protection. The soldier chief explained that he could not allow that. But other chiefs joined Little Wolf and pleaded with Tall White Man. At last he agreed.

When Tall White Man finally left them in Indian Territory and began the long journey back to Fort Robinson, a sinking feeling spread among the Cheyenne. It seemed strange to feel that way about a soldier, but his kindness would never be forgotten.

After the Cheyenne arrived on the reservation, many of their relatives among the Southern Cheyenne rode out to greet them. Buffalo Calf Road was seated on her horse when she spotted her brother and Pemmican Road approaching by horseback in the distance. She raced her horse toward the couple and three riders leapt from their mounts, embracing in joy.

Pemmican began to cry at the sight of Calf, huge uncontrollable sobs. Then they saw the baby hanging in its cradle from Calf's saddle and a great excitement broke out. At that point Little Seeker and Black

Coyote joined them and the noise of rejoicing rose anew. It was a happy moment for Calf, the happiest in many moons, worth, for an instant at least, the pain of being forced south.

The Northern Cheyenne set up camp near their southern relatives. Calf and her people lived in canvas tents now and the camp circle looked strange. Already the Moon of the Ripe Plums had arrived and the worst of the south's summer heat with it. But in the first days the newcomers thought little about it for all the feasting and rejoicing provided by their old friends.

Soon, however, the rejoicing ended. The humid sticky heat never let up, night or day. Calf quickly discovered, as they all did, that among the trees along the riverbed swarms of tiny biting insects multiplied. Like attacking bluecoats, they flew in formation against the Indians, sucking their blood.

Furthermore, a new kind of sickness struck the northerners, and one by one they fell ill. Chills, fever, aching bones, and coughing wracked their bodies, made worse by the terrible heat and dampness. Sometimes a doctor came from the agency to help the sick, but with almost no medicine for the malarial disease he could do little. Even the powers of Bridge and Medicine Woman came to nothing. During the first moon in the south, the strange sickness hit many of the newcomers.

One day, Little Seeker ran sobbing into the tent. Calf grabbed the child and held her tight.

197

"What is it?" she asked anxiously.

"Runs Ahead . . ." Her sobs broke the words.

"What about Runs Ahead? Tell me, Little Seeker!"

"Her father . . . her father is dead. From the sickness."

The crying grew more intense. Calf clutched the child.

"Runs Ahead is all alone now . . . all alone," her daughter cried.

Calf sat Little Seeker in a corner of the tent next to the baby and, kissing the child's forehead, she whispered, "Wait here."

Quickly Calf ran from the tent. The blistering sun stood high over the parched dry earth, striking her as she stepped outside. She had begun to hate that sun. It was not the sun of the north, with its warm soothing rays that healed the earth and made things grow. This sun sent killing spears against the earth and its living things.

When she arrived at the tent of Runs Ahead, the women were already inside, quickly preparing the body for burial. Runs Ahead was nowhere in sight, but Brave One met Calf at the door.

"I've seen to it, Calf. She's at my tent."

"But you have the others . . ." Calf protested.

"And you have the baby to care for. No, I can do it." Putting her arm around Calf's shoulder, she added, "Don't worry. It will be alright."

One afternoon during the Moon of the Yellow Leaves, a lone rider raced into camp. It was Wooden

Leg, who breathlessly rushed to Little Wolf as a small crowd gathered.

"I was at the agency. The talking wires have spoken today." Looking very solemn, Wooden Leg said, "The soldiers have killed Crazy Horse."

A quiver ran through the crowd. A terrible sinking feeling struck Calf.

"Crazy Horse? Dead?" Little Wolf repeated incredulously. "What happened?"

"The talking wires say he was making trouble. He was trying to escape while being dragged to prison. They say a soldier stabbed him to prevent it."

An ominous hush fell over Calf and the crowd. They knew what it meant when the army said an Indian was making trouble.

So many emotions poured over them: sorrow for the death of a brother, foreboding at hearing of a thwarted escape, a terrible emptiness for the times in the future when they would need Crazy Horse and he would never again be there. They mourned for him, but mostly they mourned for themselves.

As they walked back to their lodge, Calf said to the Coyote, "Crazy Horse is dead and Sitting Bull is in the Grandmother's country far away to the north. No one is left but us."

In the weeks that followed, the white man's fever attacked Black Coyote as well. Calf tended him as he lay shaking from chills, but soon she and the baby became ill too. With the help of Leaf, who came every day, Little Seeker tended the family as best she could.

They were among the fortunate. Though left with a terrible weakness and recurring bouts of the fever, in time they got better.

Meanwhile, other troubles emerged along with the dreaded sickness. The amount of food given the Northern Cheyenne decreased. Often there was no food. The warriors tried to hunt on the reservation, mostly with bows and arrows and the few guns from Tall White Man, but except for an occasional rabbit or eagle, nothing could be found. When they tried to slip off the reservation to hunt for food, soldiers pursued them and forced them back. In desperation they sometimes killed stray cattle that wandered onto the reservation or left the herd when a cattle drive passed through Indian Territory. But when they did this, the whole tribe suffered the punishment: even less food and a constant guard of soldiers everywhere. Hunger soon became part of their lives.

Worse yet, trouble developed between the Northern and Southern Cheyenne. Political differences surfaced. The southerners, at peace for some time, passively accepted their lot, while the northerners still smarted from recent battles. Forty winters of separation saw many cultural changes between them as well. The southerners, having adopted many white ways, looked upon their relatives from the north as wild, almost savage. Sometimes, though they had little themselves, they looked down on these people for their poverty.

Many southerners farmed now, but the warriors

from the high plains scorned this labor as demeaning. Soon the northerners came to suspect that the army rewarded the Southern Cheyenne for their docility with more and better food. Not long after they arrived, the newcomers moved their camp a distance from the Southerners.

This splitting of her people pained Calf more than the hunger. She knew that each small division, each argument, widened to a chasm the misunderstandings among the Cheyenne and strengthened their enemy's hold over them.

At the same time, Calf knew that what divided the Cheyenne was not trivial. It was the difference between despair and hope, between defeat and struggle—between two ways of life. For all the terrible confinement, Calf still knew what she wanted in life and would never settle for this death that posed as life. So each day she talked courage to those around her.

Private troubles came, too.

Yellow Hair, brother of Wooden Leg, and his two companions who stayed out when Last Bull's band surrendered, had not been heard from since they parted. However, not long after the band's arrival in Indian Territory, news came of Yellow Hair's death. Settlers had killed the young man as he hunted along Crow Creek. This, following so soon after the death of Yellow Hair's sister, Crooked Nose, left the family of Wooden Leg desolate.

In the lodge of the angry Bear Rope, the fever struck

him with such severity that everyone feared he would die. At the same time Bear Rope's son, young and strong with a family of his own, fell sick. The agency doctor never came and Medicine Woman's chants and potions failed. For a long time the two lay in their separate lodges, freezing and burning in turn, delirious and uncomprehending.

When his son died, Bear Rope, too, seemed near the end. Comes in Sight Woman was frantic at her mother's grief over the death of her only son and thought her mother could not bear the loss of a husband too, even a bad one. So, though she felt nothing for the sullen violent man who fathered her, Comes in Sight vowed to Maheo that she would cut off her little finger in offering if he lived.

Before the night passed, Bear Rope breathed more easily and the fever broke. When he connected again with the world around him, he heard of the death of his son. In a man such as Bear Rope, even grief turns to rage, and his rage consumed him. He raved like a madman at Maheo, at the Sacred Persons, at the Sacred Objects. When they tried to tell him that Maheo had saved his life because of the vow of Comes in Sight Woman, Bear Rope became livid. The yellow pallor of sickness turned red and the raging voice became a sputtering croak.

"Nothing shall be given to Maheo, nothing!" He was gasping now. "Not a finger, not a prayer. Did he save my son? Did he? No one will bleed for my sickness but the whites." Then, turning his fury on Comes in

Sight Woman, he boomed, "I forbid you to fulfill the vow! I forbid it!"

Comes in Sight lived in terror from that day, not just because of the twisted violent man in her mother's lodge, but because of the vow—the unfulfilled vow.

One day Buffalo Calf Road rode out a distance from camp to hunt for medicinal herbs over the desolate land. She searched close to the rocks, where an occasional plant grew in the sandy earth, out of the glare of the killing sun. A lizard darted from the shade now and then as Calf moved among the rocks, leading her horse by a long rope.

Then, as Calf bent to examine a strange-looking yellow plant, the sound of a horse's whine reached her ears. She stood up immediately, dropping the plant. A bluecoat soldier was approaching from the direction opposite camp. Calf's body stiffened and a cold impassive stare fell over her eyes. Her fingers tightened around the rope tied to her horse. Still the soldier came, moving directly toward her. When his horse was barely two arms' lengths away from Calf, he stopped.

A narrow smile crossed the man's lips and he began to speak. Calf could not understand what he said with his white tongue. But at one point Calf caught a gesture. The bluecoat motioned her onto his horse, the thin smile never leaving his lips. She drew back sharply and turned to leave. The man slid from his horse, the flow of incoherent words rushing out.

Before Calf could mount her horse, the soldier was

on her. His hands clamped down on her shoulders from behind. She could smell the tobacco breath hot against her neck as he pressed against her back. Fear and rage rose in Calf from some deep place in her bowels. Instantly her hand flew to the six-shooter hidden in her belt. When the yellow-haired bluecoat whirled her around, Calf's arm shot out, pointing the gun at his leering face.

The man's jaw dropped and he stumbled backwards. Calf cocked the hammer. The soldier began to gesture frantically. Without flinching, Calf aimed at the man's chest. She wanted to pull the trigger, to destroy the invader. The fear was gone and only a bitter rage boiled in her brain. But instead Calf gestured sharply with the gun, sending the man running to his horse. She never lowered the gun till he had ridden from view.

Suddenly Calf felt very drained. Leaving the small pile of herbs on the sandy ground, she mounted her horse and rode back to camp. She never told the Coyote what had happened lest it push him over some unseen cliff.

For many moons the Cheyenne hung about their soldier lodges. The idleness crushed their spirit more than the fever sickness. The men could not hunt and the women had no hides to tan, no food to prepare, no skins to sew.

Yet the women still worked hard, but not the old creative work of making a lodge and decorating it with painted scenes, sewing fine moccasins and shirts, or making a thousand tooth dress. Instead they mopped fevered brows, sat all night with the sick, cleaned the messes of disease, and frantically tried to produce meals when no food came.

And without the hunt, the men had nothing to do and no purpose for being. They hung listlessly about camp and in desperation began quarreling with each other and even hitting their wives and children in the white man's way. When the despair got too bad, they took to drinking the white man's firewater and felt better for a while, then much worse.

It was late afternoon toward the end of winter when the Princesses hurried back from the agency store, pale and shaken. Short One asked what happened, but they hung their heads and looked away. Dull Knife pressed them to speak. The oldest Princess, her hair still cropped in mourning for her dead husband, answered first, a silent rage flashing in her eyes.

"A bluecoat came to us. He offered us money to go to the soldier chiefs' beds."

It was all she said, but her fingers worked a rope in her hands, twisting and crushing it from every side.

Dull Knife leapt to his feet and flew to the agency store. The agent claimed he knew nothing. How could it be? They must have misunderstood; yes, that was it, a misunderstanding. When Dull Knife raved on, the agent said he would look into it, assuring Dull Knife it would never happen again.

Yet it did happen again. Not to Dull Knife's daughters—the bluecoats did not make that mistake twice.

But not all the women—starving and frantic to feed their children, looking for medicine to save a loved one dying of the sickness—could say no.

Sometimes, when the man of her lodge learned of her action, he cast her out, hiding his own inability to seek revenge from himself by burying the sight of her. Some of these women remained the pay women of the soldiers, but two of them, as helpless as small orphans, sought out Brave One and she took them into her lodge.

When Calf heard what Brave One had done, she saved a little food each day from her own meager supply and gave it to the two. It was not that Calf condoned what they had done, though she understood their despair. What the Cheyenne men had done by casting out their own women ate at her. She could not forgive them for that.

Calf and Leaf talked together about the women. Leaf was angry, too, at the treatment of the women.

"The soldiers who do these things are never touched," Leaf noted bitterly.

"Our men will not touch them!" Calf replied angrily. "Instead they punish our desperate sisters who were driven to do these things. Our bravest warriors, who would die in battle, will not confront these soldiers. Their false pride eats at them, Leaf. The women are punished because they have gone to the beds of other men."

Calf sat silent for a long while before she spoke again.

"In the end, it's always man's false pride. . . ."

Some days later, as the hot spring air hung oppressively over them, Calf and Leaf knelt at the river's edge pounding their lifeless clothes. Little Seeker played with Leaf's son as her brother dozed in his cradle. Her playmate seemed listless, continually rubbing his eyes, and Little Seeker pressed the child to play in earnest. Becoming irritated, he pushed her to the ground, only to be repaid with a solid whack to the shoulder.

Calf and Leaf rushed to separate the two when suddenly Leaf gasped. Her son's face was covered with strange blotches. Quickly Leaf pulled at his shirt. The red rash spread across his chest and back. He felt hot and his eyes sat in flaming raw sockets. Grabbing the sobbing child, Leaf raced back to their lodge.

Quickly Calf gathered Leaf's clothes from the rocks at the water's edge and, handing the baby to Little Seeker, she said firmly, "Take him home and stay with him."

By the time she got to Leaf's tent, the boy lay in his bed with Leaf bent over him, wetting his burning forehead with water.

"It's warm," Leaf said frantically, turning to Calf and nodding toward the water in the pan at her feet. Instantly Calf grabbed the pan, rushed down to the river, filled it with cool water, and ran back. Again and again she brought cool water.

"His mouth is filled with white spots," Leaf said tearfully as she wiped the child's nose, draining now

207

for no apparent reason. "What is it, Calf?" She whispered. "What is it?"

Calf had never seen anything like it.

"I'll get Medicine Woman," she answered, not knowing what else to say. "She will know what to do." And touching her friend's shoulder reassuringly, she ran again from the lodge.

When the two returned they found Bull Hump in the lodge, anxiously peering at his only child. Medicine Woman looked hard at the boy covered with the frightful red blotches. She felt him on the head, on the chest, on the leg.

"Fever," she said, as she probed, but she knew it was a new fever, one she had never seen before. All the old woman could do was apply the old treatment for fever, which consisted of grease mixed with pulverized stems and leaves of the make-cold plant, rubbed over the entire body. As she worked, Medicine Woman spoke many prayers and chants.

For several sleeps the child lay burning, covered with the red spots, and suffering frequent nosebleeds and violent headaches. The agency doctor refused to come—nothing he could do, he said—they must wait the sickness out. Calf helped as best she could. After six sleeps the boy began to breath with the greatest effort; after eight sleeps he lay dead in his mother's arms.

Leaf did not cry when he died. Her pain hung too deep in her bowels and her anger too close to the world. Leaf, who had protested the ritual gashing of

208

the Princess, did not gash herself. Mercifully, the exhaustion of so many sleepless days and nights tending the child plunged her into a deep sleep, like the sleep of death itself. After that, she sat for days in the lodge, feeling and thinking, and did not emerge till word came that Little Seeker had fallen ill with the mysterious disease. Then she stayed by Calf's side.

It was the same all over again. The fever, the frightening red blotches, the hacking cough, the running nose, the flaming eyes, the fierce headaches. Black Coyote hovered over the child, running back and forth to the river for cool water even when the water in the pan had not had time to warm. His silent rage against the *veho* who forced them to this place of sickness and death festered and spread to every nerve in his body. He became like the army big gun that needs only a spark to set off an explosion.

For five sleeps Little Seeker lay burning, then the spots turned to dry scabs all over her body, and with the scabs the fever broke at last. In other lodges some children got well too, but many died. By late summer the Northern Cheyenne buried fifty children struck down by the white people's spot sickness, called measles by the soldier doctor.

After Little Seeker recovered, Calf and Black Coyote sat over their water soup and their hungry stomachs, talking out their desperation. Calf saw that the Coyote was not himself, that he nursed a wound of the mind. She saw the sickness spreading around her and she heard the daily keening of the dead. She saw the empty place in the tents where the stores of food should have weighed heavy against the earth. Hunger and disease and death hung in the stifling air. Around them only the biting insects and the bluecoats grew and multiplied.

"I will not stay in this place," she said at last. Then, as if she were uttering an inevitable truth, "I want to feel the cool breezes blowing through the sweet smelling pines. I want to be where animals still live and cold streams rush through the mountains. I will die in our home country."

The Coyote's face brightened, as though she had already taken him there. How often he would have said those very words, but fearing for the children, as he had when the little band struggled to survive in the north, he held back, growing more desperate each day.

"We will go!" he said instantly, jumping to his feet as though the journey would begin at that moment.

Calf reached out for his hand.

"This time we must go with the others," she cautioned him. "It must be planned." Then, reassuringly, "They will go this time. I know it."

So, by early summer, the talk of leaving began in earnest. People continued to die through the merciless summer and each death increased the resolve to escape, to return to the high plains and the pure air. Even the old men chiefs, Little Wolf and Dull Knife, declared themselves ready to leave.

"After all," Dull Knife said, "Bad Hand and Three

Stars promised we could return whenever we wished if we were unhappy." The point was received with a certain skepticism.

But willing it was easier than doing it. Bluecoats were everywhere. It was difficult enough for a single warrior to slip away to hunt, how could hundreds leave unnoticed? And not everyone agreed. One of the old men chiefs had grown old and tired of the fight. Dirty Moccasins said he would stay in the south and die with the sacred objects, the Arrows and the Hat, which must not be defiled in another fight with the soldiers.

Dull Knife and Little Wolf decided to confront the agent with their determination to leave. He seemed a kind man—a Quaker, he called himself—who seldom received enough food from the government to give the Indians. Nonetheless, he worked for the government, and when things did not go well he said he was only doing his job and set the soldiers on them. His brow knit when they told him they would return north.

"Soldiers will follow you and kill everyone."

So the fear grew: fear of the soldiers, the lack of horses, the scarcity of food for such a strenuous journey, and only a handful of guns present. The arguments grew intense. Those wanting to go could not understand those willing to stay in the grave called Indian Territory. Those determined to remain resented the new punishments the flight of the others would bring on them. And there were others like Standing

Elk—called agency men now—whose families grew plump and had new blankets. They tried to incite the Cheyenne against the leaders who spoke for flight. Divisions arose through the summer and deepened till at last a group of almost 300, those who wanted to return north, who still hoped to save the old ways, moved camp up the Red Water River, a good distance from the rest.

Preparations for the flight began. The hungry people hoarded scraps of food. Calf, Leaf, and the other women repaired their worn clothing as best they could, especially the moccasins. The men made more arrows for their bows and a few managed to trade in secret for a gun. The chiefs and some of the men gathered to decide the way back to the north, whether to follow the old Indian trail or to plot a new trail farther west.

"We know the old way. Our people have traveled it many times," said Little Hawk, whose own pain at the loss of his precious Crooked Nose had healed somewhat in the face of his people's suffering, and who spoke again in the war societies.

"That is true," agreed Dull Knife, "but we cannot follow the path of our ancestors. It's changed now. White settlers are strewn up and down the trail like leaves in a wind storm. It's too dangerous."

"That is the reason to go!" interjected Black Coyote. "With settlers along the way there will be cattle for hungry mouths and horses and guns to take."

Dull knife looked angry.

"No one will touch the cattle of whites!" Snapping at the Coyote, he said, "Do you want to bring the blue-coats on us?"

"The bluecoats will be on us wherever we go and whatever we do," Black Coyote retorted.

"I understand how you feel," Little Wolf said to the Coyote. "But Dull Knife is right. The whites must know we do not wish to hurt them, that we only wish to go home. We will not give the army cause to pursue us."

Still, other young men would not let it go.

"No, the Coyote is right," insisted Little Finger Nail. "The soldiers have never needed cause to attack us. We leave here with almost nothing. If we are ever to arrive home, we need guns. Nothing else will save us."

Little Wolf looked sad.

"I carry with me Sweet Medicine's bundle. What is a gun next to the guidance of Sweet Medicine?'

"We will follow a new trail to the west," Dull Knife said firmly, asserting his authority.

"That will take longer," Whetstone protested. "Our people are sick and weak."

Wild Hog responded. "When we leave this place of death we can again hunt the buffalo and antelope. The meat will restore the Cheyenne to their old health and strength."

"It's settled," Little Wolf insisted. "Dull Knife and I are responsible for the safety of our people. We go to the west." Ignoring the grumbling of the young men,

213

Little Wolf added, "The time grows short. See to the preparations."

But preparations to stop the flight began too. One sleep after the Cheyenne moved their camp up river, Calf and the others watched as the troops followed them, dragging the dreaded two-bang gun that shot huge exploding balls. They came with Arapaho scouts, dressed in blue coats and doing their bidding. The Arapaho chose the best spot to watch from. The Northern Cheyenne camp sat uneasily above the Red Water, looking past the river on the south to the flat barren plains beyond. To the north and east and west sloping ridges surrounded the small village, protecting them but also closing them in. The cavalry set up camp behind the hills, out of sight of the Indians. On the top of the ridges sentries posted themselves and their guns, positioning the great gun in the center, aimed straight at the village.

The next day the agent came to meet with Little Wolf and Dull Knife.

"We cannot have this defiance. It sets a bad example for the others. Return to the main camp and give up this crazy notion of leaving, or blood will flow." The agent spoke sternly and with a sharp edge to his voice.

Little Wolf answered. "Many years ago the Great White Father in Washington said he did not want any blood spilled. For years Indian blood has covered the ground only because we wish to stay on the land of our ancestors to hunt and live in the old ways. You cannot frighten us with talk of flowing blood. Our blood does not flow here in the south, but our people die like flies before the cold winter frost. It is the death of cowards and the Cheyenne are not cowards."

The agent's voice quivered. "If you do not return to the main camp with the others, there will be no food for your people."

"No food!" Little Wolf thundered. "And have our pots been full of food till now? You will keep from us food we never get?" They were brave words, but Little Wolf knew that a scrap of food was better than none.

The agent rose.

"I will wait to hear from you," he said stiffly. And turning to go, he thought surely they would relent without food. But he did not fully understand that they were used to starvation, for every night he sat before heaping platters of food.

Now no time could be lost. The word spread quietly that they would leave any day now. Everyone moved carefully, appearing to do the same things as always, so the soldiers would suspect nothing. Those with family and friends in the main camp went quickly to urge them to come home to the north, for it was a bitter thing to leave so many behind.

Calf went to her brother, Comes in Sight.

"Will you come?" she asked, almost pleading.

His face looked tired and drawn.

"I cannot leave her," he said, sadly shaking his head as the shadow of his tall frame fell across Calf's body, cutting off the sun.

Calf knew since she arrived south that Pemmican

was not well, that she still carried the wound her father had been unable to inflict on her. Pemmican still mourned her family, her whole family, as though they were dead and she had killed them.

"Maybe the movement and friends around her might . . ."

Her brother kept shaking his head.

"Nothing will help her. She is one lost in the sorrow of her past and she will not find her way. She lives, but she has given up life. This burial ground suits her. It gives her nothing and asks nothing of her."

Calf's heart broke for his sorrow.

"And you?" she asked. "What of you?"

"It grieves me to see her so, but I love her, Calf. I cannot leave her."

Just then they spotted Pemmican walking back from the river carrying water. When Pemmican saw Calf, she hurried a little.

"Is it true?" she asked. "Will you really go?"

"Soon. Very soon." Calf paused, and then, looking into Pemmican's eyes, "I wish . . ."

But Pemmican cut her off, as though to forestall the appeal.

"Don't go yet. I have something for you." She turned quickly and disappeared into her lodge. In a moment she returned clutching a small package of meat.

"I've been saving it for you, Calf. I knew you would go soon."

Calf thought how long they must have gone without

to save this. She choked back the tears and embraced her friend.

"I'll miss you," Calf whispered. "I'll miss you both."

And she turned to her horse. Mounting quickly, she hurried back across the scorched earth that floated behind a film of tears.

That same day, Wooden Leg rode into the isolated camp, surrounded by bluecoats. He found Little Hawk and Whetstone in Black Coyote's lodge, the three of them working over their weapons—bows and arrows, a rifle, and a six-shooter. A pang of regret cut through him.

"You'll come?" the Coyote asked when he entered.

Wooden Leg shook his head sadly.

"But why?" said Little Hawk.

"Is it your family?" Whetstone asked before he could answer.

"They still grieve for my brother and sister." Wooden Leg glanced at Little Hawk and saw the young man's jaw set and his lips become a thin line. "They have no heart for the flight and I think I should stay to help them feed the young ones." He paused. Then, looking embarrassed, he added, "And I have met a Southern Cheyenne woman. I would like to marry her someday, but if I leave . . ."

Whetstone slapped him playfully on the back.

"So . . . Wooden Leg will marry."

Everyone was happy for him, and for a moment they laughed and teased him lightheartedly in the old way,

217

till it was time for the sad good-bye.

Others would be missed too: Coal Bear and Black Hairy Dog, who decided to keep the Sacred Hat and Sacred Arrows safe in the South; Box Elder, grown old from the struggles and waiting to die near the holy objects; Dirty Moccasins; and even the troublesome Last Bull, who remained behind, though no one knew why.

For three days, a few warriors, led by Black Coyote, had ridden out in the morning, appearing to head east toward the agency. A ways out, far from the eyes of the soldiers, they circled south and rode to a place west of their camp. There they left a few horses each day, but only a few and not enough to arouse suspicion.

On the fourth day after the arrival of the troops, the Cheyenne furtively finished their preparations. That night they would slip past the sentries. Bridge made strong medicine that day, praying for clouds to cover the lights of the universe and bring them darkness.

But the Sacred Persons did not favor the Cheyenne that night. Bridge's medicine brought no clouds to cover their escape; instead, the moon shone full and bright, surrounded by the far away lights of the universe that burned like a million lodge fires in the sky.

Soon after darkness began, the thin figures slowly stole from their soldier tents, one by one. As everything had been planned, they slipped through the camp, avoiding the glow of the fires left burning to assure the soldier bluecoats that they stayed. A few of their friends stayed behind, Wooden Leg among them, and circulated about the camp that night, speaking loudly and laughing, now in one empty tent, now in another, so the soldiers would suspect nothing.

Dull Knife went first, his feet as soft on the earth as those of a rabbit. After him came a number of women—Buffalo Calf Road, Leaf, the Princesses, Pretty Walker, Short One, Pawnee Woman, Feather on Head, and others—struggling with their children and the small packs that held their only belongings. All moved swiftly, fearful of breathing heavily lest the air move around them.

Next came Iron Teeth with her son, Gathering His Medicine, helping the young ones. They had spoken and decided together to try again to live in the old way. They knew the danger but Medicine said it was better to be killed quickly than to die the slow death of the reservation. Yellow Bead slipped through the pass in the ridges with her aunt, followed by Little Finger Nail and his beloved Singing Cloud, helping her old father who saw at last that he was dying and should not keep his daughter from the hope of the north. Behind them came Spotted Deer, straining to see Yellow Bead in the distance ahead and all but carrying the wasted form of Old Grandmother, who said she would go north to die under the sweet-smelling pines of the Bighorn Mountains where the wind knew her name.

Old Great Eyes, father of Leaf, walked proud, carrying the last sacred shield of the Northern Cheyenne,

219

the shield of a hundred winters, saved from the attack on Old Bear's camp and again from Bad Hand's massacre. He would carry it north once more to look on the Elk and the Tongue and the Powder Rivers. His young nephew, Red Bird, walked by his side.

From shadow to shadow they crept, hiding from the huge bright eye in the sky that seemed to single them out for the soldiers. As they slid through the pass leading west, they could hear the distant voices of Arapaho bluecoats above, laughing and grunting, sounding as though they had drunk the white man's firewater. For once the Cheyenne were glad to have Indians drink the water of stupor.

When ailing Bear Rope passed, he walked alone, followed a bit by his wife and daughter and her husband. It was good he left, many thought. The cool clean air of the open plains in the north would cleanse him of the sickness that ate at his brain. If he stayed any longer, people thought, he would surely kill his poor wife.

The old men crept together—Black Crane, the peacemaker; Old Crow, once a scout for the white man; Bridge, the medicine man; Old Bear, the old man chief; and Old Crier, the voice of the tribe. Behind them, Wild Hog led his wife and son and daughter through the pass.

A few Southern Cheyenne came too. Black Horse—who had survived the massacre on the Sappa three winters ago, and the Florida prison far away, and the wound that crippled his leg when he escaped and fled west from the stockade—crept along slowly with his wife, again in search of freedom. The widowed Yellow Woman, a Southerner too, fled with them now, carrying a baby and helped by her son, Pug Nose, already a young man. And there was Left Alone, called that now because her husband had died six moons ago of the fever sickness and she had no family anywhere. She walked heavy and slowly this night, carrying within her the weight of an unborn baby soon to see daylight. But that would not happen on the reservation, she vowed. Yellow Woman walked by her side and helped her as those swifter of foot passed them and nodded in silence.

Near the end of the line, the warriors came leading more horses. They brought as many as they could, but not half as many as they needed for the nearly 300 who fled now. The warriors slowly led the horses, their mouths bound and their feet tied with rabbit fur or cloth to deaden the sound of their steps. Black Coyote walked ahead, leading his horse and Calf's. Behind him came Whetstone, Little Hawk, Bull Hump, Little Finger Nail, Woodenthigh, Limpy, Tangle Hair, Big Foot, Bullet Proof, Left Hand, and Bear Shield. Still others followed.

Far to the rear, at the end of the moving string of people, came Brave One and Little Wolf with the lone women and children. Brave One held the hand of little Runs Ahead, frightened and looking very alone. The little ones remembered Brave One's stern commands and made no sound. Little Wolf, carrying a Winchester now, hurried them along, peering behind him every step of the way, as though his peering would keep the soldiers away.

So, early in the Moon of the Yellow Leaves, the band of undefeated Northern Cheyenne, hungry for food and life and freedom, slipped through the blue-coat sentries guarding their poor camp and began their long journey home, thirteen moons after they were brought south and forced onto Indian Territory.

CHAPTER 7

All night the broken line of people hurried through the bright darkness. In tiny strung-out groups they climbed the broken ridges, hugging the gullies and following the shadows. Their hearts ran forward while their eyes looked back, waiting for the thunder of soldier hooves and the crash of the two-bang gun. But besides the hoot of an occasional night owl, only the rustle of their skirts and the flight of their moccasins over the grass and rocks followed them.

At last they reached the open prairie, and those with horses mounted now. All the warriors rode since it fell to them to scout ahead, to hunt for food, and to guard the rear against the soldier charge sure to come. The sick—Old Grandmother, Singing Cloud's father, and others—lay on travois dragged along the ground. The line quickly organized, with the headmen leading the flight and the Dog warriors, an elite warrior society led by Tangle Hair, protecting the rear, as was their custom.

Black Coyote moved in front with the headmen. Not far behind came the young women, including Leaf and Buffalo Calf Road, who rode with the baby strapped on her back and Little Seeker in front on her saddle. Far to the rear many moved on foot and, as the moon rose and fell across the sky, the distance between the riders and the walkers lengthened. Brave One and the lone women and children straggled far behind the others, slowed by the tired and hungry legs of the children who must take two steps for every one of the adults. Just in front of them Left Alone labored with her unborn burden as she leaned on Yellow Woman.

It was not yet dawn when Yellow Woman felt her friend falter against her arm. The young woman quickly straightened herself and moved ahead. Again Left Alone hesitated, her swollen body bent under its weight. Yellow Woman looked anxiously through the darkness into the woman's shadowy face.

"What is it?" she whispered.

"I . . . I think it is time . . ." Left Alone groaned.

Yellow Woman's breath sank. Quickly she spun around searching the darkness. She could see a clump of trees outlined against the spotted sky in the moonlight. When Left Alone saw her unstrapping the baby from her back, she protested.

"No! You must go on."

But Yellow Woman kept working at the straps.

"I will not have the soldiers capture you too," Left Alone pleaded. "Please go on. I know what to do."

"The soldiers will capture no one!" Yellow Woman snapped. Then, turning to Pug Nose, she said, "Take the baby ahead. Quickly!"

The boy looked frightened.

"I will stay too, Mother."

"No," she said firmly. "Take the baby and go ahead. We will catch up."

By now Brave One and the others approached.

"Is something wrong?" Brave One asked.

"It is my time," Left Alone answered, feeling guilty. "Please, Brave One, make her go with you."

But Yellow Woman interjected, "There is no time to argue. A woman cannot leave a sister at such a time." Turning to Brave One, "Help Pug Nose with the baby."

Brave One nodded, but before she could speak, Yellow Woman grabbed Left Alone's hand and pulled her toward the trees in the distance. The anxious group watched as the two stumbled through the darkness, fading into the shadows of the prairie.

Soon the blackness turned to gray and one by one the lodge fires in the sky went out. A misty haze began to gather over the prairie as crooked streaks of yellow pushed across the eastern sky, bringing the hot southern sun once again to scorch the earth. But it was light the Cheyenne feared this day, not heat. Behind

224

them on the reservation, Box Elder prayed to the Sacred Persons for their escape, but Ox'zem lay in his lodge, far from the runners who needed its power to conceal them in flight.

The sun had already risen above the prairie grass when Brave One's group heard it: the distant noise of horses, faint at first but unmistakable.

"Quickly," she ordered. "Into the grass."

As the frightened little ones scattered and fell into the tall green buffalo grass, Brave One grabbed the baby from Pug Nose. It had started to sob. In an instant the two fell to the ground and, cupping the small one's mouth, Brave One held it hard till it seemed the baby's breath would come no more. After an endless instant the riders flew by, near enough to kick some pebbles over the huddled bodies. Only two horses had passed, but for a long time nobody looked or moved in the grass, expecting more to follow.

At last Brave One gave the signal and slowly the crumpled buffalo grass rose again around the legs of the small group as they stood and peered into the distance. Her voice was anxious.

"We must move quickly now that it is light," she urged, rushing the children ahead with a wave of her arm. As she spoke she caught Pug Nose straining to see across the distance from which they had come, his eyes searching for his mother.

Ahead the tired people kept moving through the tall grass, green and thick this year from the winter rains that nursed them. It meant food for the horses but the

225

Cheyenne went hungry, saving what scraps they brought against starvation and plucking a few wild berries and plums as they ran. The biting insects followed them all night through the sticky heat and into the morning.

When two riders approached the Cheyenne snaking across the prairie, the Dog warriors had already formed a line of defense, their weapons drawn. Still the two came. Suddenly Tangle Hair threw up his hand signaling the warriors to wait. It was two young Southern Cheyenne men, boys really, from the reservation.

"Do you bring a message from our people?" Tangle Hair asked.

They shook their heads.

"What do the soldiers do?" The Dog chief persisted.

They did not know, having left during the night as soon as they heard of the flight.

"Then why do you come?" Tangle Hair asked in exasperation.

Their answer poured out: because all of their youth had passed on the reservation, because around the campfires they heard the men tell of the old days in war, of great victory and many coups. Their eyes flashed with excitement.

"We know the soldiers will follow you. We will fight with you and count our first coup."

Tangle Hair frowned angrily.

"And will you starve with us and die with us?" He sensed trouble. Young men anxious to fight, anxious to count coup, with no experience in war. . . . It was not good to have these around in hard times.

The sun blazed overhead when Old Crier rode swiftly along the twisted line, bellowing his message of joy.

"Buffalo! Buffalo! We stop ahead to eat. We stop ahead to eat."

The heavy swollen feet lightened at the words, moving quickly across the rocks and grass, and the sleep-laden eyes opened wide at the image, rushing ahead to the feast that waited far in the distance. Sick, starving, and weak, the Cheyenne straggled up to the place in a canyon overlooking the Bull River where the butchering had already begun. Calf, Pretty Walker, Leaf, and the other young women worked swiftly preparing the buffalo meat, cutting it into chunks and throwing them on the fire for the hungry mouths to eat. Some had fallen far behind so it was late afternoon before they caught up, and then only after the warriors rode out to bring them in.

Exhausted and starving, the Cheyenne ate ravenously as they lay about the sheltered canyon high above the meandering river. A delicious coolness pervaded the hollow where a small spring spilled from the rocks, splashing ripples in a pool below. Overhead two morning doves circled, eying the intruders. As the buffalo meat disappeared into the chomping mouths of the Indians, it worked its magic in the frail bodies, nourishing and healing and strengthening every muscle and organ. The good buffalo meat, which none

227

had tasted for many moons, would cure the fever sickness, they thought as they ate. From a rock above them, Young Eagle blew his love flute and the young people giggled together. It was good being here in this peaceful place, going home.

When Black Coyote returned with the last of the walkers on horseback, shouts of joy greeted Brave One's party and people ran to get the children and give them food. In the excitement no one noticed at first, but then a squeal of surprise rose from those crowding the women and children.

"A baby! A new baby!" Someone shouted and the excitement grew louder. Everyone crushed in now, wanting to see the tiny one, as though they had never seen a baby before. But this time there was truly something special: a new life among them as they fled the place of death, a new hope among them as they headed home. A good omen, a very good omen, everyone agreed as they led the exhausted Left Alone and the baby to the fire and the food.

"What shall we call the baby?" someone asked.

"Little Comes Behind," Calf said immediately without thinking. "Yes. Little Comes Behind," she repeated, satisfied with the choice.

The Coyote laughed at that, a loud happy laugh, and Calf glanced quickly at him, smiling. She could not remember when she had last heard the Coyote laugh. Quickly the contagion of laughter, long lost but now found again, spread through the crowd and in an instant everyone roared, gasping for breath between the laughs, swaying in joy, and feeling the tensions of the mind evaporate into the hollow. At that moment nothing felt real but the togetherness, the laughter, the peace of the sheltered canyon above the earth.

Only Little Wolf looked down. He watched his people in their spasm of joy, but his eyes kept moving to the south, to the ground they had just covered that came from the reservation and the two-bang gun. He saw nothing in the distance but the open prairie, the river, and the sky, where already the sun moved quickly toward the earth. But he thought uneasily of the soldiers' far-seeing glass that could peer across the earth better than any eye, even the hawk's. The Cheyenne could not see them, yet with the fire here and the far-seeing glass there. . . .

Little Wolf moved to the fire and raised his hand.

"My people, it is good to fill the stomach and empty the mind." It pained him to speak. They needed this respite from the pain. "But we must not stay too long. The soldiers . . ." The word stuck in his throat. "The soldiers will come soon. Rest a little now. When it is dark we move again."

He thought he could see the faces stiffen again, but they understood, and one by one they eased their bodies to the ground, and weariness did the rest. No one had shelters now, but the canyon hollow felt like a great lodge circling a large family. For the moment they slept a heavy, curing sleep. Little Wolf took up the watch with the Dog warriors while Calf, Leaf, and a few women put out the fire and saved what little was left from the butchered buffalo cows, including meat and the precious hides that would be needed for moccasins.

When Calf finished, she moved to the spot where Black Coyote lay with the baby and Little Seeker, all asleep. The Coyote's face seemed placid, empty of all emotion, and each breath stole gently from his lips. It was a long time since she had seen him like that. She thought of the nights by his side on the reservation, of the flashing eyes that stared into the night while others slept, of the times she woke in the darkness to find him sitting alone consumed by his anger, and of his tortured thrashing sleep when he finally dozed.

Softly Calf dropped onto the blanket beside him and lay her tired head down. A thin strip of cloth fallen from the Coyote's braid curled on the bed beside her face. Her long slender fingers touched it tenderly, as she closed her eyes. Overhead the sun moved low in the western sky, pushing the shadows of the canyon rock across the earth. Later when voices moved over the crowd, telling them to rise, darkness already lay on the world.

All night they fought their tiredness and the heavy blackness that hid stones and crevices, thorn bushes and cacti. The Cheyenne moved mostly on the rocky benches, hoping to dull their trail for the bluecoats. Everyone but the sick walked through the darkness now, inching themselves and their horses forward, while the occasional sob or moan of a child followed them.

Even before the first streaks of morning spread across the sky, while the darkness slowly turned to gray, Little Wolf strained to see across the distance ahead, searching for a place to hide. Surely the soldiers would reach them today. But for three days they moved with no sign of the army.

For the better part of the fourth morning the Cheyenne persisted in their flight. Many still had no horses, so the walkers continued to fall behind. At last Little Wolf found a spot in some sandstone hills to the north. The reddish hills rose steeply against the sky with many ravines and draws cutting through them, good for hiding or escaping. He chose a site overlooking the approach from the southeast, still expecting the soldiers to come from that direction. Behind them a stand of trees surrounded a spring of water. Black Horse, the Southern Cheyenne, knew the place well and called it Turkey Springs, for the flocks of wild turkeys once found there. Now only a huge black raven flapped noisily into the air when they approached.

Slowly the long string of exhausted people began unraveling at Turkey Springs. Those on horseback dismounted and a few led the horses back for those still moving on foot. Calf and Leaf took some horses out to meet Brave One and her party, who had fallen far behind. Little Runs Ahead dozed in Calf's arms as they rode toward the place in the red hills. Not far from the trail leading up to the springs, they heard it— the faint and distant sound of horse's hooves.

When Calf and the others reached the top of the hill, a cloud of dust had begun to form on the horizon. People scattered everywhere. Old Bear and the Crier shouted to the women and children to hide, but the young women refused and took up positions with the warriors—Calf, who had hidden the children with Chicken Woman, Leaf, more defiant than ever, Singing Cloud and Hog's Daughter, often together these days, Pretty Walker, and others. So, on the fourth day after fleeing their camp on the Red Water, the Northern Cheyenne watched as the cloud approached and the thunder grew louder.

Little Wolf rose in their midst and spoke.

"We will not fire the first shot."

When a loud grumbling met his words, he raised his hand and continued.

"I will ride out to meet them. They will hear what I must say."

"They will kill you!" Black Coyote shouted.

"Then I will be the one killed," Little Wolf responded. "You may fight if that happens. Until then, I will try to speak and tell them we are going home, that we do not wish to fight."

The murmuring among the young warriors slowly subsided. They saw no point to the gesture, but Little Wolf was an old man chief, so they clenched their jaws and held back the words. It was midafternoon when the bluecoat cavalry formed its line on the plain below the sandstone hills. After a while an Arapaho scout, Ghost Man, galloped toward the steep rise

232

where the Cheyenne crouched. He began calling the names of Dull Knife, Little Wolf, and Tangle Hair.

"Turn back!" Ghost Man shouted, his voice climbing the hill like the growl of a rabid dog. "Turn back! You will not be harmed. The agent will feed you well."

A bitter laugh caught in their throats. At that point Little Wolf rose and, mounting his horse, he lifted the white people's signal of truce. Slowly he climbed down the hill. Behind him, at a distance, Dull Knife, Wild Hog, and Tangle Hair followed in support. When he reached the bottom, Little Wolf raised his voice to the bluecoat Indian scout.

"Tell them we will not go back. We wish to harm no one, but we will go to the land of our people."

The Arapaho growled his warning again. "The soldier chiefs will beat you back if you refuse." As he spoke Ghost Man inched his horse backward. Suddenly he snapped at the reins and galloped away toward the cavalry. Before Little Wolf could move, a volley of shots cut the afternoon air. Immediately he wheeled back to the others and the four flew up the hill.

When the warriors saw that the chiefs were safe, they jumped on their horses, and making a terrible din, charged the bluecoats from the front and sides. The unexpected counterattack left the cavalry horses rearing and shying in terror. The shrieking warriors pressed against the soldiers, swinging hatchets, shooting arrows, and firing guns. In the melee, Black

Coyote went straight for Ghost Man and, taking dead aim, he brought the Arapaho down as he screamed, "Death to the white Indian!"

Above on the hill, Calf fell naturally into a leadership position as she and the women guarded the approach to the springs, firing when a soldier got too close. At one point a group of bluecoats reached the foot of the hill and their rifle fire flew overhead, striking the trees and the rocks. Calf aimed in her slow careful way and when she shot the soldier starting to climb the hillside, the others pulled back.

Suddenly above the noise of wounded and dying, she heard Brave One call out.

"Come quick! Help."

Calf whirled in time to see Brave One dragging the limp body of little Runs Ahead from behind a bush. The child whimpered softly as the blood gushed from her foot.

"Someone get Medicine Woman or Bridge! Hurry!" Brave One pleaded as she comforted the child.

Calf rushed back among the rocks and draws calling for the healers. Bridge came first and as they rushed back to the child, a bugle sounded from below. Calf knew the signal of retreat and her breath eased a bit. Quickly Bridge went to work, praying and moving his rattle over the bleeding wound while he sprinkled medicine on it.

"How did it happen back here?" Calf whispered to Brave One.

The older woman thought a bullet had struck a rock

above them and bounced off, striking the child's leg. Bridge interrupted them, talking so the girl could not hear.

"A bullet is lodged in her ankle. I will have to cut it out. Carry her back to the spring."

Calf groaned inside at the thought. Carefully they lifted the child, who never cried out but sobbed quietly, her chest heaving under the short gasps and her eyes pleading with Brave One and Calf. Bridge gave the women some dried leaves of the yellow medicine plant from his pouch, instructing them to boil the leaves in a little water.

"It will put her to sleep," he said as the child watched in fright.

When it was ready, Brave One coaxed Runs Ahead to drink the sedative. Bridge began to chant a hypnotic prayer and after a while the child began to doze. While the medicine man worked over the girl, preparing to cut out the bullet, Calf returned to the rocks overlooking the fight. The soldiers, at a disadvantage in the open, had already retreated to a deep gully where they lay entrenched behind rifle pits, surrounded by Cheyenne warriors. Little Finger Nail and Woodenthigh had captured a mule and two bluecoat horses and were leading them up the hill. The young women met them as they ascended the rise.

"What will the warriors do now?" Singing Cloud asked.

The Nail frowned.

"We should attack and destroy them all. As long as

235

they live, their shadow will darken every step we take."

"We would," Woodenthigh interjected, "but Little Wolf forbids it."

For the rest of the afternoon and night the warriors moved back and forth between the camp fires on the hill and the watch below where they kept the soldiers pinned down in the ravine without water or help for their wounded. Though some warriors had been hurt, the crippling of little Runs Ahead enraged them most. Throughout the evening the arguing continued between the young men and some of the old men. Little Wolf insisted they save their ammunition and allow the soldiers to save face.

"Another defeat such as that against Long Hair will bring the whole army against us," he said.

"If we do not kill them," Little Hawk answered, "they will pursue us all the way."

"And how will you kill them?" Wild Hog asked. "With pebbles and sticks?" Even with the guns they had managed to bring, ammunition was scarce.

"No!" the Coyote spoke angrily. "We will use what we have to get their guns and bullets."

But in the end they grudgingly gave in to the wishes of the old man chief. Instead of covering the enemy with bullets, they covered the soldiers with noise, chanting and whistling, howling and singing all night, till the bluecoats would have dropped from exhaustion. On the hills above, the sounds of their warriors spooking the enemy lulled the Cheyenne to sleep, a

236

long sleep for the first time in three nights. Little Wolf had chosen well a place of safety for his people, while the bluecoat chief, Red Face, had led his men into a hopeless position in the open, impossible to defend.

The next morning, the people at Turkey Springs watched in relief as the soldiers, thirsting and low on ammunition, mounted their horses and withdrew south as the Cheyenne warriors offered no resistance. After the cavalry left, pulling litters carrying their wounded, the Indians found the body of Ghost Man and three bluecoats, as well as a number of dead horses. As Calf and the women quickly skinned the dead horses and cooked the meat for a hasty meal, the men and children fanned over the battlefield collecting cartridges and the occasional weapon left behind by the soldiers. Others tended the wounded, five warriors in addition to little Runs Ahead with her shattered foot, now called Lame Girl by everyone.

Calf's people headed north after that, crossing the Bull River and moving over the broken prairie that stretched far ahead till it touched the sky. They trudged through the thick grass as they went, picking their way around the great buffalo wallows of herds slaughtered by the far-reaching guns of the white hunter.

Calf held Little Seeker on the saddle in front of her while the baby dozed on her back. Leaf rode by her side but the two only exchanged glances when they passed near the signs of the white settlers spilling over the plains: the wounded earth torn into long furrows, the cattle roaming freer than any Indian could roam, the strange dirt houses in the ground. Everyone sensed how vulnerable they were in the open, surrounded by the hidden eyes, so they moved quickly, though it was as hard as ever now with the wounded on travois and the walkers struggling to keep up.

Toward evening they rested a bit and ate the last of the horse-meat strips. They talked with apprehension of the white settlers everywhere.

"We will have to move in small groups and scatter," Little Wolf said. "Then the enemy must follow many trails. We will move at night and hide by day when we can."

"What of food?" Black Coyote asked.

"Some of you warriors must continue to hunt while others scout ahead and behind," Dull Knife responded.

"Hunt!" the Coyote retorted. "Here where the whites have scarred the earth and killed the game?" He gestured toward a heap of bones drying in the sun.

"We will have to kill some cattle," Little Finger Nail interjected.

"No!" insisted Little Wolf. "I have told you we will not touch what belongs to whites."

"What belongs to the white spider?" cried Black Coyote jumping to his feet. "Does the land belong to whites? Does the game they slaughter and leave for vultures belong to whites? Nothing belongs to whites, I tell you, nothing! I take the cattle in payment for destroying our food and our homes!"

238

Black Crane stepped forward quickly, seeing the Coyote slip into one of his rages.

"The old men chiefs must think of the safety of the people," he said, thinking to pacify Black Coyote, but the young man became angrier still.

"And I do not think of the safety of our people?" He glared at the peacemaker.

"My brother, sometimes you do not think at all," the old man said gently.

"Fool!" the Coyote cried. "If you do not feed the people, you can save them from nothing! Or perhaps you hope to keep them safe in their graves." With that he pushed past the old man and stormed away from the talkers as Calf watched from a distance, her spirit apprehensive at the thought of the Coyote's sickness of the heart.

Little Hawk was angry now.

"Black Coyote is right. What good is safety when you starve to death?"

"Must we always slink from the white man?" Little Finger Nail added. "He keeps food from our children for many moons, but we must not touch one of his cows. He imprisons us, but we must sit quietly. He pursues us and shoots us when we escape, but we must not kill him. He takes the land of all people and calls it his own, and we must hide in it, creeping about like strangers in our own land."

Little Wolf's face tensed. He understood the passion of the young men, but he understood too the power of the white man.

239

"No one will starve," he said simply, ignoring the rest.

Calf followed the Coyote to the spot far out in the grass where he sat alone. She touched his shoulder softly and sat beside him. For a long time neither spoke.

Suddenly Black Coyote blurted out, "They are white Indians!"

"You are too hard," Calf said, looking at the grass.

His face grew darker. "You too?"

She sat quietly, still looking down while her fingers pulled at the green blades. There was something in him these days she could not understand. Not just the moods, but the quickness to turn on his own people. He had always been hot tempered, quick to disagree. It wasn't that.

"You don't trust them anymore," she said quietly, almost as a question. When he did not answer, she said, "The old men are not your enemy."

"Who starves us, then?" he snapped.

Calf looked quickly at him, puzzled.

"We have just eaten."

He seemed not to hear.

"The old men keep us from the food we need."

"They keep us from trouble with the *veho* so we can get home," she corrected him.

"They blame me for the trouble," he persisted.

"But why would they blame you?" Calf asked, becoming uneasy.

"Because they know I can lead the Cheyenne home.

They know I can destroy the whites who try to stop us. And they cannot."

Calf stared at him with a sinking feeling. What had she hoped, she wondered, that the clean air of the plains would purge the darkness of his thoughts, that the buffalo meat would give him strength to fight the sickness in his mind? She brushed his forehead with her fingers. Around them the grass and the sky darkened. Slowly the deep caverns in the Coyote's forehead disappeared under her soothing touch. He reached up and took her arm, pressing it against his cheek. Calf brushed away a tear and saw that the people in the distance were beginning to move. Slowly they rose and together walked back across the grass to the others.

For two nights they pushed north in the darkness, sometimes hiding in the daylight, sometimes moving. There was little food again, only the berries hastily plucked as they ran or the roots dug when they stopped. Many still suffered from the chills and fever that had plagued them on the reservation. The walkers were exhausted and suffered from blisters on their feet. Some of the riders took their turn on foot, giving up their horses periodically, but the warriors continued to ride, scouting, looking for game, and guarding the rear.

The Cheyenne kept moving. There was no place to hide now, only great open prairie in all directions. Suddenly the long tattered line broke, its figures melting into a crushed circle with no place to hide.

From the east, horses rode hard and gunfire echoed across the plains. A small formation of soldiers pressed against them as warriors took their stand around the people. Not nearly as many bluecoats as at Turkey Springs charged them and in a short time the warriors pushed them back. A momentary relief spread through the crowd when the horses retreated, but their anxiety quickly returned as they imagined the next onslaught of soldiers.

The movement became frantic as everyone tried to move more quickly. Singing Cloud's old father threw himself off the travois onto the grass, wanting to lighten her load so she could escape. But the young woman and Little Finger Nail dragged the old man onto the travois again. Brave One and her party still trailed far behind. Lame Girl's foot festered and flared as the child rode feverishly on a travois, her painful whimpers barely audible. Iron Teeth led her children forward, though chills and fever struggled within her as she slumped on the horse dragging Lame Girl's travois. The ailing Bear Rope stormed at everyone, at the old men chiefs, at his daughter, but mostly at his wife who tried desperately to make him comfortable. His wife had slipped away to Bridge several nights before, begging him to make medicine for easing the sick man's mind. But nothing seemed to help. That afternoon they stopped to camp beside Bluff Creek having moved all night and all day.

They must get horses, Little Wolf told the men, so they could move more quickly. The warriors chose

Black Beaver, a calm peaceful man, to buy some horses at a ranch with the green paper found on a dead pack mule at Turkey Springs. He left immediately followed by several warriors, including Little Finger Nail, Woodenthigh, Whetstone, and Black Coyote, who mumbled as he left that no white person would give horses to an Indian.

As they neared the ranch, Black Beaver asked the others to stay back and wait. Slowly he approached the cabin on horse, but as he neared the house, the door burst open and two white men opened fire, killing first the Beaver's horse, then him. The warriors made a rush toward the Beaver's body but a rain of bullets kept them back.

Black Coyote screamed to the others. "We take the cattle!"

And with that he raced howling and screeching toward some steers, stampeding the small herd away from the ranch. The others followed, except for Woodenthigh, who stayed behind to wait for a safe moment to bring away Black Beaver's body for burial.

That evening in camp, no one criticized the warriors for taking the cattle. Instead the bitter talk of revenge salted their food while the relatives of Black Beaver keened their sorrow. Some could speak only of the evil whites who had shot a man come in peace, while the others understood that the settlers were now frightened at the mere sight of an Indian. Little Wolf said nothing, but he refused to eat the meat that Quiet One coaxed on him.

243

Calf and the women quickly skinned the remaining cattle, cutting the meat in strips, and before midnight they moved again, pushing their tired feet and horses across the hilly prairie. The horses were exhausted from the constant moving and the heavy burdens of two or three people. Many were near collapse, yet all the next morning they moved, stumbling and straggling. Around midday, another charge flew against them, this time mostly cowboys.

The Cheyenne huddled together against the onslaught with no place to hide on the prairie. Many adults threw their bodies over the children while the warriors pressed the enemy back. Clearly outnumbered, the cowboys soon pulled back, leaving behind one dead and taking several wounded. One of the elderly Cheyenne, Old Sitting Man, took a bullet through his thigh bone. Bridge worked feverishly over the old man, setting the bone with the fresh hide of a dead horse.

There was no holding back the warriors now. They rode out in small parties looking for cattle and horses and blood. One party ran into a cow camp and killed four men, coming away with horses and mules. Little Wolf was furious when he heard of the murders but nothing he said would stop them. The next day, two warriors left behind to scout were found shot to death and scalped. Little Hawk and Black Coyote carried their bodies to a rocky grave and their rage to the Cheyenne.

For days they moved north, more of them on foot

now than when they left the reservation. The few captured horses and mules could not replace those worn out ones left as bones along the trail, their flesh feeding the hungry people. During these days of running, an unexpected boost came. Several young men rode to them from the south, wanting to join them now. Word had spread over the reservation of their success in driving back the troops of Red Face. They were pleased that their people in the south wished them well and cheered them on.

Darkness had already fallen when Little Wolf finally gave the signal to make camp for the night. For four days they had not been bothered, but occasionally they caught sight of a horseman or a group of settlers watching in the distance or hurrying their stock to safety.

Several small fires burned already when Buffalo Calf Road walked into camp leading the tired Little Seeker by her hand and stooping under the weight of her sleeping baby. Her horse had given out that day, so she moved on foot now like so many others. After a while the Coyote joined her and together they rested on the cool ground while the baby nursed hungrily at Calf's breast.

One by one they fell into camp and collapsed, hardly speaking, hardly moving. The delicious smell of cow meat roasting over the spit rose to greet them as they came, while the haunting love flute of Young Eagle drifted through the air. Even the aroma of coffee bubbling in the open kettle filled the camp, the first they had for many moons, gotten by the young men, though no one asked how.

Little Finger Nail sat beside one of the fires, sketching again with his colored pencils in the ledger book brought all the way from the Little Bighorn. People came to peer at the figures emerging on the paper, proud figures from the old days—warriors in colorful headdress counting coup on the enemy or riding their great stallions into battle or turning aside a volley of bluecoat bullets with their strong medicine. They were pictures of a brave people, a great people, everyone thought. In the eerie moving light that licked at the darkness, the figures with their sacred lances and shields seemed alive and moving among them. Those who gazed long at the magic of the Nail's fingers forgot for a moment the camp with no lodges, the stolen meat and coffee, and the horseless people dressed in shabby torn clothes.

Spotted Deer made Old Grandmother comfortable on the ground and brought her a slab of roasted beef, coaxing her to eat though she felt poorly. The young man kept stealing glances at Yellow Bead off to the right with her aunt, but she seemed not to notice, looking instead toward the place where Dull Knife's beautiful people sat, though she dared not look directly at Little Hump.

Iron Teeth's chills seemed to have eased as she sat surrounded by her children, drinking the hot coffee that spread its warmth to every bone. Even sad-faced Lame Girl sat up tonight and nibbled a little meat. The women had bathed her swollen foot in hot water and it seemed less angry after that. Singing Cloud and Hog's Daughter giggled a secret together as they followed Medicine Woman on her rounds treating the sick. The old men sat together as always, puffing on their pipes, full of tobacco brought to them by the young men, and planning the future as though it were the past. Overhead a tiny sliver of the bent moon moved from behind a gray cloud, watching the small fires spread over the black earth.

Calf had just finished nursing the baby and placed it on a blanket next to Little Seeker, who was dozing already, when a horrible scream jolted the camp. Immediately shouts cut the air and more screams, tortured and full of pain. Calf leapt to her feet and raced toward the noise. Everyone was running toward the terrible roar.

Calf was one of the first there. For an instance she could not take it in. Next to the small dying fire, Comes in Sight Woman slumped over the ground, naked to the waist, her clothes hanging in shreds from her arms and around her torn skirt. Her right hand clutched a butcher knife covered with blood. Beside her on the grass her father lay, groaning loudly in pain, his stomach cut open and his entrails spilling over the ground as his fingers, twisted into great claws, tried to close the gaping wound. Behind them, Bear Rope's wife sat stunned, holding her head as blood covered her face.

Rushing forward, Calf grabbed a blanket on the

ground and quickly wrapped it around Comes in Sight, whose body had begun to tremble violently. Calf held the woman tightly as some others crowded around, tending to her mother and helplessly watching as the pallor and silence of death slid over Bear Rope, draining the man once and for all of his violence and sickness.

At that moment Comes in Sight's husband pushed through the crowd, stopping in terror at the sight. In an instant he understood that Bear Rope had tried to rape his own daughter. The hatred of many moons struck at last at this unforgivable act, and he began pounding the dead man with the bloodied rock by his side. Black Coyote and Little Hawk pulled him from the body already turning black.

As the crowd looked away in shame, the women, used to death in their midst by now, moved in to dispose of the corpse. Feather on Head, Quiet One, Pawnee Woman, and Short One quickly mopped up the gore and wrapped the body tightly in a blanket, tying it with pieces of hide. One of the young men led a horse pulling a travois and the women lifted the heavy wet bundle onto a litter as a low painful keening rose from the crowd.

As the horse dragged away the body, Little Wolf stepped forward with the Sweet Medicine bundle strapped on his back. As keeper of the sacred bundle, it fell to him to enforce the laws of their great hero, and no law was more serious than the injunction against a Cheyenne killing a Cheyenne. Little Wolf spoke, all the while looking away from the trembling figure staring at the ground.

"Cheyenne blood has been spilled and the law of Sweet Medicine requires the guilty party to leave our people. No one may speak to the murderer for at least four winters and then . . . ."

"Murderer!" Calf interrupted in a heartsick rage. "You call her a murderer!"

"Cheyenne blood has been spilled," Little Wolf insisted.

"It was spilled in self-defense!" Calf answered. "What would you have had her do?"

Old Crier spoke then. "Never has a woman spilled Cheyenne blood. Never in my lifetime . . . and her own father."

"Our people will be cursed by this deed," Old Bear added.

"She is innocent!" Calf insisted. "There is no curse in helping the innocent. You cannot drive her away in this place of the enemy. *That* would be murder."

Dull Knife had listened quietly, his eyes shifting from the mother to the daughter. He thought of the long suffering of these two good women, of the unfulfilled vow, of the white man's persecution that drove Bear Rope mad.

"Yes," Dull Knife said. "Calf speaks the truth. A Cheyenne woman must defend herself from attack. That is a holy law too."

"Yes! Yes!" Voices rose in the crowd. "Let her stay!"

249

"I will make medicine," Bridge said, "to purify our people and to keep the anger of the Sacred Persons from rising against us."

"It is done then. The woman may stay," Little Wolf said, deferring to Dull Knife. "Now we must put this evil night behind us. Rest, my people! At dawn we move again."

Slowly the crowd broke and the weary figures melted into the darkness. Comes in Sight's husband touched Calf on the shoulder and nodded his gratitude.

"I will take care of her now," he whispered.

Reluctantly Calf backed away from the three, huddled together before the glowing embers of the dying fire. Together she and the Coyote walked back to the sleeping children, whose exhaustion had saved them from witnessing the ordeal.

"The white man has killed another Cheyenne," Black Coyote said, then added simply, "I will make him pay." Calf stared into the darkness.

Before dawn, the women prepared to flee again, moving quickly, wanting to leave that place of death behind. When Calf and some others went to check on Comes in Sight and her mother, they found the three gone. Only the ashes of their fire and crusts of blood remained on the ground. In the days that followed they learned from their scouts that Comes in Sight, with her husband and mother, trailed far behind. Caring nothing for herself anymore, she did not want to bring a curse on her people. The women took to leaving food for them along the trail whenever there was any to spare.

It was the twelfth day since leaving the reservation, although it seemed like twelve moons. Anxious eyes searched the ground to the north as they moved, hoping to find the Arrowpoint River known to lie ahead. White people called this place Kansas, Bear Shield told them, and they were not too far from a white village named Dodge. They had not gone far that day, most still struggling on foot, when their scouts rode hard into their midst.

"Soldiers! Soldiers not far behind!"

A frantic run began. The broken canyons of Sandy Creek lay ahead, other scouts told them. That would be a better place to meet the bluecoats than here in the open. As they fled, dragging the children and sick and stumbling over their packs, Little Wolf signaled the hunters and warriors in. Those with horses picked up those on foot, riding double and triple, whipping the poor beasts into a frenzied run. Most of the day the Cheyenne fled, helping each other as best they could, moving relentlessly north. When the burdens of their packs became too great, they dropped them beside the trail; when their horses collapsed, they left them to die.

By late afternoon they reached the twisted canyons of Sandy Creek. Without stopping, they burrowed deep into the ravines and gullies, the old men herding the women and children into a long draw, though many of the young women refused to go and took positions instead with the warriors. Buffalo Calf Road and Yellow Woman took their babies deep into the draw and left them there with Chicken Woman before joining Pretty Walker, Leaf, the Princesses, and the others in their makeshift rifle pits.

Toward evening the troops appeared in the distance and set up camp farther down Sandy Creek. Indian scouts who watched up close said they were led by Red Face, the same soldier chief from Turkey Springs. About 150 soldiers followed him, as well as many cowboys. For a while small parties of soldiers charged in and out of the canyon draws, pushing the Cheyenne warriors steadily back. Most of the Indians shot arrows to save what little ammunition they had. At sundown, Red Face's troops pulled back to make camp and wait for daylight.

Little Wolf lost no time in spreading the word to move out, to push on north, to try to elude the soldiers. So again the exhausted people dragged themselves on, stumbling and falling in the rocky darkness. Toward morning, unable to go farther, they positioned themselves on a high ridge in small pockets of hollowed-out earth and waited. Behind them a small spring bubbled from the ground with two rifle pits guarding it.

By late morning the column of bluecoats appeared, dragging their supply wagons. Slowly the charge began again as the foot soldiers moved forward, dropped to the ground, fired, then moved again. Behind them, the cowboys rode their horses, keeping at a distance. Closer and closer they came, slowly through the early afternoon as Little Wolf and Wild Hog went among the warrior men and women cautioning them not to fire, to save the precious bullets. The men and women in the rifle pits found it hard to wait with the soldiers nearly upon them. Far behind them, the other women and the old men sang their stout heart songs.

Powers help us!
Powers that live in the winds of the storming,
In all the great directions, and in the earth and
    the sky,
Help us!

Over the hills the songs spread.

All the things of our life are here,
All that are left of our people.
It is a good day to die!

Closer the soldiers came.

"Do not fire. Wait," Little Wolf kept urging the people.

Then, as the bluecoats rose again to make the final run, he gave the order.

"Fire!"

A great rain of arrows and bullets flew against the soldiers, and the clutching and falling began. Before the soldiers could recover themselves Little Wolf cried out again.

"Charge! Charge!"

In an instant the whooping, screaming warriors lunged as one great body toward the soldiers trying to help their wounded. The blue line crumbled down the hill, stumbling over itself. More arrows and bullets followed the confusion of retreat and more soldiers fell. As they moved, warriors designated for the task quickly gathered what they could from the battle-ground: their own arrows, rifles from the dead, bullets dropped in the haste of reloading, even a precious box full of cartridges lost in the panic. Before they went too far Little Wolf blew his eagle bone whistle, signaling their return. From the hill they could see the blue specks below milling around the great wagons, while two soldiers rode out to the east, probably to get help.

After a while small groups of soldiers and warriors skirmished around the hill, but without much enthusiasm for the fight. The ridge was too well chosen and virtually impossible to penetrate. By evening the soldiers had pulled back again to the supply wagons in the distance Little Wolf called the people together.

"We were lucky today with only a few wounded. These soldiers from the south are not like those in the north. They are not used to fighting Indians and they turn away too quickly. But we cannot stay here. Their numbers will swell when the riders who left get help; then they will swarm over us without the need of discipline. Soon the sun will disappear and we must also.

Eat quickly now; we leave after dark."

So the weary bodies ate a hasty bite and built up their fires for the soldiers to see and think they remained. It was still dark when Calf and the others reached the Arrowpoint River, meeting there the chiefs' sons, Woodenthigh and Bull Hump, sent ahead to prepare the way across. Everyone felt an ominous chill standing there in the darkness, listening to the current and the gentle splashes. Surely there would be soldiers nearby, perhaps on the other side, waiting to pounce on them, Calf thought.

But beside the fear, they felt something deep within, tying them to this place, this river. Next to these waters, long ago, a woman had come to the Cheyenne from a far-away place. It was this woman who gave them the form of government they used to this day and in gratitude they named her the Great Mother. Each of them thought of that sacred beginning, of the debt to that woman, of their desperation now to preserve Great Mother's ways.

Dull Knife made the first splash into the river, following the willow reed path laid by the two warriors. At intervals, willow reeds had been thrust into the river bed to guide the people across a shallow part of the river. One by one they struggled against the current, the children crying and the horses lunging, until everyone was across but the invisible party of Comes in Sight Woman. Once on the other side, they came to the strange wooden road that carried the great smoking metal snake filled with whites. But there were no soldiers and no snake tonight, only the noise of the crickets.

While the warriors helped people across the river, Buffalo Calf Road led the women ahead, taking them up Punished Woman Creek, looking for a place to camp in the gray light of dawn. The place she selected was a dry riverbed, emptying into Punished Woman Creek when the rains came. The ravine climbed upward, cutting into solid canyon walls. At a point towering above the creek, Calf told the women to make camp. When the others began to arrive, small fires already burned their welcome.

First Calf instructed the women to build breast-works, so they chopped the earth with their knives and scooped hollows in the ground. Surely the soldiers will come again, Calf thought, and it was a good place to fight. After resting a bit in the quiet canyon, the women began to repair moccasins and clothing and to search the riverbed shrubs for berries. The old men made arrows, Medicine Woman and Bridge gathered herbs and roots for their treatments, and the warriors hunted for game. Even the children helped by collecting buffalo chips for the fires.

By late afternoon the hunters returned jubilant, having found a small herd of buffalo. A great cheering climbed the dark stone walls, growing fainter and fainter as it spread across the blue sky above the riverbed. Soon the delicious aroma of roasting meat rose out of the canyon and vanished into the great space above the earth where the sun moved indifferently in its endless circle. Alone in a gully to the south, Comes in Sight's grieving party butchered a buffalo cow left for them by the warriors. That night the Cheyenne slept soundly, secure in their rocky fortress. The decision had been made to rest here for two or three days and to make a stand if the soldiers came, since only more prairie lay ahead.

Before she opened her eyes the next morning, Calf heard the chirping of birds in the morning coolness. Overhead a circling cliff swallow flew into sight, its brown wings extended in front of its short squared tail, its white forehead cutting the air in a graceful slice. Above the swallow the early morning light stayed in the sky, its horizontal rays unable to enter the shadowy canyon. Calf glanced from the soaring bird to the sleeping children beside her. Gently she ran her fingers over their soft dark hair. Little Seeker had known some good times, briefly, but the baby, the baby with no name, had never seen a time of peace.

Were it not for the fear of the bluecoats, the next two days would have been like the old days. The children played games; the young men courted the young women with their reserved ways; the warriors hunted or worked over their weapons; old friends visited; and married couples made love again. A new spirit came over the village with no lodges and a new strength filled their bodies as they ate the good buffalo meat. Even a quiet wedding took place in the canyon above Punished Woman Creek—Broad Faced One, always with her parents, had consented to marry Limpy, though she did not untie her chastity rope for several days.

Early on the third day, scouts returned with news. Many soldiers approached from the south, not far away. Immediately Little Wolf called the warriors together, this time with Calf and the other women who fought now in the rifle pits with the men. Quickly he laid his plans for ambush. The Dog warriors would wait in rifle pits on the cliffs above the point where the dry riverbed ran into Punished Woman Creek. Below them at the entrance, several warriors would remain hidden in the willow trees to build a fire in the narrow opening to the riverbed after the soldiers had all passed through, preventing their escape. Two others would hide just past the entrance to gather the rifles and ammunition of the fallen bluecoats. Deep up the ravine, the rest of the warriors would wait in their rifle pits mounting the ambush from the front, while the Dog warriors fired from the rear. Little Wolf cautioned them again and again to stay quiet, to give no sign of the ambush. Meanwhile Dull Knife led the rest of the women and children and the sick and old ones far back into a twisting gully.

Slowly the bluecoats worked their way along Punished Woman Creek, dragging their wagons and pack mules over the rocky ground. Little Wolf moved among the warriors, urging them to hold their fire. He said nothing to Calf and the women in their pits for he knew their patience, they who had no manhood to prove and no need to count the first coup.

At last the big soldier chief, whom no one recognized, led his men toward the canyon. A spasm of tension passed over the silent cliff. Suddenly, before the soldiers reached the juncture, a shot rang across the canyon from the gun of one of the Southern Cheyenne boys who had come after them from the agency. A moan of despair passed through the pits at the betrayal.

The soldiers began to charge the canyon in a fury, spilling back and up the cliffs from all sides, like a raging river bursting its banks. In a frenzy Little Wolf dispatched some warriors to protect .the retreating Cheyenne on the cliffs. Then, grabbing his quirt stick, he wheeled around, lumbering like a great angry bear toward the guilty young man, and raising his stick, he slashed it across the boy's face. The great plan had crumbled, their lives put in danger, because of an impetuous and undisciplined youth.

Already one Indian fell from his horse in the retreat and was trampled in the crush. The soldiers kept coming up the ravine and along both cliffs, sending a volley of bullets ahead. The Cheyenne answered with bullets and arrows and the bluecoat charge fell back for a moment to regroup. But more soldiers and wagons and horses kept arriving below, covering the ground like a plague of blue beetles.

Little Wolf ordered those in the first rifle holes to fall back. Calf and Leaf waited in their gravelike pit with the other women—Singing Cloud, Hog's Daughter, Pretty Walker, the Princesses, Yellow

Woman—all with their guns and bows poised. When a second charge got close, they let fly their missiles. Two bluecoats fell to the ground as their comrades dropped back to reload. Little Wolf ordered the women back.

Meanwhile the soldiers crawling over the cliffs made a discovery. Hidden carefully in a deep gully, the small pony herd of the Cheyenne, loaded with precious buffalo meat and fruit, moccasins, and the other poor things they owned now, had been found. Calf grabbed Leaf's hand when she saw the bluecoat commotion by the hidden gully and the two clung to each other in despair. The warriors were far back now, pushed nearly to the place where the children and the others crouched, sobbing in fear. Brave One ran among the children shouting.

"We are Cheyenne! Do not shame our people. Be brave!"

At last, when it seemed hopeless and the final charge just moments away, Black Coyote rose in their midst.

"I will not die like a gopher trapped in his hole!"

Then he stepped forward defiantly and stood waiting for the last charge, clutching his rifle in front of him. In an instant Calf was on her feet. She rushed back to where Chicken Woman held her baby, and quickly strapping the infant to her back, she rushed forward and stood beside the Coyote, her six-shooter in her hand. Whetstone came too, then Black Horse limped up, followed by his wife. The others watched dumbfounded as Chicken Woman raced to the side of Whetstone, and the proud group stood impassively waiting to fight and die.

Suddenly Wild Hog rushed before them like a great angry boar.

"No!" he shouted. "Do not waste yourselves. Something may happen. The Cheyenne are not dead yet!" With his great hulk of a body and voice, he pushed them back, though he never touched them.

Little Wolf rushed in.

"My brothers and sisters. We will keep fighting. Sweet Medicine guides us."

Chicken Woman took the baby from Calf again, and the young woman returned to Leaf and the others just as another charge flew against them. The sight of the six brave ones had deeply moved the Cheyenne and they fought with a new heart. This time many bluecoats crashed to the ground, so the others pulled back. Little Hawk got the attention of Little Finger Nail and motioned toward some boulders. Quickly they crawled out of the pit and over the ground, and together they shoved the great boulders over the sides, sending one after another crashing among the startled bluecoats.

Still the charges came. At one point the old men entreated Little Wolf to surrender to the *veho*, but he refused. Others urged the chief to send a few strong men and women out of the canyons to preserve the seed of the Cheyenne, lest everyone be killed. Again he refused, urging patience and courage.

"Something will happen," he kept saying, clutching the Sweet Medicine bundle strapped to his chest.

By late afternoon many soldiers had fallen along with many wounded Indians, though only two Cheyenne were killed. Then something did happen. The noise and the charging seemed to fade even as the light in the canyon faded. No one understood it until Bear Shield rushed into their midst.

"The big soldier chief has been shot! The bluecoats move back to their wagons!"

A gasp of disbelief and relief rose from the crowd.

"You have done it, my friends. You pushed back the soldiers!" Little Wolf praised them generously. Then he added quickly, "We must go from this place now. There is no time to lose. Make no sound, but gather together the hidden ones."

So the tired band set out again, running on foot through the long, twisting ravines that opened to the north. With bad hearts they ran all night, unable to mourn out loud for the dead warriors or for the father of Singing Cloud, found dead in his hiding place. The few remaining horses carried the wounded. By morning they found themselves without food and without a mother and son, lost somewhere in the night flight and never found.

During the next morning they discovered that Comes in Sight's party had somehow gotten ahead of them and was leaving markers indicating the way to avoid places where whites lived. By afternoon they had crossed the Bunch of Trees River and another wooden road for the metal snake that smoked as it ran over the timbers. With their people hungry and exhausted, the young warriors took to raiding again, looking for horses and cattle.

Always north they raced, dragging and carrying their tired children, hardly stopping to rest, hungry and cold now in the chill fall nights. When Black Coyote and the others rode a herd of horses into their midst a great cheering rose from the tired lips. But an anxiety rose with the cheers. If they were caught stealing horses, all would be hung.

First the headmen and their families got horses, then the others. Bull Hump offered the rope of a black and white mare to Short One, struggling with her packs. The horse seemed calm enough and Short One began loading her packs. Suddenly two Dog warriors rode among them from the rear.

"Soldiers! Soldiers are coming!"

In a nervous fluster, Short One threw on the rest of her packs and tried to mount the mare, but her skirt, slapping in the prairie wind, and the agitation all around, caused the animal to lunge and buck. Short One clutched the mare, digging her fingers into the horse's skin to keep from falling. Before Leaf or anyone could help, Short One slipped from the horse and landed under the pounding hoofs. Dull Knife rushed to the side of his wife, her body already lifeless and her face bloody.

"The soldiers!" someone cried out. "The soldiers are close."

For a while they dragged the body of Short One on a makeshift travois, everyone riding double and triple, even quadruple now, to escape the pursuing bluecoats. But the travois was slowing them down, so Brave One and the Princesses insisted on staying behind and burying the woman they all loved. From their hiding place on a rocky hill, the women with their corpse watched as one great cloud of dust disappeared to the north and another moved in from the south. When both clouds had passed they buried Short One in a rocky grave and keened their sorrow to the silent prairie while Short One's men, Dull Knife, Bull Hump, and Little Hump, rode in lonely silence among the fleeing people through the lengthening shadows of the late afternoon.

Toward evening, Cheyenne scouts reported that the army had stopped to make camp for the night. Little Wolf kept them moving though the horses were near exhaustion and several had fallen already. Ahead of them lay the Sappa Creek, and the memory of the massacre there darkened the Cheyenne faces worse than the blackening night.

Around midnight Little Wolf signaled them to stop and rest a bit, but they sat about listlessly, thinking and talking about the killing of their Southern relatives at the Sappa just three years ago, remembering how the whites had clubbed their babies to death and thrown them on the fires of their burning lodges, how they had shot to death the old Keeper of the Sacred Arrows, how they had cut down the women who leapt

264

against them so others could escape. Little Wolf saw the blood of the warriors boil at the words and sensed trouble, so he went among them, warning the men that their people would pay dearly if they sought revenge. He ordered them to take only horses and food if they rode out and to leave the white women and children alone. But the few Southern warriors among them would have none of Little Wolf's orders, and together with some Northern warriors they left the moving people at dawn to raid among the settlers, determined to kill one white man for each Indian man left dead at the Sappa.

Buffalo Calf Road was angry at all this, angry at the thought of innocent people being killed by men too quick to use the gun. The warriors were needed among their people, for finding food and horses, she said hotly to Leaf, as they crossed the Sappa. Afterwards, when she heard that a small white boy watching sheep had been killed, she was furious.

Later two southern warriors returned with two girls captured from one of the strange dirt houses of the whites. What was left of their clothes hung in shreds from their bodies and their blue eyes were frozen in terror. Calf leapt from her horse at the sight of one of the warriors parading his prize as he yanked a blond mass of disheveled hair.

"Let her go!" Calf cried in a rage.

The young man laughed.

"She is mine! I will keep her as my woman!"

"Let her go!" Calf said again, pulling her pistol from

her belt and cocking the hammer of her gun. "Let her go!"

Leaf stepped forward and stood beside Calf, her hand resting on the gun in her belt.

As Calf straightened her arm to fire, the youth let the yellow mass fall and the girl crumbled in a heap, like so many twigs from a broken bundle. Her sister rushed to her side and the two clung together in desperation.

"Get some blankets!" Calf said to the people with no blankets standing behind her.

Somehow two blankets appeared and were handed to Calf as the two warriors glared in hatred. Little Wolf arrived, and seeing the white girls, began quirting the two young men as the crowd looked away in shame. Calf wrapped a blanket around each of the frightened girls, gently touching their yellow hair as Little Wolf ordered one of the Southern youths to give his horse to the girls. After the blond ones rode away, the group began moving again, some riding, some walking to save the horses.

Next they crossed the Red Shield River where they slept for a short while in a deep draw along its banks. But Little Wolf would not let them stay long, for all that saved them from the pursuing soldiers was the fact that they kept moving while the bluecoats rested. In the days that followed the crossing, the warriors brought in some game, but it was too little to satisfy all the empty stomachs. They had better luck at capturing horses and managed to seize about 200 ponies.

However, before three days were out, half of the horses collapsed from the constant running, and several old and sick Cheyenne fell and died in the rush.

Again the soldiers came, but not as many as at Punished Woman Creek, and the doubling and tripling on the horses were repeated as the warriors put themselves between the bluecoats and the fleeing people. This time the run was frantic, the bullets killing and wounding children and adults. When the soldiers fell back and the Cheyenne stopped at last to breathe, they discovered in horror that two babies hanging in the sacks on their mother's horses had been banged to death in the furious run from the soldiers' bullets. That same day Limpy's father, Buffalo Chips, was shot to death by some cowboys as he followed a stray horse over a ridge.

At last they reached the great, wide, shallow river called the Fat River. It was the fourth day of the Moon When the Water Freezes at the Edges and the waters should have been covered with great flocks of geese making their way south from the Grandmother's Country. In the old days great herds of buffalo and antelope drank at the Fat River, but now only a few ducks floated quietly over its muddy waters and a thin line of geese honked far overhead as they flew in arrowhead formation away from the cold high plains and the coming snow. Calf had always loved the sound of geese, but today they seemed ominous in their escape south. Ahead of them lay still another wooden road for the metal snake, which they quickly crossed, and that same day, a small way from there, they crossed the Moon Shell River.

That night they rested around a big fire, fed well with piles of logs to keep away the frosty night air. Dull Knife, whose tongue had fallen silent after the death of his wife, spoke some unexpected words.

"We must make our way to our friends the Lakota—to Red Cloud."

Little Wolf started. "Have we fled one reservation to die on another?" he asked in disbelief.

"And no one has died off the reservation?" the Knife snapped back.

"My friend," Little Wolf said, hearing the anguish in the old man's voice, "we planned to go north."

"We are north now!" the other interrupted.

"Yes, but not on the Powder River or the Elk River or the Bighorn Mountains of our ancestors."

The tired rough voice of Dull Knife continued.

"Smell the air. It's wet and cold. The white grizzly will be on us in days."

"Yes," Old Crow nodded in agreement. "Winter is almost here and we have nothing—no lodges, no blankets, no food."

"And the soldiers," Sitting Man put in, "we cannot run from the soldiers forever."

Buffalo Calf Road could stay silent no longer.

"Little Wolf has brought us safely all this way," she said. "We cannot go back to the reservation."

"The soldier chiefs on the reservation promised," Dull Knife said to the woman who dared speak among

268

the men. "They promised we could return if the South did not suit us."

"You believe them?" Calf asked. "You believe Three Stars and Bad Hand who led the army against our people?"

Dull Knife turned away.

"I believe them. They could have forced us south without the promise."

"You make too much of the idle words of the *veho,*" Little Wolf said quietly, not wishing to rouse the old chief to anger.

But the crack in their midst had begun, and it widened.

"You deceive yourself," Dull Knife sputtered. "Our people cannot go on. Red Cloud is our friend. He will take us in."

"I beg you not to do this," Little Wolf pleaded. "We must stay together."

"Then come with me to Red Cloud!" Dull Knife said.

Already the warriors were muttering in the background, taking sides. Little Wolf sensed the ominous division and spoke.

"I will not lead my people into the spider's web a second time. I will take them home!"

Dull Knife's anger boiled over.

"Fool!" the Knife shouted. "You will take our people to starvation, to the bullet, to the freezing death! Enough!"

The grumbling grew louder. Calf looked around in

alarm. How had this happened? Were they still not of one mind after all? Little Wolf saw what it would come to if they continued to argue. The tension would erupt among the warriors, frightened in spite of their show of bravery, pitting them against each other. He touched Sweet Medicine's bundle on his chest and the prediction of the Cheyenne hero came to him:

You will lose respect for your leaders and start quarreling with one another . . . You will forget the good things by which you have lived and in the end become worse than crazy.

Little Wolf stood up and spoke slowly.
"I will step aside. Everyone who wishes to continue north with me is welcome."
A quiet hush settled over the people and for a shocked instant, no one moved. Then, as one mind, Buffalo Calf Road and Black Coyote rose, and picking up their children, followed Little Wolf. Then Wild Hog and Tangle Hair stepped behind Dull Knife. Slowly, painfully, the people separated into two clusters as the night thrust a black wedge between them and the wind spoke their names.

CHAPTER 8

By morning Dull Knife's band had disappeared into the dense fog that hung like tears all around. Behind them a gesture of love lay on the cold, bare earth: a rifle, a little ammunition, and a buffalo skin from a recent kill. An unspeakable sorrow weighed on the people left behind at White Tail Creek, who felt a paralyzing loneliness like that of a rocky grave. A sense of finality, of permanent end, followed the separation of those who had lived together in good times and seen death come among them in bad times. The pale figures moving about in the hollow white mist shuffled around like ghosts, packing their meager belongings for a last departure.

Calf was despondent on this morning that blocked out the sun. Little Seeker stayed near the red-eyed woman sorrowing in silence. The homecoming was not to be for the Cheyenne, scattered now in the south and the north, pushed apart by the white takers multiplying in their midst, exerting their influence even from afar.

Quickly, despite the burden of sorrow, a gaunt and haggard Little Wolf went among them, even now urging them on. There was still the army to worry about, even in grief. So the band of proud holdouts, shrunken now to 126, set out again, vanishing into the swallowing fog as their kin had done earlier that morning.

Dull Knife turned his people northwest in the dark mist. His breath came heavy from the weight of loss that crushed his chest as he slowly worked his horse through the plum and chokecherry thickets, stooping under their unpicked fruit. Little Wolf will make it now, he thought, without the slow ones keeping him back. All of the sick and wounded, all of the very old except Old Grandmother, and most of the children followed in Dull Knife's procession. No one spoke as they moved through the shroud of gray fog wrapping them in sorrow.

Leaf stared at the shadowy figure of her husband riding ahead of her, now real, now unreal, as the thick earth clouds came and faded and came again. She loved Bull Hump and she had little choice but to follow him when he chose the path of his father rather than Little Wolf. But it gnawed at her, this separation. Dull Knife was wrong, she felt, and she cringed to think what Bad Hand would do when they returned to the agency. And she thought of Calf, dear Calf, who would lead the women home or die trying. Already she missed her friend, only so many moccasin steps away. I will never see her again, Leaf thought, as the path in the thicket grew narrow and the first rays of the hidden sun made the fog look heavier.

Hog's daughter and her friend, Singing Cloud, still mourning the death of her father, rode quietly together on a horse. She knew that Singing Cloud wanted to stay out with Little Wolf and Calf and the others, but she was a young woman without family now, and

Wild Hog had offered to take her in when they fled Punished Woman Creek. She wanted to reach up and comfort Singing Cloud, to reassure her, but the words would not come.

Behind them Little Finger Nail rode, unable to comprehend the separation. On his back the ledger book hung, full of colorful drawings depicting the glorious Cheyenne past. The scenes often crowded into his thoughts, but today they seemed just so many lines on paper, so many unreal images gone forever. He cared for Singing Cloud more than anyone, so he followed her now, concluding in his fatalism that he could die as well here, in the place whites called Nebraska, as in the Bighorn Mountains.

Brave One came in Dull Knife's party too, leading her small group of women and children. The little ones' blistered feet limped along, their arms and legs as thin as the twigs that fall from trees in the first winter wind. With them came Lame Girl, carried mostly, once so full of life and chatter—had they really once called her Runs Ahead?—but now wasted and silent. By herself, Brave One would have gone with Calf and Black Coyote, but with the suffering children she could not.

Iron Teeth and her young ones, too, followed Dull Knife. All the way she had carried the southern fever and chills and her children feared for her in the brutal winter of the high plains. Her son insisted she go with Dull Knife to seek the help of the great Chief Red Cloud. Besides, her oldest daughter and youngest son had left with others some days before to find the reservation, and Iron Teeth wanted the family united again.

Medicine Woman and Bridge came too, both of them needed to care for the wounded, sick, and old. Great Eyes, still carrying his sacred shield and tended by his nephew Red Bird, chose to stay with his daughter, Leaf. The Dog warriors followed Tangle Hair, the old men followed Dull Knife, and the women followed their husbands and fathers. The newlyweds, Limpy and Broad Faced One, came too, hoping for a lodge of their own and some privacy. Yellow Woman, fearful for her son and baby, followed the rest. In all 149 followed Dull Knife, all of them sad at the parting, none of them certain they had chosen the best trail. Like sleepwalkers in an endless night they moved, never stopping but barely conscious that they moved.

By late morning the damp fog began to lift. In fluffy pieces it rose, like the feathered seeds of the milkweed pod blown in the wind, the drying rays of the sun taking their places. After a while, the shrill cry of a Dog scout bringing up the rear pierced the air. "Soldiers! Soldiers on the trail!"

Wild Hog looked quickly at Dull Knife. The old man looked exhausted, dispirited. He made no move, so Hog flew out. He sent the warriors to guard the rear and ordered the others to scatter into the sand hills and build rifle pits wherever they could. Meanwhile Leaf, Singing Cloud, Little Finger Nail, She Bear, and

Hog's wife raced to make a decoy. They circled around a hill in the direction of the army approach and quickly made a wide false trail away from the pits. It took most of the day for the slow-moving soldiers, whose wagons sunk into the sand, to catch on, and by then the Cheyenne had slipped away.

For several days they kept moving northwest, just a little each day, resting in sheltered places along the way. They went slowly because an invitation had not yet come from Chief Red Cloud, although they had sent three people to tell the Oglala of their plight. Within a day's ride of the Agency, Dull Knife hid his people in a rocky canyon past the Sudden River. When still no one came, Hog and Dull Knife sent a formal mission to the old chief at Pine Ridge—Bull Hump, Tangle Hair, and Young Hog, and since tradition required two women to prove no evil intent, Leaf and one of the Princesses went too.

The haggard people settled uneasily in the chill to wait some more. They lived on roots and berries, a little wild game, and their horses, daring not to touch the white man's cattle and make known their presence.

One night while scouting, Black Coyote and Little Hawk found the cold camp of Dull Knife's people and warned them soldiers were everywhere, that Red Cloud's reservation crawled with the white spiders.

"Come back," they pleaded as everyone watched Dull Knife for a sign.

But the old man tightened his lips and spoke the

275

frozen words, "Red Cloud will help my people," so Black Coyote and Little Hawk said good-bye.

At last the huddled people spotted the party returning from the reservation, their bodies hunched over their horses against the growing cold. When Bull Hump approached his father, his face was tense and drawn. Quickly a crowd gathered.

"There are bluecoats everywhere. The Lakota are ordered about like the pay soldiers themselves." His eyes fell to the ground.

Hog's son stepped forward.

"The soldier chiefs have ordered Red Cloud to surrender any Cheyenne they see to the army." He spoke softly, ashamed to tell of the once great chief, now commanded by whites. "Many Lakota warriors scout for the white man. They are searching for us now." And then, "The three you sent before us to Red Cloud are captured."

"Red Cloud is beaten," Leaf added. "He tells us to surrender to the bluecoats. He would have us trade our freedom for a cup of water soup, as he has."

"That is not the worst!" Tangle Hair added, sensing the reluctance of the others to let the words out. "We are to be sent south again, back to Indian Territory."

Dull Knife's head jerked at the words. His face blanched and his fists clenched. He looked very old, this peace dreamer, as a small fire leapt over the deep crevices covering his face. He could hear the stifled moans and the soft crying around him. He could see the mothers clutching their little ones, though his eyes stuck to the ground. He heard the silent despair of the young people. Slowly they all rose, out of deference for the old one who meant well, leaving him alone with his sorrow and anger.

Wild Hog tried to take charge. Fourteen precious sleeps had been lost in the Sand Hills waiting for an invitation from their Lakota brother. The weather had grown cold, the time of the first snow already overdue. Where could they go now? Bearcoat had offered them a place at the fort on the Elk River. But that was long ago, before they surrendered at Fort Robinson, before they were sent south. There was Spotted Tail on his own reservation. But there were no ties with Spotted Tail's people as there were with the Oglala. Nonetheless Wild Hog decided out of desperation to seek help from Spotted Tail.

The next morning the band set out to find Spotted Tail, to suffer the shame of begging for food and supplies if he could not take them in. Their horses limped, weak from hunger, and many people walked. Another damp mist had risen among them during the night, but by dawn the air turned bitter cold and the wind sent a driving freezing rain against them. The children clung to their mothers who had no warm blankets or buffalo robes to draw about them. Walking was hard as a fierce wind shoved them over the slick earth. The air got colder still and the icy rain turned to snow, falling fast and hard and rising everywhere in sharp mounds on the frozen ground. The wind stabbed them with icy spears and drove the snow so thick that the world

277

turned white and empty of all but pain.

Then, in an instant, out of the blinding swirl, Lakota figures appeared in their bluecoat finery. The Cheyenne gasp lost itself in the howling wind as the ragged people found each other again in a desperate huddle. A wall appeared behind the army Indian scouts, a wall of mounted soldiers and pointed muzzles. The Cheyenne warriors who rushed up met the wall.

Quickly Dull Knife and Wild Hog urged their stooping ponies forward.

"We are hurting no one," Dull Knife said. "Let us pass."

American Horse, an Oglala who was once their friend, addressed them now behind his garish army buttons.

"It's no use. Stop now. The soldiers will feed you and make you warm." His voice rose to a shout against the howling wind.

At that point a soldier chief, one they did not recognize, came forward.

"No one will harm your people." A fierce gust threw the words back at him. "We want to shelter you!"

Dull Knife moved next to the talking bluecoat and leaned into the snow driving between them in an effort to be heard.

"My people were dying in the south," he cried over the wind, in a plea for understanding. "We are going to Spotted Tail!"

"I'm sorry!" the soldier chief shouted, the effort of

speaking in the blizzard draining his patience. "You must come with us." With that he gestured the soldiers forward to herd the freezing Cheyenne with guns drawn.

Quickly Hog spoke, raising his hand.

"I will ask the people what they wish," he said in his gruff way, as though they spoke in the great councils of old and everyone had a choice.

In a moment he returned, proud and tall on his shabby mount.

"The people have decided to follow you."

Straight into the wind the soldier chief pointed them, soldiers in front, soldiers in back, soldiers alongside. On foot they moved, through the swelling drifts, dragging their stumbling horses and children and rag-bound feet. When they fell, the bluecoats extended a furred hand, prodding them on and on. At last they reached the army camp where a huge fire and food waited in a sheltered place among the hills. Some of the old ones cried at the smell of coffee boiling on the fire, while a few of the young soldier recruits stared in disbelief at the wretched poverty of the frozen Cheyenne. Everywhere a low moaning could be heard as the burning needles pierced the swollen frostbitten limbs extended toward the flaming warmth.

That night they slept in makeshift lean-tos, shivering in fear under the piling snow, watched by a guard of bluecoats. By early morning the soldier chief appeared among them again, giving his orders through an interpreter.

"Give up your horses and your weapons!" he shouted.

So it begins again, Hog thought to himself, but immediately he began a long talk, a stalling talk, with others joining in, stalling, stalling, so the people could hide a few of the guns. Brave One heard and quickly dismantled a rifle, hanging the trigger from a leather thong around Lame Girl's neck, attaching the lever and hammer on the belts of two other children, strapping the barrel to her leg and giving the butt to her friend to slip in her blouse. Leaf and some other women did the same, hiding the guns in their skirts or taking them apart. No one would search the women.

When the soldier chief lost his patience, they came forward with the horses and a few guns, a very few. The bluecoat looked skeptical, but Wild Hog insisted that was all.

"We hunt with bow and arrow," he said innocently.

"Bring me the bows and arrows!" the soldier said, and reluctantly the warriors threw down the weapons of their ancestors, crafted by the old men in their midst.

The next day more soldiers came with empty wagons to carry the Cheyenne to Fort Robinson.

"Fort Robinson!" Dull Knife gasped, as he thought of the place from which they were sent south.

The Indians refused and threatened and vowed to die on the spot, but in the end the two-bang gun and the many rifles pointed in their direction spoke louder, and the people were carted away like bundles of hay

280

thrown on a farm wagon. All the way to Fort Robinson the men and women chanted their prayers and their death songs.

"Sacred Persons, help us."

"Sun, smile on your sons and daughters."

"Cheyenne, it is a good day to die."

Only Little Finger Nail sat tight lipped and silent, looking straight ahead.

The bitter cold day hung over the wagons. No more snow fell but the drifts had grown as tall as the tallest Cheyenne in places and the way had to be cleared, a narrow trench wide enough only for a single file of horses and wagons. Along the trail high mounds of snow covered the hollow underbrush, spraying its frozen crystals as the wagons pushed against its branches.

The moving branches caught Leaf's eye. She waited and watched. They were near the fort, but night would cover them before it came. Finally she caught her chance in a narrow place of great drifts, with the lights of the fort shining ahead in the darkness. One of the Lakota scouts rode behind her wagon, but she moved anyway. Quietly and quickly, as though she were mounting a touchy wild steed, Leaf climbed over the side of the wagon and threw her body into the snow-laden underbrush, falling in an instant through the snow, through the branches, and into the hollow place beneath. As she fell, the Lakota scout's horse pushed against the bush, its hoofs nearly touching her, but nothing more happened.

The wagons rolled by, the bluecoat horses passed, but still the Lakota on the horse waited by the bush. When everything had gone, the Lakota reached his hand into the bush and motioned her out, swiftly lifting the woman behind him on the horse. Slowly, letting the others get far ahead, he trailed the caravan and took her straight to the lodges reserved for the bluecoat Indian scouts.

While her people were being counted and herded into a long empty barracks, Leaf disguised herself as a Lakota scout, braiding her hair like a man and wearing the bluecoat clothes of her new friend. Perhaps out of guilt, perhaps out of shame that a woman was driven to this, perhaps out of fear for their Lakota brother who had brought her among them, everyone kept quiet, letting her come and go as one of them. In the days that followed, Leaf went among her people, motioning them to make no sign, all the while watching to see what would happen.

Meanwhile, Little Wolf's band had learned of the capture and their scouts watched the fort from a distance. Many sleeps after their arrival at Fort Robinson, Leaf spoke to Black Coyote in the cliffs above the barracks. The gaunt husband of her friend looked more agitated then usual as he pressed Leaf for details. The Coyote spoke wildly of attacking the fort and freeing the band, as though he could do it alone. He raged against the old men for their weakness and it seemed to Leaf he blamed them for conspiring to bring about the capture. The Coyote alarmed her. His words betrayed erratic thoughts; his behavior must be the same she fretted, thinking of Calf.

During the sleeps that followed, Little Wolf's scouts carried a few supplies to the cliffs above the fort, hiding them in a cave against the day when Dull Knife's people would leave the whites' long wooden houses. Berries and strips of deer meat multiplied in the spot and Leaf learned that Little Wolf's band hid at Lost Chokecherry Creek, where the game was plentiful. Not long after she had spoken with Black Coyote, Leaf found Calf waiting high in the cliffs with Little Wolf's warriors.

The two women embraced tearfully, but the tears quickly turned to laughter as Calf looked over the bluecoat disguise. For a long time they sat in the crisp air against the sheltering rock ledge, talking softly as Leaf related conditions at the fort.

"The soldiers have all our horses and what guns they could find. But the women have managed to hide a few still."

"How are they treated, Leaf?" Calf interjected.

"Quite well, at first," she answered. "Our people were allowed to move about the fort freely and in the beginning one of the small soldier chiefs gave us a great deal of meat. He is called Chase and he feels a kindness for Lame Girl. It is the first she has laughed in many moons. Some of the white women have been kind too."

Calf listened intently.

"One woman especially, the wife of a soldier chief

283

named Lawson, came everyday with her daughter to comfort the women and bring them things. Even one of the owners of a great cattle herd visited often with the men, bringing news and tobacco. Bronson, this cattleman, has become good friends with Little Finger Nail and is greatly interested in the Nail's drawings of our people. And since I am a scout for the army," Leaf laughed, "I too have been allowed to visit the Cheyenne."

Then her face became serious.

"But all this has changed. Several sleeps ago a new soldier chief took over the fort. He ordered our women to work about the grounds—they must unload the grain wagons and pick up the horse droppings and trash."

An old anger crept into Calf's eyes as she listened silently to this new indignity.

"He has stopped the white women from visiting and Chase no longer plays with the children. Even the Lakota scouts cannot talk to the Cheyenne." She paused, looking at the ground. "I have not spoken to Bull Hump or my father for days."

"Who is this man?" Calf asked, thinking it might be one of their old enemies—Bad Hand, Three Stars, or Bearcoat.

"I have never seen him before," Leaf answered. "The soldiers call him Captain Wessells. He is a funny man—short, always moving, always darting about like a rat."

"What does it mean?" Calf asked.

"The bluecoats insist we return south," Leaf said.

"Surely Dull Knife will not agree," Calf answered in dismay.

"Dull Knife sits quietly with his thoughts. It is Wild Hog who speaks for us now."

"And he . . . ?" Calf asked.

"He will not agree. But . . ." Leaf hesitated. "Soon we will have no choice."

Calf looked deeply into the young woman's face. The same strength was there, yet a fatalism had crept into her eyes.

"We will go south or we will die," Leaf prophesied simply.

Calf took her friend's hands.

"Come with me to Lost Chokecherry. There is nothing you can do here now."

Leaf smiled at the thought of the lodges tucked in the small valley far to the east.

"How are the little ones? And Black Coyote?"

She saw Calf's face stiffen.

"You saw him," Calf answered. "What do you think?"

Leaf shook her head sadly.

"He is ill. A sickness claws at his mind. But why, now that you can rest and hunt a bit and are safe?"

"Yes. The rest is good and it heals the body, but it cannot cure the sickness of the mind. He's not well, Leaf, and I fear for him. He has followed a trail and he will never return. None of us will."

As she spoke Calf stared at the ground where

285

patches of snow partly covered the dead box elder leaves. Overhead the green cedars stood dark against the sky of The Moon of the Big Freeze. It was midafternoon when Calf said yet another tearful good-bye to her friend.

Calf and the others had gone a good distance from the cliffs above the fort when the distant report of gun-fire suddenly reached them. It seemed to follow them directly over the twisting trail left behind. Without thinking, Calf whirled about on her horse, urging the animal back over its own footsteps as the scouts fol-lowed. The shots had stopped as quickly as they began.

As they neared the cliffs again, the small group moved cautiously. A strange quiet hung over the frozen earth as the cedars continued to tower indiffer-ently. Calf dismounted and tied her horse to a naked box elder as the others followed. Slowly she picked her way through the rocks and trees, searching every-where with her darting black eyes, till at last she reached the edge of the cliffs near the spot where Leaf had stood watching her leave. Then she saw them.

Four bluecoats moved on horseback toward the fort across the fields below, flanking two figures on foot, their hands tied behind their backs. With a sinking heart Calf immediately recognized the tiny figures walking in the distance, though she only saw their backs. It was Leaf and her husband, Bull Hump.

A furious army chief ordered the two into the prison barracks, where the rest of the Cheyenne already sat crowded together. The relative freedom of Dull Knife's people to move about the grounds had disappeared with Bull Hump's escape two days before. The first day the young warrior hid himself well, but when he tried to find Leaf at the cave she had told him about, the bluecoats picked up his trail.

The log prison consisted of one room holding the prisoners, about thirty paces on each side, and a smaller adjoining kitchen. What little light found its way into the dark prison entered through two small windows. Rough wooden floor boards covered the damp earth and through the timber walls the cold penetrated to the blanketless people. A potbelly stove provided a little heat. The prisoners sat about on the floor and on wooden benches lining the room. The men used a makeshift toilet closet while the guards herded the children and women out to the snow-covered fields in small groups to relieve themselves. The Cheyenne still wore the tattered dress they arrived with; neither clothing nor blankets had been provided by the army.

For days the Cheyenne sat locked in the room, crowded and cold. They were asked repeatedly if they would return south. Always the answer was the same, "We will die before we go south."

The coldest part of winter arrived, the Moon of the Frost in the Lodges. Then the order came, four days into the new moon: The Cheyenne must prepare at once to move south to Indian Territory. Through his interpreter, Wessells told Wild Hog, Tangle Hair, and

Dull Knife to take one day to get ready.

"We will never go south," Hog snorted at Wessells.

The day of preparation came and went. Hog and the others stood firm on the land of their ancestors. The message to the hated soldier chief was simple, "We will die first."

The fidgety Wessells was furious at Hog and had the warrior brought to his office.

"It is the will of the Great White Father in Washington. It is not for me to decide such things. I must obey orders and you must too! We want no trouble. Your people must go quietly," Wessells said.

Hog sat impassively as the words passed through the interpreter and would speak no more. Pacing back and forth Wessells issued an order to Lieutenant Chase: no more food, no more fuel for the Cheyenne! Chase looked stunned and began to stammer a protest. But Wessells bellowed the command again. "No food! No fuel!" Chase saluted and left immediately. The pacing captain peered at Hog, but still he did not move or speak.

"Take him back!" he shouted at a guard with a nervous wave of his hand.

After Hog returned, the loud thud of the metal bar fastening the double door of the prison sounded through the crowded room. The young men spoke angrily in a group as they assembled the rifle pieces hidden on the women and children. Others tore up the floor boards and began fashioning crude clubs. Some of the women still had knives.

288

Outside the bitter cold slowly forced its way into the barracks. The women managed to keep a small fire burning in the stove by using the animal chips they had gathered and by breaking up the wooden benches for firewood. But it was a losing battle, and the frost grew thicker and thicker on the windows. A little food remained hidden—grain and some beef tallow the women had taken while unloading the soldiers' wagons.

Early the next morning the sound of the moving bar on the door banged through the room. Instinctively everyone moved back. Hog cautioned the young men to stay calm as the doors swung open. Dressed in a great warm buffalo coat, Wessells strode into the cold room surrounded by guards, their bayoneted rifles drawn.

"Well, now," he said, moving about the room. "I trust you have seen the wisdom of obeying the Great Father. You will go south now?"

No one stirred as the interpreter remade the words into Cheyenne. Wessells seemed surprised that they were not ready to capitulate. Then he saw the torn floor boards and the broken benches and his face grew dark.

"I can wait!" he stammered as he whirled and disappeared behind the crashing door.

The next morning Wessells sent word that he would feed the children if they were sent out of the barracks. But no one moved. When Lieutenant Chase implored the little ones to follow him, they clung more tightly to their parents. The Cheyenne had grown sullen and menacing and the officer was driven from the room.

On the fourth day Wessells gave the order to withhold all water from the prisoners. By now the hidden bits of food and the wooden benches were gone and the people were reduced to scraping frost from the windows. The young men took over now, planning to break out, the young women plotting with them too.

Late the next morning the interpreter tried to enter the prison but the young warriors kept him out. So he shouted his message through the open doors, surrounded by armed guards.

"Wessells wishes to speak to Hog in his office."

A tumult broke out.

"No!" Little Finger Nail shouted. "It's a trap."

Others joined in the protest. Hog stepped forward.

"The soldier chief may speak to me here, before my people."

"Yes! Here!" some shouted in agreement.

Seeing that Hog would not leave, the interpreter offered a compromise.

"You may bring a man with you. Wessells only wishes to speak about the situation."

Old Crow stepped forward at once.

"I will go with you."

Again a loud protest arose.

"No! It is a trick of the *veho!*"

Hog, seeing the warriors in a frenzy, thought better of bringing Wessells before them. Motioning Old Crow forward, the two passed quickly through the open door. A line of bayonets closed behind them as the menacing warriors surged forward.

In Wessells' office, the captain again put the question to Hog.

"Are you ready to go south now?"

When Wild Hog stated once more that the Cheyenne would die before they returned to Indian Territory, Wessells signaled to the guards, who immediately fell on Hog and Old Crow. While his companion made no resistance, Hog fought back. He managed to pull a hidden knife from his belt and lashed out, wounding one of the guards. In the struggle Hog crashed through the door, howling war whoops as he fell. When he saw that it was hopeless, Hog tried to turn the knife on himself, but the soldiers fell on him in the snow and in an instant the irons closed on his wrists.

A crowd gathered to watch and, in the confusion, a Lakota visiting from Red Cloud's reservation ran to the prison barracks, shouting that Hog lay in chains. When the Cheyenne heard, they went wild, pushing through the door onto the grounds. It was all the soldiers could do to keep the Indians from breaking through their line. Left Hand did manage to rush through, but he was immediately taken and dragged off to Wessells. Before long word came that the families of Hog and Old Crow were to step forward. Another great murmuring arose in the crowd. After a scuffle the wives of Hog and Old Crow emerged from the group, but Hog's daughter and son shouted that they would die with the others; neither could be budged. Then, with bayonets drawn, Wessells's men forced the angry Cheyenne back into the dark barren room and slammed shut the doors, banging the great bar into place. Within moments the bluecoats moved around to the side door leading into the kitchen and began nailing it shut with wide boards. Then the sound of heavy chains latching the door still tighter rang through the room.

Suddenly, rising above the angry talk, a moaning voice grew louder and louder.

"They have sealed us in a wooden tomb to burn us all."

Over and over the lone woman in a dark corner cried the words till her voice became shrill and wild. Brave One ran to her side and tried to calm her, remembering that the bluecoats had thrown the woman's baby into the fire at the Sappa. But it was no use. She would not stop. A few children whimpered at the frightening cries and the sound of the little ones brought the woman to her feet. A knife flew from her skirt as she lunged for the children.

"We must kill them quickly. Hurry, they must not suffer the flames," she screamed as the women tried to hold her back.

Something in this spectacle woke Dull Knife from the strange paralysis that had immobilized him since the rejection of Red Cloud. He pushed his way to the woman and shouted angrily at her till she fell to the ground sobbing. Quickly Brave One wrenched the knife from her hand as Medicine Woman and Bridge

292

moved in to use their sleep medicine and chants.

Little Shield spoke first to the warriors.

"There is no time left. We must move tonight."

The Nail nodded in assent.

"Already the sickness is taking hold of our people."

So they began their preparations. Leaf, Singing Cloud, and the other young women went among the people and urged them to get ready, while the warriors made what medicine they could. About fifteen guns had emerged, and these together with the makeshift clubs were divided among the warriors. There were few cartridges, however, so the guns lacked the power they might have.

Carefully the plan was laid. Little Finger Nail and Little Shield each were to lead the way out of one of the windows. The men without guns and the strongest women would carry the small children. Dull Knife and the other old men would help the women and children and Tangle Hair and his Dog warriors would follow behind, holding back the soldiers while the others escaped. The fastest runners would race to the ranch of Bronson, the cattleman who had befriended Little Finger Nail, for horses, without which they could never hope to escape. Leaf would lead a few others to the cave with the hidden food brought by Little Wolf's scouts. Everyone would try to make it to Lost Chokecherry to find their sisters and brothers, though in their hearts they doubted they would.

Husband and wife, parents and children, brother and sister, and young people in love found each other for perhaps the last time as dusk covered the gaunt thirsting people in their wooden prison. They sat together for a few moments, their fingers only touching, fearful of holding tight lest they never let go.

Limpy and Broad Faced One, never in a lodge of their own since they married, looked anxiously at each other through the growing darkness. Little Finger Nail and Singing Cloud, who had loved each other as long as they could remember, said good-bye in the darkness, without any words, only their hands touching. Iron Teeth huddled with her three remaining children, Gathering His Medicine and the youngest daughters, wondering if the other two had made it safely to Red Cloud. It was agreed that her son would carry the smallest child and she would run with her other daughter.

Brave One, thinking of all those other flights, whispered final instructions to the thin haggard children staring at her through large hollow eyes. Lame Girl sat crumpled in a heap with the others, her foot healed now but in a twisted way that left her limping when she moved. Yellow Woman, who came to the north to escape reservation life, clung to her baby and her young son in the crowded wooden tomb. Hog's Daughter and Little Hog thought of their father, taken away in chains, and their mother, ordered to follow him. The young woman had grown hard and angry during the ordeal, brooding in her rage at whites.

Leaf wondered if she would ever see Calf again as

she watched her father call Red Bird to his side. Great Eyes still had the sacred shield saved from the attack on Old Bear's camp two winter's before. The old man stared at the shield in the faded light, his eyes passing over its red face adorned with a crescent moon. Gently he touched the grizzly claws, the turtle tail, the owl and eagle feathers as if for the last time.

"You must carry the shield of our ancestors to safety," he said to the tall, young boy. "It must not fall to the enemy. Run fast and protect it with your life."

Red Bird stood awed at the charge as the old man slipped the leather strap over his arm and shoulder. The weight of the great shield pulled at the thin body but the frightened boy stood straight and proud. Medicine Woman prayed to the Sacred Persons for their safety, while Bridge chanted to Maheo for the delivery of the Cheyenne. Little Finger Nail frowned at the praying and muttered that Winchesters and lots of bullets were needed, not words.

Dull Knife lingered with his family after the frigid room turned dark, touching each in turn—Pawnee Woman, Bull Hump and Leaf, Little Hump, and the Princesses. Then he moved about the room urging his people to have courage, to live or die as Cheyenne. Outside a bright moon and a great cold rose over the freezing snow as if to emphasize that once again things would not go easy. At last only a few guards still walked the cold night air, their feet crunching the icy snow as a lone coyote wailed to the moon.

When the time came, Little Finger Nail took his post

at one window, Little Shield at the other. Slowly, without a sound to warn the white spiders with their web, the Cheyenne rose and, lifting their small packs and children, moved in line behind the two warriors. Then, after a few endless moments, the Nail gave the signal and he and Little Shield fired at the guards outside the prison. Three bluecoats fell and in an instant the windows were crushed to bits as people poured from the gaping wounds in the log prison. Two more shots, two more sentries dead. Grabbing the weapons of the fallen soldiers, the warriors circled for the cliffs west of the fort as they ran southeast toward the river, the moon lighting the way and their escape for all to see.

The gunshots had boomed across the night and almost instantly the door of the guardhouse opened, spewing its inhabitants clad only in their white underwear and carrying their rifles. Within moments the soldiers opened fire and the fleeing people began dropping in the snow, their crimson blood looking blue in the moonlight. Everywhere men, women, and children in the desperate racing line fell dead or wounded.

Old Sitting Man with his hurting leg was one of the last to jump from the broken window. But as he leapt to the frozen ground, his leg shattered again. When a soldier in his strange white nightclothes rushed forward, Sitting Man began swaying in the snow, chanting a death song to the spirits. Slowly and deliberately the young man raised his rifle to the old one's

296

head and pulled the trigger, tearing off the top of his skull.

As the survivors continued their run below the barracks toward the river called White Water, Tangle Hair and four Dog warriors made a stand, trying to hold back the swarm of spiders crawling over the land after them. Very little time passed before all five lay wounded or dead in the snow. Tangle Hair managed to crawl away and cried out in Lakota to a passing soldier who took pity on the bleeding Indian and had him carried to the doctor. But the others did not fare so well. The soldiers went from body to body strewn over the white ground and poured bullets into each. Only a few of the wounded, recognized as women or children, escaped the finishing onslaught. But otherwise the hot lead did not discriminate in its mark.

By now a trumpet blew and soldiers dressed in the hated blue coats came charging on horses. Still the people ran, dropping for a drink in the river, chancing the bullets to ease their raging thirst. Some stayed at the water too long and ended their lives by pouring their blood into the icy stream. Others fled across the bridge or plunged into the freezing water, their clothes turning to ice about their running legs. Still they fell under the relentless onslaught of the soldiers.

A few warriors made a stand at the sawmill a short ways down river on the south side. But the soldiers poured over the grounds of the mill like water from a broken dam and in a short time all the resistors in the mill lay dead. Already half the warriors were lifeless.

The remaining Cheyenne scattered in small clusters, but the cruel moon followed them across the snow, lighting the bluecoats' way with shining moccasin steps.

Two women hiding in a draw near the saw mill suddenly found a soldier on them. They leapt at him with knives as he fired his pistol again and again. One woman fell, but the other kept coming long after the bullets had ripped through her body. The young soldier fell back as he shot, sickened at the sight, till finally the woman lay dead in her shredded blood-soaked clothing.

Dull Knife led his family—Pawnee Woman, his sons, the Princesses, Leaf, Great Eyes, Red Bird, plus some women and children who stuck by the old chief, thinking his medicine would save them—toward the distant bluffs. The freezing cold cut through their poor clothing and weakened the starving people further, numbing their feet. It was a night as bitter and full of pain as that other terrible winter night when Bad Hand had set his troops on their village in the Bighorn Mountains. Dull Knife thought of that night, of the killing of his son and his son-in-law, and he urged the stumbling group on toward the safety of the cliffs. There was no hope now of reaching the cave of Little Wolf with its food, no hope now of getting the horses from Bronson's ranch: the fleeing people could not choose their path, as they had hoped, but instead scattered from the driving bluecoats.

One of the Princesses had been hit in the first round

298

of shooting and now she could run no more.

"Go on! Leave me!" she whispered breathless on the snow.

But her young brother would not leave her, so he urged the others on.

"The chief of the Cheyenne must not die here like a great buffalo brought down by the white hunters. Take him!" Little Hump shouted.

When Dull Knife did not move, Leaf tugged firmly at his arm till he started again. So the small party began their running once more, except for the youngest Princess who stayed to help her sister and brother. Little Hump ran a short way back toward the advancing bluecoats to hold them off. Nearby a baby began to cry, dropped in the snow near its mother's body, fallen from a great hole in her side. The wounded Princess clutched her sister's arm as the soldiers rode closer.

"Quickly! Take the baby and run. I cannot go on."

With the tears freezing on her cheeks, the youngest Princess rushed to the shivering baby. As she scooped up the child who seemed to have turned to ice in the bitter cold, a small group of four women and three children came running from the direction of the river. So the Princess, clutching the emaciated baby, joined the party as they ran for a nearby slope.

In the old days they would have run up the hill in a few moments, laughing as they went. But now, weakened from days without food or water, stiff from their long confinement, numb from the freezing air, they labored over each step, gasping for breath over a pounding heart, falling and dragging themselves on again. At last they made it to the top of the hill covered with a stand of thick tall pines. A sweet fragrance swept over the women and children, the old familiar fragrance from the days of freedom on the high plains. One of the women wept for joy at the scent and for an instant they were back in the Bighorn Mountains, breathing the good air and looking up through the thick pine needles to the clear star filled sky beyond as they lay panting on the ground.

The Princess sat against a pine trunk, holding the baby in her arms and watching the others resting on the ground where they had fallen. She thought of the women with Little Wolf's band—Pretty Walker, Buffalo Calf Road, Yellow Bead, and the others—safe at Lost Chokecherry, breathing in the good pine fragrance everyday, watching the sun set and rise. She smiled at the thought of some of her people secure from the bluecoats, for a while anyway.

Then a loud, deep voice covered the sound of their exhausted panting.

"Come out now. It's no use. Give up and you will not be harmed."

They recognized the voice of the officer called Chase, though none of them understood what the white man's words meant. No one moved.

"Surrender or we shoot," the unfathomable voice said again.

But it did not matter what the words meant. They

would not surrender. They would not go back. So they clung to each other in the dark pine grove that had taken them home for a moment. And they waited.

One more word from the officer Chase rang through the crisp air and the firing began. When no shots were returned the men charged the defiant stand of pines. The baby in the Princess' arms was the first hit, but the young woman sat still as the blood flowed over her body.

"It is a good day to die," she thought to herself.

And in a few brief instants they all lay dead under the gentle spreading pines. Chase did not wait to see if they were dead or wounded, but he ordered his men forward after the rest of the survivors. Just beyond the bottom of the slope, the other Princess lay unconscious and her brother dead, Little Hump's body thrown over his sister in a protective gesture.

Iron Teeth and her son, Gathering His Medicine, each with one of the little girls, had followed the tortured trail down to the White Water, but soon they scattered like the rest, he one way, she another. Iron Teeth and her daughter made it at last to the far bluffs west of the fort. Scrambling over the rocks they discovered a cave behind some snow-covered brush and crawled in, trying to cover their tracks with a branch as they went. Another Cheyenne, a man named Crooked Nose, found the cave too, and together they waited as the sound of gunfire echoed through the bluffs and the freezing cold bit their weary limbs.

Meanwhile, Gathering His Medicine had stumbled

on a deep pit partly hidden by thick chokecherry and plum bushes. Quickly he jumped in with his little sister and covered them both with the dead leaves filling the deep hole. The worry for his mother and sister, the loud noise of the firing all around, and the bitter cold kept the young man awake all night while the child, light as an autumn leaf from the long hungering, slept in his arms. So the darkness passed.

At the fort a crowd of civilians from the area gathered after the shooting began, hungry for blood. On horse and on wagons the men moved out from the barracks riding over the bodies strewn across the ground. Out of sight of the officers, they began their grizzly work, looting and stripping the bodies, scalping the dead, mutilating the women. They too chased the fleeing Cheyenne and killed those they found as though they were killing game for the sport of it.

At the post hospital, the wounded who were not shot to death or frozen where they lay were carried in and stretched out in rows on the floor. Some died soon after arrival and the attendants hauled them out to a wagon piled with the dead. By morning the room was filled with the wounded brought in by a few soldiers not hardened enough to kill defenseless people lying in their own blood. Outside the corpses on the wagons accounted for almost a fourth of the Cheyenne confined in the barracks only the day before. Many more, especially children, must have frozen to death in their hiding places, the officers speculated. At any rate, it was early and the dead were still being carried in.

The first light of dawn found soldiers spread everywhere—along the roads leading from Fort Robinson, along the White Water, around the cattle and horse ranches in the area, on the bluffs to the west—everywhere save the steep cliffs behind the bluffs. The slippery straight cliffs ‾prohibited horses, so the army would have to travel very far around to approach them from behind.

During the night about thirty-five Cheyenne had helped each other up the steep rocks, moving from crevice to crevice, clutching at the jagged pieces like mountain goats. This morning they were strung out along the top of the cliffs, some daring to warm themselves at small fires. When the sun rose, Little Finger Nail and Roman Nose moved the long distance over the cliff's edge, gathering the small groups of three, five, six together, the last of Dull Knife's people.

As the scattered Cheyenne on the cliffs found each other, the survivors below waited in their hiding places, hoping to escape notice until darkness came again when they might try once more to reach safety. Most did not. Under the bright sky of day all the moccasin prints leapt into view and the soldiers, dressed now in their boots and warm coats, hats and gloves, riding on fresh horses, made easy work of following the remaining Cheyenne to their end.

When Gathering His Medicine heard the approach of horses' hooves in the distance, he woke his little sister from her deep sleep, hugged her tightly for a moment, and instructed her to lie flat in the pit. Furi-

303

ously he raked the leaves over the whimpering child as he told her to keep still till the soldiers left.

"I will draw them away from the pit, Little One. When they are gone, you must look for the others, for Mother."

In an instant he leapt from the wound in the earth and, brandishing his empty gun, flew at the bluecoats riding hard at him. His body caught a burst of fire, enough to kill many great buffalo, but still he ran away from the pit and the hidden child. When at last he fell, the soldiers stood about for a few moments, marveling at the strength of the young man that made him run so far after he should have died. But there were more such men to find, so they threw the corpse on an empty pack mule and went on.

The little girl lay all day in the open grave, sobbing in silence. The next morning when she crawled out of the ground, soldiers saw her almost at once and carried her back to the fort across the river.

Others beside Gathering His Medicine were shot to death the day after the escape: Yellow Woman and her baby, killed before the hidden eyes of her son; Bridge, shot as he tried to reach the Princess and her party in the pine grove, thinking some had survived and wanting to minister to their wounds as he had all night for others; two more Dog warriors, fired on in a ravine when they refused to surrender; four members of Pumpkin Seed's family hiding in a cave on the slopes, riddled with bullets till all died except a young boy; and many more.

Still others, mostly women and children, were captured in their hiding places, many nursing wounds and frostbite from the night before. These were brought back to the prison or the hospital to join those already there, like the Princess who had been dragged, barely breathing, from under her dead brother, and Medicine Woman, shot in the eye, and Little Buffalo Girl, wounded in the thigh.

Seven nights passed before Iron Teeth and her daughter were discovered in the cave. Somehow they had survived the cold and hunger, nibbling a few berries and a little dried meat they had hidden before the starving began. Iron Teeth's eyes searched frantically among the captive Cheyenne, looking for Gathering His Medicine and Little One. She dared not ask for fear of alerting the bluecoats to their absence. At last Little One was brought to her by one of the women.

"Where is your brother?" the desperate woman whispered to the child, hugging her.

The child said nothing but stared at the ground.

"Where is he?" Iron Teeth repeated, the words catching in her throat.

Suddenly the child burst into tears, sobbing uncontrollably. The woman, gaunt and haggard, looking old beyond her winters, knew at once that he was dead.

Only two groups remained out now, neither dead nor captured: the party of Cheyenne who had reached the safety of the cliffs the first night, and the last of the beautiful people of Dull Knife, gone like the hot bub-

bling water that vanishes into air. Wessells asked
everyone brought in for news of Dull Knife, but no
one knew or would say. It ate at the nervous little man
that after seven days he could still not account for all
these pathetic Indians. But plans went forward to
punish the warriors who had done this thing and
brought this embarrassment on the soldier chief. The
only men left at the fort—Hog, Old Crow, Left Hand,
Porcupine, Tangle Hair, Old Man, Blacksmith, the
Lakota, and Stubfoot—would be sent to Fort Leaven-
worth, Kansas, to stand trial for murder.

The Cheyenne on the steep cliffs had a little time
now. The soldiers could not get to them directly over
the cliffs and it would take a while for them to circle
around to a place where their horses could climb.
Little Finger Nail and Roman Nose had gathered
together the remnants of their people the morning
after their escape. Miraculously, Brave One had
dragged and coaxed the children, including Lame
Girl, up the slippery rocks, along with Hog's
Daughter, who mourned her brother's death. Singing
Cloud was with them too, and Small Woman,
wounded that night on the plain below, and other
women and children, fifteen in all. Besides the Nail
and Roman Nose, the men present were Pug Nose,
Young Magpie, Bear, Young Elk, Young Medicine
Man, Bullet Proof, wounded now, and others, twenty
in all. They would try to reach Little Wolf or Red
Cloud, but without horses and with the wounded, it
would require the help of the Sacred Persons, who

seemed to have forgotten the Cheyenne.

By the second day after the escape, the tattered group had moved a good ways, considering their hunger, wounds, and frostbite. But that morning they spotted the bluecoats far in the distance coming in a straight neat line, so they found a good spot up on a hill and spent the day in a standoff. Only one soldier was killed and some horses, and unexpectedly the troops withdrew to the fort before dark. Wessells had not expected the capture to take so long and had brought few supplies. After they left, the starving people ate the dead horse, quickly taking strips of meat and skin for new moccasins. All night the Cheyenne walked and by midmorning the soldiers returned. A group of bluecoats scouting from the main line came upon Bullet Proof and Roman Nose looking for horses, and before it was over Bullet Proof lay dead and the Nose wounded, though he was able to get back to the others.

But still the soldiers could not get to the hurting people, refreshed a little now by food, water, and some rest. For days Wessells pushed them to the west along the cliffs covered with pine and box elders, cutting off their trail to Red Cloud and Little Wolf. The steep rock ledges stretched like a thick, long, bending island between Hat Creek, from which they got their name, and the White Water, which flowed past the place of their imprisonment. Cutting out from the bluffs, dry riverbeds full of snow ran like white twisted fingers over the earth.

At one point the Cheyenne sat trapped for a day in their rifle pits, burrowed deep in a ravine as heavy fire filled the air above them. With their ammunition almost gone, the warriors crouched in their pits like gophers surrounded by dogs, pained in their pride to sit and wait for death. But there were the little ones to think of. That night the soldiers threw up a guard, but Little Finger Nail, thinking of the many times Little Wolf had led them to safety during the flight north, decided to dare an escape.

By morning, when no shots came from the ravine, Wessells cautiously led his men forward, only to find empty rifle pits mocking his attempts to bring in the ragtag bunch. The captain raged inside as he waited for the supplies to arrive from Fort Robinson, but they never came. The army wagons had tipped over on the steep slippery hills and crashed to the valley below, so the busy little captain was forced back to the fort once again, having failed for six days to round up the running Indians. When Wessells left Robinson again, it was with many troops, a pack train of supplies, and a vow not to fail again.

While they were on the move, the desperate band killed a few cows to eat, dried a little meat as they slept, and made crude moccasins and blankets from the skins. They managed to accumulate enough meat to hold them for many sleeps, and in the skirmishes that followed they replenished their weapons and ammunition off of a couple of dead soldiers. But some of their own died too—Pug Nose and Small Woman,

308

both shot to death—and those who survived walked on bleeding blistered feet, carefully on rocks and thick grass, avoiding the snow or the mud that would betray their trail. But with many children and wounded it was hard, and Little Finger Nail saw that something more was needed to escape.

For days they kept to the cliffs, pushed west by the troops following below. The distance between them and Red Cloud and Little Wolf grew longer each day. They must turn eastward, the Nail agonized. But how? On the open plains there was little shelter, almost no chance of escape, and yet they could not continue going nowhere. Little Finger Nail looked around him at the tired, suffering people sleeping on the ground, huddled together against the cold. His eyes fell on his beloved Singing Cloud sharing her thin blanket with three orphans who clung to her, one of them the child of the dead Small Woman. It pained him to think of their life together, of the proud time when they might have lived in a lodge of their own under the open sky of the great plains, loving together and making a family.

But the thoughts fled quickly for there was the present to deal with. A flaming sky to the west signaled the approach of darkness. The Nail knew it was time to decide as the great chiefs would have decided. They must try to reach their friends, the Lakota. Lost Chokecherry lay too far to the east now. He knew what must be done, yet he feared for these brave ones who could not live forever fleeing. At first darkness

Little Finger Nail led them quickly down the steep slope and away from the rocks that had been their salvation these past twelve days of running.

By dawn the Cheyenne had reached Warbonnet Creek, only a dry riverbed now, deep for hiding till darkness returned. Hastily the women dug into the crested snow and ground with their knives while the warriors piled sod and sticks and dirt around the deep wide hole for breastworks. When they lay in the pit, they could only be attacked by someone standing on the edge and firing into it. So they sat waiting for darkness so they could flee again, eighteen men and fourteen women and children. By midmorning the troops, led by an Indian scout, picked up their trail and the Cheyenne, buried in the earth, watched as the long columns moved forward. Without speaking, the warriors painted themselves with sage and earth. The Nail looked deep into the eyes of each person, lingering on the dark eyes of Singing Cloud, who reached out her hand and gently touched his arm. Slowly the scouts advanced up the creek bed, closer and closer, at last making the motion of discovery to the troops behind. The warriors opened fire, hitting a scout and a soldier.

Immediately Wessells signaled his troops into position, spreading them around in all directions. Steady gunfire continued for a long time. At last Wessells signaled them to stop and instructed a Lakota scout to order the Indians to surrender. But the order met with silence. The fidgety soldier chief drew his men closer and the firing began again. In the pit the children

310

whimpered a little, but silently, to themselves, like disciplined Cheyenne children. Several of the warriors fell as they rose to fire and finally the women had no more bullets to hand those who lived.

At last Wessells heard the silence from the pit over the soldiers' guns, and signaling Chase to move his men in, they charged the hole in the ground. Wessells leapt to the edge of the pit, his gun drawn and cocked, and ordered the survivors to surrender or be killed. A last single bullet flew from the hole, striking Wessells on the side of his head. Immediately the bluecoats opened fire into the pit, shooting and shooting, a great smoke rising over the dry creek bed. Little Finger Nail, bloody and wild looking, leapt over the breast-works with a knife in his hand. In an instant he fell dead.

Finally Chase ordered the firing stopped and the soldiers crept to the pit, gazing at last on the pile of corpses below. Slowly the bodies were hauled out. Seventeen men lay dead, and another fatally wounded. Brave One and Singing Cloud lay lifeless on the top of the pile of women and children, their bodies shielding the others. Under them, two more women and two children were shot to death, but eight women and children still lived, some of them badly wounded, like Hog's Daughter, who had been hit in the neck. From the heap Lieutenant Chase sadly pulled out a child of six winters, shot in the side, the little girl he had ridden about the fort on his horse, little Lame Girl.

When the soldiers hauled away the body of Little

Finger Nail, they felt something hard on his back, a ledger book fastened to his body with a wide leather strap. One of the men removed the book out of curiosity and, flipping through the pages, saw the colorful pictures of fine Indian warriors brightly painted and in full headdress, riding to war, hunting the great buffalo, riding free on the plains. . . .

But a bullet hole ran through the pictures of the great Cheyenne past.

CHAPTER 9

On the morning of the silent parting of Dull Knife's band, Little Wolf quickly led his people north under the protection of the thick fog. Soldiers were near at several points, but the Sweet Medicine chief slipped them through the thickets toward the deepest part of the great sand hills. On and on they moved, scattering when danger approached, coming together again when it passed.

At last they arrived at the Sudden River with its deep hills beyond. Carefully, everyone riding double and triple on their horses to hide the moccasin prints, Little Wolf led them along the river to a place north of the fork where the headwaters of the Snake River flowed.

One by one the horses rode into the hidden valley rich with grass and trees surrounding a lake covered with honking geese and mallard ducks resting on their flight south. Great cottonwoods, their leaves already on the ground, and hackberry trees sheltering the sand hill cranes, stood at the water's edge. Behind them climbing up the hillside, thick stands of brush, painted for fall, merged with naked box elders higher up. Beyond the gentle slopes, steep hills dark with cedar stood guard. In the water, frogs played among the rushes. Overhead a graying sky extended from hill to hill, touching the land and trees wherever they rose.

Buffalo Calf Road stared at the peaceful spot in disbelief. Had the bearer of the Sacred Bundle truly brought them home, then? Behind her the women came, still following her lead—Feather on Head and Quiet One, Chicken Woman, Pretty Walker, Yellow Bead and her aunt, the mother of Little Comes Behind carrying the baby, Ridge Walker, Swallow, and the others.

When Old Grandmother saw the valley from her place behind Spotted Deer, she slipped from their horse to the ground and in a gesture of embrace, she hugged the earth, calling up to her grandson.

"I am home. Here I will die."

The men filed in too—Black Coyote, Whetstone, Young Eagle, Old Crier, Black Crane, Woodenthigh, Little Hawk, Vanishing Heart, Thin Elk, Bald Eagle, and the rest. Most of the people dropped wearily from their horses, too tired to notice the beauty and peace of the place. They had traveled fast through the Sand Hills, resting little, always anxious because of the troops searching for them. It was hard, even here in this hidden valley, to forget the soldiers for a moment, though scouts stood guard.

Back against the hills, the women built hasty lean-tos of brush and started small fires under their thick branches so the smoke would not travel far and betray them. Game roamed the valley in abundance and the warriors lost no time in bringing down antelope and deer with their bows and arrows for the hungry mouths. That night the band slept more soundly than it had for a long, long time under the watchful eyes of Little Wolf and his Elk warriors.

Buffalo Calf Road and Black Coyote lay together under their lean-to with the children beside them.

"I think the snows will come soon," Calf said softly.

"This place is not safe," he answered unexpectedly. "We will have to move tomorrow."

"But why?" she said. "It seems so hidden."

"The white people's trail runs close by here. It is the way that takes them to our Black Hills." He stopped and she could feel the old rage in the darkness. "Many will pass this way, crazy for the yellow metal."

"Winter will come soon and fewer people can travel the road then. It will be good here for a while, camped together like the old days." Calf tried to soothe his anger.

"But the children," he protested. "We endanger them here."

"We endanger them more by moving about. The bluecoats can pick up our trail, especially when the snows come." Touching his arm, she added, "Our people cannot run anymore. We must rest for a while."

"The old ones have brought us to a trap," he said sullenly.

Calf frowned to herself. *Again he complains of the old ones,* she thought.

"Please," she said as she gently rubbed his brow. "Do not blame the old ones. Little Wolf has led us home. Tomorrow we can see how it is here. Besides," she said softly, "tonight we are in a great lodge together."

Her touch quieted the Coyote, and the furrows on his forehead relaxed. The Coyote smiled weakly, drawing her close.

As the days passed without trouble, Black Coyote and Little Hawk rode toward Red Cloud Agency in search of Dull Knife. When they returned Black Coyote spoke angrily of the stubborn old man.

"Red Cloud's land is crawling with white spiders, yet the Knife waits for an invitation!"

"There is no possibility he will make it to Red Cloud," Little Hawk added sadly. "But he would not return with us."

"Foolish old man!" the Coyote put in for emphasis.

Little Wolf sat quietly through the news, thinking of the little ones and the wounded and the aged. He touched the Sacred Bundle on his breast.

"They have nothing," he thought to himself. "Not the Sacred Hat or the Sacred Arrows or Sweet Medicine's presence."

The people who had gathered around the pair of news-bearers worried silently for their relatives and friends. Dusk was falling and a bitter wind was kicking over the lake as heavy gray clouds hung in the darkening sky. All the ducks had left Lost Chokecherry for the warm southern places, all except a few late geese, scrawny and sickly looking, clinging to the choppy waters of the northern lake.

"By morning it will be too late for the geese to leave," Calf thought as she watched them bobbing about on the waves.

During the night a freezing rain drove down on their lean-tos and by midmorning the sleet turned to a raging snow, the first blizzard of the winter. When it was over at last, the Cheyenne emerged from their snow-laden shelters like a great grizzly shaking off the heavy winter sleep, and the business of life began anew. The warriors brought in game which the women skinned, drying the meat and curing the hides for much-needed clothing and blankets.

Everyone seemed better, happier at this camp. Old Grandmother, thinking for so long she would die when she got home, came to life instead, busying her-self with the meat and skins. In the evening Young Eagle blew his love flute softly for the young people who began again the old courting ways. Spotted Deer looked longingly at Yellow Bead, watching her carry the water, too shy to approach her in the joking way of one in love. For her part, Yellow Bead thought of the absent Little Hump, daring to believe that Dull

316

Knife's son would someday marry her. One night the young people started a small dance in a clearing, with low singing only and no drumming lest it carry over the hills.

Old Arrowmaker and the other elders fashioned bows and arrows with colorful feathers and pipes for smoking the tobacco they hoped to have again. The young children took up their games once more and the medicine of laughter made them whole. Little Seeker played with a ball again, one made by her father from the skin of a young doe. Like the other children she seemed to have forgotten the ordeal of the flight. Even her small brother moved about now, crawling and tottering, looking healthier because of the rest and food.

Still things were not as they should be. Buffalo Calf Road watched the youngsters playing in the snow and thought of the three winters past—of the many endless flights, of the lost ones, of the slow breaking of the tribe. It was good living here in the old way again, and yet it wasn't really the old way at all. The sheltered valley hid them and fed them, but it held them like a prison. Only a few scouts came and went, carefully hiding their tracks, riding only the shod horses taken on the flight north so no one would suspect Indians were about. And life in the valley came hard. The warriors hunted with bows and arrows and traps to keep from firing a gun. The women had few of the tools needed for their work; only one kettle had fled north with them. Not a single lodge stood at Lost Chokecherry, only the branch lean-tos blending with the land, and when the snows started, many moved into the shallow caves dotting the slopes.

But mostly Calf thought of the changes in Black Coyote. She remembered the serious young boy who grew to a serious young man with his keen sense of pride and his fierce belief in the old life. As long as she could remember the Coyote always resented the white man and his taking ways. And she did too. But with the Coyote it was different. His rage had somehow turned inward, eating at his mind like an evil spirit gnawing at his brain. His obsession with the white man grew—how could the hunted help being obsessed with the hunter? But the frustrations, the defeats, the inability to get at the white enemy rising everywhere boiled over against his own people. Increasingly Black Coyote took issue with decisions of the old chiefs and he fell to quarreling with them and blaming them. Black Crane, the peacemaker of the tribe, found himself having to contain the young man's anger on several occasions. Not only did the quarrels disturb the peace of the camp but they left the Coyote depressed and listless for days. Yet at other times, he was happy and contented, strangely so. All of it worried Calf.

Calf knew the women had begun to pity her, but they did not understand. The Coyote's rage was a righteous rage, the primitive inarticulate anger in all living things, like that of a swallow watching its nest plundered. His was the rage of a helpless one who is wronged, thrashing about in self-defense, the rage of a

318

decent one in an indecent world, the rage of fearless self-respect. Had he been alone, unmarried and childless, he would have fought the invader in the open to the death. Buffalo Calf Road understood that kind of death, the suicide of courage, of control of one's life. She too would choose to die so. But Black Coyote held back, afraid not for himself but for the little ones, and this holding back was destroying him, twisting him. He is a heroic person, Calf thought, driven mad by an unjust world.

The news of the capture of Dull Knife's people disturbed the camp at Lost Chokecherry greatly, especially Black Coyote. When Calf returned from her visit on the cliffs and reported that Leaf too had been captured, many thought it a bad sign. As the Moon of the Frost in the Lodges appeared, the bitter cold and snow and the weakened winter condition of the horses made it difficult to travel to the cliffs above the fort. So the Cheyenne, camped in the ring of hills, settled in to wait for the worst of winter to pass.

One day, after the bitterest of all moons had passed into the Moon of the Snowblind Eyes, Cheyenne scouts whistled the approach of someone. People scattered anxiously into the bush and caves, but after a while the scouts signaled all clear. The growing crowd by the frozen lake stared in disbelief at the emaciated limping boy in their midst. It was Red Bird, staggering breathless under the weight of a burden on his back.

Quickly Buffalo Calf Road led the young boy to a small fire as the women brought hot red tea and dried meat. No one spoke as the shivering boy wolfed down his food while the great, painted, leather carrying case lay in the snow by his side. His torn blood-crusted moccasins hung about his swollen feet, while the long forked branch that helped him walk lay on his lap, taking its turn to rest. When the youth spoke at last, a stunned crowd listened in disbelief.

Red Bird told of the escape of Bull Hump, of his capture with Leaf, of the imprisonment, of the starvation and the thirsting, of the taking of Hog and Old Crow in irons, of the desperate flight through the smashed windows. The boy's voice quivered as he described the white figures emerging from the troop houses, shooting at people who dropped around him like flowers at the first frost. He told of the Princess shot, of Little Hump and her sister staying behind to help. Yellow Bead's face dropped at the name of Little Hump, and she felt immediately, without the telling, that he was lost to her forever. She rose from her listening spot in the snow and walked quickly away, Spotted Deer watching her go.

The boy continued. After the Princess dropped, Dull Knife's party struck off away from the main body of Cheyenne. When the soldiers picked up their trail, Great Eyes rushed out into the open, shouting war cries at the troops, stumbling about, confusing the trail, leading the bluecoats astray till Dull Knife got them away and Great Eyes dropped dead under the bullets.

The boy fell silent for a while, staring at the ground

320

with his hollow eyes, then he went on. He himself had been hit in the leg by a bullet bouncing from a rock when Great Eyes drew the soldiers away. For ten sleeps after that they hid in a deep cave, nibbling on some berries and roots, nearly starving to death. When it became clear everyone would die in the cave unless they left, Bull Hump led them away, carefully, their moccasins leaving no trail for the snooping white eyes. But Red Bird, his leg not healed, had to be left in the darkness.

It was Leaf who told him how to find Little Wolf, Leaf who had spoken with Calf, the Coyote, Little Hawk, and the others. She had whispered before they left that she did not think Dull Knife would go to Lost Chokecherry, the burden of guilt heavy on his shoulders. So the boy had waited a few days till he could stand on the leg and slowly, dragging himself and his precious bundle the whole way, made it to the hidden valley, eating rose hips and berries and roots as he went.

When he finished speaking, Red Bird opened the leather case and drew out the great shield of one hundred winters, the last Sacred Shield of the Northern Cheyenne. Sadly he handed it to Little Wolf who sat motionless and speechless, his face taunt and frozen.

"I do not know if anyone else is alive," the boy said in a barely audible whisper.

Black Coyote rose now, his face dark and ominous. He motioned to Whetstone and some others, and a small group of warriors pulled off by themselves. The

321

others hardly noticed in their grief, but Calf anxiously watched them ride out of the valley.

The next morning Old Crier ran up and down the poor camp with Little Wolf's message.

"Make ready your things! Make ready! Tonight we leave this place."

That day Little Wolf sent his son Woodenthigh to Red Cloud to find out if anyone from Dull Knife's party still lived. Beyond the grief of the news, the preparations lay heavy on the Cheyenne. For more than three moons they had found a small peace, even here in the shadow of the army, a peace they had not known in a long time. Buffalo Calf Road was assigned a place of honor again, leading the women, something the old chiefs would have done in another day.

When Black Coyote returned, Calf saw that the pain in his face had eased, but she did not ask what he had done.

No one wanted to leave but they understood the necessity. With Dull Knife's people no longer posing a problem, the army would turn all its attention to Little Wolf's band. If they waited till the winter passed, it would be harder to elude the bluecoats, whose wagons stuck in the snow.

So, when the last rays of the cold sun fell over the western hills, Little Wolf gathered his people onto the horses recently captured by the warriors and led them out of the valley. The party headed northwest toward the Powder River country between the Bighorn Mountains and the great Elk River. With the warriors gone most of the time hunting game and horses, Little Wolf relied heavily on Buffalo Calf Road to help lead the people safely through.

A few days later Woodenthigh, back from Red Cloud, rejoined them, carrying with him the full story of the massacre. The names of the dead were given to their relatives and the last days of Little Finger Nail's band, slaughtered and wounded in the pit on Warbonnet Creek, were told. They learned of the special horror of Wild Hog's family—of his son killed in the escape, of his daughter barely alive and shot through the neck, of Hog's wife who tried to kill herself with scissors, of Hog himself who also attempted suicide so his wife and daughter could go to Red Cloud with the remnants of their people. He failed, Woodenthigh told them, and had been sent to Kansas with Old Crow and the remaining warriors to stand trial for murder.

Trial for murder! Little Wolf clenched his fist and a bitterness spread across his face. At that moment he understood the rage of Black Coyote, the killing rage that drove the Coyote to murder the cowboys on the Sudden River the day Red Bird brought news of Dull Knife's band.

The people tried to take it in—so many dead, so many wounded. And not even a proper burial for the lost ones. They shuddered and looked away in shame at the account of the burial at Fort Robinson in a mass grave, bodies lying together in a dirt trench dug by the bluecoats. But somehow the news of Brave One's death with the children hurt most of all, especially the wounding again of Little Lame Girl whose long suffering, like that of the tribe, went on and on and on.

Calf walked off by herself after hearing about Brave One, her heart on the earth beneath her feet. The gray sky and the freezing wind and the barren trees gave no sign of spring. She felt in an instant the endless winter of life upon her and she wept bitterly as a tiny snowbird watched from a twisted branch overhead.

When Woodenthigh was left alone with his father, the older man asked what he had hesitated to ask in front of the others.

"What of Dull Knife?"

"Dull Knife and the rest of his family are alive, but no one must know," the young man answered.

"With the Lakota?"

Woodenthigh nodded.

His father drew a deep breath in relief.

"Will he come home with us?"

The young man avoided looking at Little Wolf.

"No, he will not come."

"He will not come?" the older man repeated. "Even now, after everything?"

The Bundle Bearer of the Cheyenne wanted to cry out his words of anger against the old man, but he kept silent, the rage rising from his eyes.

"Even now . . . ," he muttered instead.

For days Little Wolf and his people pushed northwest, skirting the Black Hills and plunging through the desolate badlands where few ever ventured. The cold and the snow still drove against the Cheyenne, but less so as the time passed and the Moon of the Light Snows came upon them. They were approaching the Antelope Pit River where in the old days the Cheyenne had hunted antelope by driving them over steep drops. Now no game had been seen for a long distance and the people ate from their diminishing store of dried meat.

Then it happened.

Black Coyote thundered into camp with a small herd of army horses, plainly sporting the government brand. Buffalo Calf Road watched in dismay as the young men boasted about the Coyote, but he never looked at her. An angry Little Wolf called a council, a shrunken council now that so few remained. For a long time, it seemed to Calf, the chiefs sat talking about the theft.

When at last they rose from their small circle, Black Crane, keeper of the camp's peace, spoke for the others.

"This is a dangerous thing you have done," he said to a defiant Black Coyote. "Everyone is endangered because of it. The soldiers will come for us now."

"The soldiers come for us anyway!" the tall young warrior interrupted, his face dark and his eyes flashing.

"You must take back the stock, all of it," the peacemaker continued as though he had not heard the Coyote. "The chiefs have decided and it must be done to save the little ones here from attack. My friend, take the horses back and nothing bad will happen."

The Coyote's rage boiled at the false reasoning.

"Nothing bad will happen? And the people at Robinson? Did bad things happen to them because they stole army horses?"

"Take back the horses," the old man persisted, "and we will forget that it happened."

"No!" Black Coyote shouted. "I have taken the horses of my murdering enemy. They are mine."

Black Crane saw things going badly, but it was impossible that a council be disobeyed. Slowly, calmly on the outside, he spoke the words.

"The council must be obeyed. Return the horses or you will be whipped."

A wild fury seized the Coyote now and his pistol flew from his belt.

"Let someone try. I will kill him."

Immediately Whetstone ran to the side of his friend, his revolver drawn too. Calf lurched forward instinctively to intervene, but it was too late.

The old man seized his quirt stick and before the crowd could look away in shame, he struck the young man in the old way, full of authority and a sense of each person's place. Black Coyote fired at Black Crane, without thought, from a pent up bitterness and hatred, not at the old peacemaker, but at the agency Indian taking the side of his enemies. Black Crane fell dead, the bullet ripping through his heart. His son, Red Robe, rushed to the old man's side.

A cold quiver passed over the people. Calf froze at the sight. The Coyote stood crazed, as though he did

326

not comprehend the event, as though someone else had pulled the trigger. Other warriors rushed forward, their knives and guns drawn in confusion against Black Coyote, against the old chiefs, against each other.

Red Robe rose in rage and sorrow from his father's body and, raising his revolver, shot at Black Coyote, hitting him in his arm. The sight of his bleeding limb triggered some new fury in the dark brooding Coyote and he fired again and again, out of control now, shaking violently, the bullets flying wildly about. Red Robe fell to the ground.

Suddenly Old Crier stood in their midst, raising the sacred pipe of the Cheyenne for all to see, its long stem cold over Black Crane's body. But in the melee, he stumbled. The crowd pulled back in a great widening circle as the long peace pipe shattered when Old Crier crashed to the ground. A breathless gasp rose from the people of the long suffering as Black Coyote staggered like an agency Indian drunk from the white man's firewater. His arm bled from the gunshot wound and he turned away from the wounded Red Robe at his feet, tottering and pitching as he went.

"Let him go!" Little Wolf thundered. "Spill no more Cheyenne blood."

Even as he spoke a low keening rose from the women. Buffalo Calf Road stood paralyzed in horror, Little Seeker clutching her skirt and sobbing quietly. The worst of all had happened—one Cheyenne killing another Cheyenne. Calf knew immediately what it meant.

"It is the law of Sweet Medicine . . . ," she heard the Sacred Bundle bearer saying. "The murderer must leave our people."

Black Coyote stood off by himself, dazed. Whetstone had already flown to his side in a gesture of solidarity. Anyone wishing to go with the offender into exile from the tribe had to leave now, before the assembled crowd. Quickly, with the greatest sorrow of all, Calf picked up her son. Pretty Walker saw her move and hurried over to help, wrapping Calf's few things in some hides. The two women's eyes met, tearfully. Then, with the roll under her arms, the baby tied on her back, and Little Seeker clinging to her hand, Calf ran toward Black Coyote.

A new gasp rose from the stunned people at the sight of their brave warrior woman leaving them. All through the bad times, Buffalo Calf Road stood in their midst, a source of strength and courage, a sister and a friend.

"No!" Quiet One called out, Quiet One of the silent tongue. "Stay with us, sister."

"Yes, stay!" another woman cried out.

"Do not go with him."

Little Wolf watched as the women kept on pleading and thought in despair, "Another great one is leaving us. . . ."

Before this newest separation was complete, eight Cheyenne stood alone as outcasts. With Black Coyote went Buffalo Calf Road, their two children, and their relatives, Whetstone, Chicken Woman, Vanishing Heart, and Ridge Walker. The chiefs took all of their horses except for seven. As the tiny band rode west across the desolate prairie, the rocks fell over the body of Black Crane and a medicine man tried to heal Red Robe's wound. Sadly and without heart, the last of those who had fled from Indian Territory, numbering little more than a third their original number, moved north again, heading for the Elk River.

But before the Moon of the Light Snows was out, the soldier chief White Hat, led by Cheyenne scouting against their own people, including Two Moons, had discovered the whereabouts of Little Wolf. The Sweet Medicine chief, seeing Two Moons with the blue-coats, thought to himself as he surrendered, "Perhaps it is time. . . ."

Meanwhile, the last of the hostiles, the last of the free Cheyenne, the band of eight, made their way toward the Powder River and the plains beyond. No one spoke, no one looked into the eyes of another as the enormity of the exile settled over them.

Black Coyote rode ahead of the others as they left their people, his shoulders slumped, his head weighing on his body. He kept apart for the rest of the day, as though to prevent some contagion from spreading to the others. Though he led the party, the Coyote seemed not to notice where he went and he moved forward aimlessly, following his horse. The others let him go, saying nothing, in deference to his grief and guilt. Even his arm wound went unattended, the stream of blood playing itself out.

Behind the Coyote rode Whetstone and Vanishing Heart, the bonds of kinship and friendship strong in adversity. In both a tangled underbrush of worries surfaced, though neither said anything. They saw how it was with Black Coyote and knew it fell to them to keep the band alive, to hunt, to scout, to protect, to keep them hidden from the far-seeing glass of the bluecoats.

The three women, the girl, and the baby rode together alone, each with her special loss and her own fears. For years Chicken Woman, childless herself, had helped Calf and Coyote with Little Seeker and the baby, caring for them when the two rode to battle. She felt close to the children and close to Calf, but mostly to her brother, though he had grown so strange and moody these past moons. The familiar places as they rode toward the Powder River stirred happy childhood memories, but the sight of Black Coyote slumped in his saddle darkened the images and they fled. A flood of pity and sympathy for him rose in her chest, but with revulsion and anger. He had brought this disgrace on the family, and they would wander in exile for four winters before he could rejoin the tribe.

Ridge Walker thought mostly of her niece. She felt old and played out, but Calf and the young ones had their lives ahead of them. She felt the pride of a woman in Calf—Calf of the fearless walk, Calf of the tall strength, Calf of the good earth. Already

Cheyenne talked of her brave deeds around the camp-fires and in times to come everyone would know her story. But now the telling would be tainted with a bad end. A stigma had fallen on Calf, a loss of standing in the tribe. Little Seeker and the boy would pay for the offense too, no matter how brave or prominent their family had once been. Anyone wishing to marry them would suffer part of the disgrace, and the talk of the killing would follow them all of their days.

For Little Seeker, the other children were gone, and her father, now so strange, frightened her sometimes. No one laughed anymore, except a little bit at Lost Chokecherry. Now her father had killed a man and suddenly they were alone and no one was speaking. She tried to understand, but big people confused her and she was scared. She remembered the other time when her mother and father stayed out with a small band and everyone got sick and nearly starved. But it was a bigger band and they had lodges then. Frightened at the thought, she turned anxiously to look at her mother.

Buffalo Calf Road sat straight on her horse, her eyes fixed ahead. A quiet dignity still marked her demeanor. Behind her fixed gaze a rush of thoughts and emotions crowded together—the sudden parting with no farewells, the homecoming in the north gone forever, the breaking again of the tribe, the horror of Little Seeker watching her father kill an old man, the pollution of this most horrible of acts, the grieving family of Black Crane. And Black Coyote, who for so long had hung over the edge of a cliff, had fallen now. A sorrow and anger fought inside her, but the anger had no object, no one to blame—not the peacemaker, not the soldiers, not Black Coyote. She almost wanted to blame the Coyote, but he had lost himself somewhere on the long trail, and she could not. Instead she stared at the slumped figure with pity and love and sympathy.

The western sun began to melt red across the sky, spreading its garish light over the frozen expanse. A line of early geese already honked their way north overhead, going home. Calf rode up to Black Coyote and gently touched his arm indicating they should stop. The healing touch restored contact somehow and the Coyote grasped the hand, holding it tight for a moment.

That night they camped beside a clump of juniper trees around a small fire. It was a calm and peaceful night with the stars very close, so quiet it was hard to think of the day just past or the days yet to come. Holding Calf's hand, Black Coyote fell into a deep healing sleep, a sleep that went on long after dawn, long after the others had risen. But they let him sleep. When he woke at last the sun had already traveled half way to the top of the sky and the Coyote seemed to have found himself again.

That day a warming thaw came and they found a better camp near a small stream. The three men went out for game and returned with an antelope, their excitement like that of a youth bringing home a prize catch after his first hunt. The Coyote, unusually animated, even talked about getting enough skins for a lodge and played with the children. Calf was pleased to see him this way, but she worried about the sudden shifts of mood.

For several sleeps they traveled about, seeing no people and few tracks. Despite the bad memories it was almost a good time, moving about freely on the home ground again, hunting a little game, seeming to have lost the soldiers. But after they crossed the Powder River, signs of the settlers grew more frequent. Most disturbing of all were the vast areas covered with buffalo bones and sometimes freshly killed carcasses left by the buffalo hunter to rot under the big sky.

The last of the great herds of buffalo on the plains now roamed the huge expanse between the Antelope Pit River to the east, the Elk River to the north, and the Bighorn Mountains to the west. The Coyote's face darkened at the sight of the dead animals and the old wounds opened again.

"They have destroyed the buffalo in the south—wasted them all! Now the white man comes for the rest." The Coyote fell silent, then added, with the prophetic wisdom of the cynical, "When the last buffalo is gone, the last Indian will go too."

The Moon of the Greening Grass came on the tiny band in their wanderings. One day Black Coyote brought Calf the skin of a huge buffalo for a fine robe, like the robes of the old times. They had begun to accumulate a few buffalo skins and would soon have lodges again. But they had to be careful all the time in their moving and camping because of the *veho* about in the land.

On the fifth day of the new moon, Black Coyote, Whetstone, and Vanishing Heart were hunting along a creek that emptied into the Powder River when they stumbled on two soldiers repairing the voice of the white people, the talking wires that stretched across the plains. The man on the tall timber fumbled and nearly fell at the sight of the Indians, while the soldier on the ground reached for his rifle.

Immediately the Coyote drew and shot the soldier dead. At the same time Whetstone fired on the pole man, who crashed to the ground. In an instant it was all over, the three men hardly realizing what had happened. Vanishing Heart motioned toward the horses of the fallen men and together with Whetstone went for the well-fed animals.

Black Coyote dismounted and walked to the bodies. When he saw that one man, the pole climber, still lived, he raised and cocked his pistol, pointing the barrel at the man's face. But there was a look in the eyes, a desperation such as the Coyote had come to know in himself, so he hesitated and finally dropped his hand. Signaling the others, he climbed on his horse and turned back the way they had come.

When Buffalo Calf Road saw the horses with the government mark she stood impassive, remembering the scene almost a moon ago when the Coyote last rode into camp with government horses. "It is a sign," she thought to herself, "that the trouble has only begun."

This time there were no chiefs to order the return of the horses and no one to complain except the women. But it was not their way. When the women heard of the shootings and understood that the talking wires would soon whisper across the plains, they made ready to leave, to get the children away.

Five sleeps passed quietly, but on the fifth day, as they moved southwest over rugged terrain, they rounded the base of some bluffs dotted with sage brush and junipers. Suddenly before them, stretched in a curving line, a contingent of bluecoats on horseback emerged, twenty-two men with pistols drawn. In front of the line, a soldier chief stood, flanked by two Cheyenne scouts.

CHAPTER 10

After two days of riding, the soldiers led their tiny captive band away from the Tongue River toward an opening in the tall gray bluffs to the west. In the distance to the north a string of cotton-woods, newly covered green, ran into the line of trees stretched along the banks of the Tongue, meeting at the place where the Tongue emptied into the Elk River. Thick gray clouds rolled over the soldier fort in the distance, surrounded by a wide arc of rugged bluffs open to the east.

As they drew closer, Buffalo Calf Road saw the canvas army tents neatly in rows a short distance from the wooden barracks. Then she spotted them—her own people—and realized in a sudden rush that it was all over, that she and the Coyote and the others had been the last of the Cheyenne out.

No one ran forward to speak, no one made welcoming gestures for their returning people. Instead they looked away in shame at the sight of the exiled man. When the prisoners reached the barracks, one of the soldiers motioned them to stop while another rode off quickly. Little Seeker looked frightened so Calf reached for her and lifted the child onto her own horse. The infant whimpered on her back. As they sat on their horses waiting, white people from the fort came and went, staring at the party. The Coyote held himself erect, his face motionless, his hands tied.

At last a soldier chief returned and spoke briefly to the bluecoat in charge of the prisoners. As the chief left, the bluecoat shouted some strange *veho* words and an escort of troops surrounded Black Coyote, Whetstone, and Vanishing Heart. When the Coyote saw that he would be taken without Calf, he turned his face to her and looked deep into her eyes.

Calf spurred her horse forward, pushing through the soldiers surrounding him and, laying a hand on his, she whispered, "We have done our best. Remember, only the stones stay on earth forever."

Little Seeker leaned over and hugged her father, her eyes filled with tears. The Coyote reached out with his bound hands and gently touched all three of them. The soldier in charge shouted another command and the bluecoats started away with their captives, leaving Calf and the two children rooted to the spot. The men were not taken far, only to another part of the fort where the guardhouse stood.

Calf, the children, and the other women were put into a stark log room in one of the barracks, where several cots lined the walls and a small window rationed the light. Outside a soldier stood guard at the doorway. On entering the dark room, Calf thought of Red Bird's description of the room at Fort Robinson and a new flood of grief overcame her. The five were fed, given blankets, and allowed to see the Cheyenne women who asked permission to come. Pretty Walker and Old Grandmother came first, and for a while the women exchanged news of the time of separation, of their capture, of life in the soldier tents.

"What of Black Coyote?" Calf inquired at last, hesitant to ask them to speak of him.

"He is in the prison house here in the fort," Old Grandmother answered.

"Is he well?" Calf pressed wearily.

Old Grandmother looked down at the plank floor.

"We are told he is in irons . . . to keep him from running away."

"Running away . . ." Calf repeated numbly. "And where is there to run now? To the mountains, up the

337

Powder River, to the Black Hills? It's all over—soldiers are everywhere."

Pretty Walker looked at the young woman, the bravest woman she had ever known, sitting now in a squat prison, talking without hope. It filled her with pain.

"There is more," Old Grandmother added, thinking Calf should know. "He will be taken from the fort."

Calf looked at the old woman, her brow knit tightly and her lips taut.

"He will be taken to the white people's town across the Tongue."

"But why?" Calf blurted, alarmed.

"I do not understand it fully," the woman answered. "But white people have their way of judging the guilt of someone. The Coyote must appear before white men who will decide if he is guilty."

"Guilty of what?" Calf asked incredulously.

"Of the murder of the two soldiers working on the talking wires."

Calf slumped back on the cot and tried to take it in: the Coyote in irons, the Coyote taken to a village of white people, the Coyote standing in judgment before his enemy.

Turning to Pretty Walker, she asked faintly, "Will your father help?"

Pretty Walker shook her head sadly.

"He is furious at the Coyote. He has not forgotten the killing of Black Crane, and Red Robe still suffers from his wounds. I'm afraid he will not help."

The young woman fell silent, not daring to tell Calf that Little Wolf had urged the bluecoat chief to send Black Coyote to a prison in the south.

"You must forget the Coyote," Old Grandmother said a bit sternly. She had had no trouble in her life forgetting many men. "Think of yourself now and the children."

Forget the Coyote, thought Calf, the friend of a lifetime, the father of her children, the warrior who fought by her side, the companion of like mind?

"I could more easily die," she said to herself without the words.

"Little Wolf is urging the soldier chief to set you free to join us in our camp," Pretty Walker put in.

"And are you free in the camp?" Buffalo Calf Road asked, trying to be kind. "Can our people leave when they choose? No, Pretty Walker, one prison is as good as another!"

"But, Calf," the young woman protested, "surely it is better in camp. You will be outside under the sky, not in a wooden box. You can breathe the air and see the trees along the river, and your people will be around you."

Calf smiled. Perhaps it is good, she thought, that the young can settle for so little.

Two days after her arrival at the fort called Keogh by the *veho,* Buffalo Calf Road, her children, and the two women were taken from the dark room and brought to the small tent village of the Cheyenne. The women and children were given a large tent of their own marked with the sign of the government and though no soldier stood guard at their door now, they were not free to leave the camp. Within days Calf learned that Black Coyote and the others had been taken to the white village across the Tongue named for their old enemy Bearcoat, a place called Milestown by the *veho*. It was a cruel thing, and Calf mourned for her husband as for one dead.

Little Seeker seemed better back with the children, but for the adults the days stretched into long empty times with nothing to do, each the same as the last. There was food to eat and the weather was more agreeable, but otherwise little was different from the days in Indian Territory. Calf thought bitterly of the long flight having come to this.

Most of the time Calf stayed in the canvas tent away from her people. She ate very little, she tended the children methodically, and she took joy in nothing. Chicken Woman and Ridge Walker tried to cheer her, but their hearts grieved too. Slowly the Moon of the Greening Grass passed away and with it the last of the snows and the bitter cold. The season of new life came upon them and with it the Moon of the Strawberries, but it came unnoticed to the Cheyenne people in the tents in the arc of bluffs.

Pretty Walker visited Calf often these days to bring whatever news of Black Coyote she heard from her father. One day she sat with Calf in the sunshine outside the tent, assuring her the Coyote was well in the stockade where they kept him. Calf frowned slightly but did not speak. Pretty Walker looked at Calf harder than she had for a long time. Her face seemed gaunt and tired, her eyes blank and sunken, her body thin, almost wasted.

"Do you feel well, Calf?" the younger woman asked with concern.

Calf nodded weakly.

"My throat is a little sore," she half whispered indifferently. "It will pass."

"You don't take care of yourself," Pretty Walker said gravely, chiding the woman. Then, when Calf did not respond, she added in exasperation, "You will kill yourself!"

Calf turned to the younger woman, looking intently at her.

"Nothing lives long, Pretty Walker. Nothing except the earth and the mountains. There is a time for dying." Calf's eyes came alive for a moment. "This is my time."

"But you should want to live! Everything wants to live!" Pretty Walker protested.

"Not everything," Calf corrected her. "You're young. It is good for the young to want to live."

"And are you old, Calf?" the young woman asked, nearly in tears. "You are barely ten winters older than me!"

"Ten winters and a lifetime," Calf smiled. When she saw that Pretty Walker was on the verge of tears, she laid her thin hand on that of the chief's daughter, who felt it as the touch of a feather. "You must not

341

fret for me. I will have it my way."

"Your way? But how can you have it your way?" Pretty Walker asked.

Calf's face brightened and came to life.

"I have fought for the old ways from the beginning and I would have died for them. I have not become a white Indian. I have remained Buffalo Calf Road and I will die Buffalo Calf Road. That is having it my way. It is the only thing in life that truly matters." Then, looking deep into the young woman's eyes, Calf smiled with pride. "I am not defeated, Pretty Walker. I will have it my way."

The determination in Calf's voice jarred the woman and she pushed back the tears.

"I don't understand," Pretty Walker said sadly. "I know it is bad now, but my father says we will get a reservation of our own." She paused. "And we are home, Calf. We fought our way from the place of death in the south. Surely that means something."

"It means a great deal," Calf answered, pressing her friend's hand.

"It's not what any of us wants—to live on a reservation," the younger woman replied. "But we will be at peace now. The fighting has stopped."

The words of Pretty Walker sent Calf's mind drifting back over the old arguments that had plagued the Cheyenne for so many moons. She remembered the day before the great battle at the Rosebud. The old peacemaker, Black Crane, had tried to stop them from fighting the soldiers at the Rosebud. Calf recalled his

342

prophetic words as if they had been spoken a moment before:

"Do you think you can stop the bluecoats? Always there are more and more. If you beat them on the Rosebud, more will come. If you kill those, still more will rush in. They are like drops of water in the great Elk River. Always more water comes from the melting snows of the mountains. No, you cannot stop them, no matter what you do. The only course for us is to make peace with the *veho*."

And she heard again the words of Black Coyote's reply, proud and indignant. "Peace! On whose terms? Shall we become sheep watched by the herders. . . ."

Then her own passionate voice came back to her.

"We know what they ask of us! That we live on small islands surrounded by a great white sea. That we give up our old ways and our religion and our freedom! Yes, we would be at peace then, but that is the peace of death. The day before *that* peace comes is a good day to die."

"It is a good day to die," she uttered aloud to herself.

Pretty Walker frowned at the words and protested, "We must try to build a different life. We must try . . ." Her voice trailed off.

"Is it true what I heard?" Calf asked.

"What did you hear?"

Calf hesitated. "That Little Wolf will scout for the soldiers."

Pretty Walker's head dropped and she stared at the ground.

343

"Then it's true," Calf sighed in despair. She leaned her head back against the canvas tent and stared at the blue sky, her hands limp in her lap.

"What else could he do?" Pretty Walker asked defensively. "You are too hard, Calf, too hard," she blurted out, wishing quickly she had not said the words.

Buffalo Calf Road continued to stare at the blue sky covering the earth.

"Do you remember the prophecy of Sweet Medicine?" Calf said, as much to herself as to the Walker, and the words began to flow, the words of Sweet Medicine spoken long, long ago, a recitation of the future and the present.

Many things will change in the time to come. First an animal will come among you, a fine animal with hair covered neck and hairy tail and round hoofs. It will carry you everywhere you wish to go. It will help you hunt the buffalo that will give you life.

Calf kept speaking, as one in a trance.

Many things will change. Strange people, Earth People, will come among you. Their skin will be fair and their ways great with power. They are different from you and they speak no Cheyenne. They will want you to follow them and will give you things, beads and mirrors and sweet white

344

sand for your drinks. Do not follow these Earth people. Preserve the old ways, the good ways of your ancestors.

But the Earth People will never stop. They will push forward and spread over the land and bring sickness and death. They will tear up the earth, drain the water, kill the trees and grass, destroy all the buffalo, and spoil the air. They will take the lightening from the sky and grab for the moon.

And finally you will not remember. You will change your religion. You will lose respect for your leaders and start quarreling with one another. You will marry into your own families. You will take after the Earth People's ways and forget the good things by which you have lived and in the end become worse than crazy.

Then Calf turned to the young woman.

"No, Pretty Walker. I will have it my way. I will be free."

Calf fell silent and the two women sat under the sun in the soldier camp for a long time without speaking. By sundown Buffalo Calf Road lay burning with fever. Chicken Woman boiled the ground leaves and stems of the make-cold medicine, brewing a strong tea which she coaxed on the sick woman. But morning came and the fever grew worse and with it the raging throat.

Ridge Walker tried what she had—a hot liquid made

from the powdered roots of the black medicine plant to ease the bad throat—then followed with a chunk of the root for chewing, its cool salty taste stimulating the saliva. She mixed the make-cold-medicine powder with grease and rubbed it on Calf's body to bring down the fever. Nothing helped.

Chicken Woman took the children from the tent and called a medicine man, one not as skilled as Bridge or Medicine Woman, but they were gone now. For a long time he prayed and purified, rattled and chanted. Still Calf burned, her skin red with the fever, her mouth raked by a cough.

At last they called the army doctor to come. When he looked into the sore throat, he frowned gravely and shook his head. A gray membrane had begun to form far back in Calf's mouth and on the tonsils, a membrane that would creep along the throat blocking the air passages.

"Diphtheria!" he mumbled, though no one knew what he meant by the strange word.

Yet they knew it was bad, for the doctor hurried to the door and shouted something to a soldier outside who rushed away. When he returned, an interpreter followed him and spoke hurriedly with the doctor outside the tent. Then they motioned to Ridge Walker and Chicken Woman and the interpreter told them that no one should come into the tent or the illness would spread like fire in the dry grass. The women insisted they would stay with Calf, so the doctor explained through the interpreter what to do for her. He gave them medicine, told them how to administer it, and left.

News of Calf's sickness spread through the camp. When Little Wolf heard, he grieved for the brave warrior woman and sent one of the Cheyenne scouting for the army, Two Moons, to tell Black Coyote.

The jail house stood at the edge of the small town named for Bearcoat. Two Moons went first to the man in charge of the jail and got permission to speak to Black Coyote through the narrow slats in the windowless building. At first the Coyote would not talk to his old friend, now working as a pay soldier for the army, but when he heard that Two Moons had come about Calf, he moved to the narrow opening, dragging the irons around his legs.

"She is ill," Two Moons said. "Very ill."

Black Coyote's face darkened and his eyes grew anxious.

"The white people's coughing sickness . . ." Two Moons spoke to the face behind the metal bars.

The prisoner stood stunned, clenching the bars, as he took in the words, repeating them in disbelief. "The white coughing sickness? Calf?"

"Ridge Walker and Chicken Woman are with her." Then Two Moons added, "They are both well," for Vanishing Heart and Whetstone stood in the shadows behind the Coyote.

Black Coyote seemed suddenly frantic.

"I must see her," he said to Two Moons, his voice hoarse and cracking.

"No one is allowed near her, but I will speak with White Hat." The scout nodded at the three and left through the stockade door.

At the sick tent not even the power of the white doctor's medicine helped Calf. She could not eat and barely swallowed the herb teas that Ridge Walker forced down her throat. The tough gray membrane had spread, intensifying the cough, and her breathing became more labored. Each day Calf lost weight, and a terrible weakness overcame her. Still the fever continued unabated and with it the dry, flushed, burning skin, the rapid heartbeat, the chills, the restlessness and nausea. Periodically, though she could barely speak, Calf asked after the children and Black Coyote. Otherwise she said nothing.

When her husband got the news that he would not be allowed to visit Calf because of the dangers of spreading the disease, he flew into a bitter rage. After that they lied to Black Coyote to keep him calm, telling him that Calf was getting better. But she did not get better. Slowly she wasted away under the poisons spreading through her body.

As she lay ill, the time came for the trial before a white judge in a hostile white town. Before the proceedings began, a white man came with an interpreter to the dark cell and told the prisoners he had been appointed to defend them. When he tried to question the Cheyenne, they sat impassively and refused to speak. He tried several times, to no avail.

Early in the Moon of the Ripening Juneberries

Black Coyote, Whetstone, and Vanishing Heart were taken from the dark jail, handcuffed and squinting at the sudden light. Under heavy guard, the trio was led down a wide dirt road lined on both sides with squat wooden buildings fronted by a boardwalk. On many of the structures the strange writing of the whites stood proclaiming inscrutable messages. As the party moved down the road, people began to gather on the boardwalks and with them a low murmur that rose to an open grumble. A group of children followed the Indians, taunting them in the strange language. One picked up a stone and flung it at the three, hitting Black Coyote on the shoulder. Immediately the crowd surged forward in an angry gesture, and only the rifles of the guards kept them from charging the Cheyenne. Through it all Black Coyote and the others never flinched, never reacted, never spoke.

At last they arrived at the courthouse, a small cabin made of rough logs standing at the edge of the wide dirt road. When the prisoners entered, several pine benches near the doorway were already filled with spectators. At the front of the room a platform held a crude wooden table covered with a red cloth at which the judge sat. Below the platform in front of the judge, a long table stood where the prisoners were seated with the man defending them. On the walls, sheets of cotton covered the rough-hewn logs.

It was a hot day, and the Coyote felt stifled in the crowded room and found it hard to breathe. All day the proceedings droned on, first their accusers, then

349

the witnesses, then their defender, everything turned into Cheyenne for them by an interpreter. Periodically the judge asked the prisoners if they wanted to question the speaker seated in a chair beside the judge's table, but they kept silent, making no sign, showing no emotion, seemingly indifferent to everything.

Through the open windows crowded the noise of horses' hooves on the dirt road, the shouts of the stage driver, the squeaking roll of the loaded wagons, the thud of grain sacks being unloaded, the hollow sound of hard-soled shoes on the plank boardwalk, the whistle of the fireboat on the river. So different from the sounds of camp, thought Black Coyote. Inside the courthouse the stale smell of tobacco mixed with the pungent odor of sweat. From behind him, the sweet flowery perfume of a white woman brought the memory of Calf to the front of his thoughts, a place she seldom left. But these days the thought of Calf filled him with a terrible foreboding, a fear of something dreaded and unknown.

For three sleeps the trial continued and on the fourth day the Cheyenne were convicted of murdering one soldier and wounding another as the men worked on the talking wires. For the last time, the judge asked the Indians to speak in their own defense, but the warriors refused to recognize the questions. So the judge passed sentence to the enthusiastic cheers of the spectators: On the seventh day of the Moon of the Reddening Cherries, Black Coyote, Whetstone, and Vanishing Heart would be executed by hanging.

Buffalo Calf Road was never told of the trial of Black Coyote as she lay dying the worst death, the slow wasting death. The rest of the women came now that the danger of contagion had passed and mourned over her, though she seemed not to recognize anyone.

Then one day Leaf came from Spotted Tail's Reservation, riding hard when she heard of Calf's sickness. The appearance of the familiar face with the flowing black hair stirred something in Calf. Her fingers crept to the hand by her side and a rush of images flooded her mind—a vast plain of tall green grass moving in the wind, giant cottonwoods stretching their limbs over a clear stream, a single bald eagle soaring over a snow-capped mountain, a herd of buffalo thundering over the dust covered earth, a mountain range sacred and black against a cloudless sky, the cascading waters dropping above and below over a rocky cliff, the smell of sage, the laughter of children . . .

Leaf closed Calf's eyes when she stopped breathing, and cried inside, as she had only once before. She picked up the old, worn elkhorn flesher lying by Calf's side as Chicken Woman and Ridge Walker began the low keening of death behind her. For a long while Leaf stared at the flesher, marked by generations, before she noticed that Calf had not recorded the second year of her baby's life, the second year of the unnamed child whose birthday came during imprisonment. Leaf took out her knife and scratched the second year of the infant onto the flesher.

News of Buffalo Calf Road's death spread quickly through the camp and a great keening rose to Maheo. Many women came to help prepare the body, bringing a soft deerskin dress, the best that could be found. A pair of moccasins, beaded white to signify an active life, were placed on her feet. After dressing Calf, the women gently lifted her onto the great buffalo robe given her by Black Coyote, the robe of the last buffalo hunted by the last free Cheyenne on the Great Plains. Carefully the women folded the buffalo robe over the body, wrapping it tightly and fastening it with leather strips.

When the body was ready, Little Wolf, Old Man Chief of the Northern Cheyenne, came to the tent of the dead and sang an old-time song to the Great Spirit who had made all people, a song of honor for the great one departed. After a prayer, the lifeless bundle was carried outside and lashed onto a travois.

Slowly the mourning procession moved through the camp with the remnants of the tribe following. Behind the horse drawn travois, a grieving Little Seeker, the elk-horn flesher hanging from her waist, walked between Chicken Woman and Ridge Walker, with Leaf following behind. Little Seeker walked with her head held high, as her mother had taught her. The twisting stream of people worked its way past the cottonwoods lining the Elk River and onto the sage-covered plain leading to the bluffs beyond.

A distance away, in his quarters at the fort, the enemy soldier chief, Bearcoat, listened at a window to the wailing and keening hanging over the land in the arc of cliffs.

When the trailing party reached the distant hills to the west, they carried the body of the brave one up the rocky slope to a shallow cave high above the plain, looking down at the place where the two rivers joined and flowed as one. Beyond the Tongue River the tiny village of white people dotted the landscape with its wooden stockade rising at the edge of town. It was a still day, with barely the whisper of a breeze, and without a cloud in the big sky that seemed low enough to touch. Overhead a small flock of starlings flew, the sunlight making rainbows on their feathers. Around the cave opening, thick clumps of plains prickly pear grew, its purple fruit almost ripe among the long sharp needles. The air hung heavy with scents of juniper and sage.

While the place in the cave was being prepared, the mournful keening of the women grew louder and more painful. The few remaining men who had fought with Calf against Three Stars, Long Hair, and the others unbraided their hair in a gesture of grief and let it fall loose. As the body of Buffalo Calf Road was lifted into the hollow grave, Little Wolf stepped forward with her pistol, retrieved from the bluecoat chief who had taken it from her. Gently he laid the gun of the warrior woman on her body in tribute to her bravery in battle. One by one the mourners piled rocks in front of the cave till the light was kept out and the darkness kept in.

Two Moons was assigned the chore of telling Black Coyote of the death of his wife. Dreading to speak the words, Two Moons rode slowly toward the stockade, its great branchless trunks rising in a tight line from the ground around the prison. Behind the wall of timbers stood the hanging platform and the scout thought with revulsion of the coming execution of Black Coyote and the others. The hated hanging was the worst way to die—it was the way Indians killed dogs when they needed food.

When Two Moons approached the log jail, the Coyote already stood by the narrow opening, his face at once sullen and anxious, Whetstone and Vanishing Heart hanging back behind him.

"How is Calf?" he asked even before Two Moons could speak.

The messenger glanced at the ground in a gesture that betrayed the unspoken words. The Coyote's face filled with alarm.

"My brother," Two Moons said, "it grieves me, but Calf is dead."

Black Coyote's eyes froze in disbelief.

"She died of the sickness yesterday and we buried . . ."

"You lie!" the Coyote screamed. "You lie!"

The man in the yard shook his head sadly.

"It's true," he said.

"No!" Black Coyote was becoming frantic. He tore at the thick timbers around the narrow opening as though he could widen the empty space and crawl out. "Bring her to me," he screamed.

"I cannot," Two Moons said. "Calf is buried on the cliffs."

Whetstone moved forward and made a gesture of sympathy, placing his hand on the Coyote's shoulder. But his brother-in-law, stricken with grief, shouted at him.

"Leave me! Leave me!"

He swung wildly at his friend and began clawing at the walls and the door, the blood running down his hands.

"Let me out!" he screamed. "I must go to her!"

When the door did not open at his command, the Coyote flew into an uncontrollable frenzy, smashing cots and throwing whatever came into view, while Whetstone and Vanishing Heart ducked as best they could. By now the guards came running, first two, then seeing the state of things, they called for more men. It took four men to bring the Coyote down and shorten the chains on his leg so he could not move far from the bull ring to which he was fastened. After it was over, Two Moons left, deeply moved by the sight of the great warrior come to this.

In the days that followed no one could get near the Coyote, sick with grief at the loss. He spoke to no one, he ate nothing, he sat wild-eyed as the others slept.

A few days after the incident, the white man who undertook their defense at the trial appeared in the cell again with the interpreter. Black Coyote sat impassive and indifferent as the man spoke.

"Many believe the verdict was unjust," he told the three. "There is great pressure from some quarters to pursue an appeal. I am prepared," he added emphatically, "to appeal to Governor Potts for pardon on your behalf. After all," he said, watching their faces for some reaction, "the Cheyenne have been at war with the army and if you were killed instead of the soldiers, no one would have been tried."

Still the trio sat impassively. No one spoke, no one acknowledged the words.

"Please," the lawyer asked through his interpreter, "Won't you let me help? Tell me what really happened."

Only a great silence answered him. At last the man rose, his shoulders stooped in a gesture of helplessness. He stood for a while looking at the three Indians in chains.

Then he said simply, in a half whisper, "There are white people who care."

When the man turned to leave the dark oppressive cell, Black Coyote's eyes moved slightly after the man, his head and body perfectly still. But he said nothing and listened quietly as the thick log door slammed shut. After the man had gone, Black Coyote turned to Whetstone and Vanishing Heart and spoke for the first time in days, his voice calm and deliberate.

"I will not let the white man hang me."

The two looked intently at the Coyote, under-standing immediately.

"How will you do it?" Whetstone asked, his voice quivering a bit.

"I will find a way . . . tonight."

Vanishing Heart sat quietly, a momentary panic clutching him, but it passed quickly, and he said, "I will do it too."

"And I," Whetstone added softly.

The Coyote was moved and a deep sigh, almost of relief, passed through his chest. He could think of Calf as she was again, alive, not as a lifeless bundle strapped on a travois. He choked a bit, thinking of Little Seeker and the baby left behind, but it was not the way of Cheyenne to abandon their own and he knew his sister would take them in. It was their life in the future that frightened him, an empty life of con-finement. So he tried to think of Calf, set free at last.

When the last faint rays of last light faded from the room, Black Coyote slowly removed his belt made of thick leather tongs. Vanishing Heart touched his arm and spoke in a cracking voice.

"Let me go first."

The Coyote hesitated a moment, then nodded, pointing to a metal bar that ran alongside and over the edge of the door. The ceiling of the room hung low, almost touching their heads when they stood. Van-ishing Heart puzzled for a moment, then quickly fas-tened a noose to the metal bar. Then he stopped and stood as one paralyzed. Black Coyote put his hand on his friend's shoulder, sensing his revulsion at the act that was always shunned by the Cheyenne.

"Remember," the Coyote said, his voice hard and determined, "we all wanted to live, but they would not let us."

When the guard came to feed the prisoners the next day, he found them, two lying on the dirt floor, their bodies stretched out, their hands at their sides, and Black Coyote, the troublemaker they called him, still hanging by the neck, his knees almost touching the ground. The guard stood amazed and puzzled till he saw the rope-burned necks of those on the ground and realized they had died in turn, swinging by their necks in the cramped room.

Outside, the town in the shadow of Fort Keogh began to stir in the hot summer sun. A burly buffalo hunter hauling his rich load of hides past the stockade commented that this had been a good year.

Overhead, unnoticed, two cliff swallows joined in flight above the stockade, fluttering briefly as they met. Then, in unison, they rose, free and unfettered, above the prison, above the town, above the great plains, soaring higher and higher, disappearing at last into the great blue arms of the universe.

EPILOGUE

The bravery and sacrifices of Buffalo Calf Road and the Cheyenne people bore fruit at last. The survivors of the Fort Robinson massacre were not forced south again and were allowed to join the group at Fort Keogh. On November 16, 1884, President Chester A. Arthur signed an Executive Order creating a reservation for the Northern Cheyenne in southeastern Montana, known as Lame Deer Reservation. Those Northern Cheyenne remaining in Indian Territory in Oklahoma were allowed to come north.

So, after years of heroic struggle, the Northern Cheyenne were reunited as a people on land of their own on the beloved high plains.

A CHRONOLOGY OF THE CHEYENNE PEOPLE

1830s: *Separation of the Cheyenne people*—Large numbers move south to the Arkansas River in Colorado to trade at Bent's Fort and Fort St. Vrain on the South Platte, while most Cheyenne remain north, trading at Fort Laramie.

1840s–1850s: *Troubles begin*—A period of growing hostilities between the Plains Indians, the U.S. Army, and settlers as thousands of pioneers began to move through Cheyenne and Lakota lands, bringing disease, killing buffalo and game, and occupying Indian campsites.

Summer, 1858: *Gold discovered in Colorado*—Within a year, about 50,000 whites had entered Plains Indian country. Whites traveling the South Platte route made north-south movement hard for the Cheyenne, further dividing the Northern and Southern Cheyenne.

November 29, 1864: *Sand Creek massacre*—The Southern Cheyenne camp of Chief Black Kettle is attacked by Colonel Chivington of the Colorado militia, who ordered his men to "kill Cheyenne whenever and wherever found." On that day, 137 Cheyenne, mostly women and children, were slaughtered, dismembered, and mutilated. A mass Indian uprising resulted.

October 28, 1867: *Treaty of Medicine Lodge*—Established a reservation in Indian Territory in Oklahoma for the Southern Cheyenne who, in return, agreed to relinquish all land outside the reservation. Not all Indians complied.

April–May, 1868: *Treaty of Fort Laramie*—Ended hostilities between the U.S. Army and the Lakota, Arapaho, and Cheyenne. Established the Great Sioux Reservation housing the Lakota, Cheyenne, and Arapaho and created unceded territory in the Powder River country where the Indians could hunt freely. Several Lakota and Cheyenne chiefs refused to sign the treaty.

November 27, 1868: *Battle of the Washita*—Lt. Colonel George Armstrong Custer attacks a Southern Cheyenne camp of fifty-one family lodges off the reservation, killing men, women, and children, including Chief Black Kettle who had escaped the Sand Creek Massacre.

July 2, 1874: *Black Hills expedition*—Custer leads 1,000 troops into the Black Hills, which was part of the Great Sioux Reservation, ostensibly to find a site for a fort. Gold is discovered and word spreads as miners rush to the area.

April 23, 1875: *Sappa Creek attack*—Lieutenant Henely's troops trap a group of Southern Cheyenne attempting to reach the Northern Cheyenne and kill twenty-seven men, women, and children. This marked the last of more than two dozen battles known as the Red River hostilities.

December 3, 1875: *Indians ordered onto reservations*—The Commissioner of Indian Affairs orders the Northern Cheyenne, Lakota, and Northern Arapaho Indian agents to inform all off-reservation Indians they must come into their agencies no later than January 31 or "military force would be sent to compel them," despite the Indians' right by treaty to be off reservation.

March 17, 1876: *Attack on Old Bear's Camp*—General George Crook attacks the peaceful Northern Cheyenne camp.

June 16, 1876: *Battle of the Rosebud*—Fearing another attack, Cheyenne and Lakota warriors attack General Crook's troops moving down the Rosebud Creek.

June 25, 1876: *Battle of the Little Bighorn*—Custer attacks the Northern Cheyenne and Lakota massed on the Little Bighorn River.

September 23, 1876: *Black Hills Agreement*—
Although it violates the Fort Laramie Treaty, a government commission coerces the reservation chiefs to surrender the Black Hills and unceded Powder River land.

November 26, 1876: *Attack on Dull Knife's Camp*—
General Ranald Mackenzie attacks the Northern Cheyenne camp on the Powder River.

Spring, 1877: *Northern Cheyenne surrender*—Crazy Horse and the Oglala also surrender. Sitting Bull leads his people to safety in Canada.

May 28, 1877: *Northern Cheyenne ordered south to Indian Territory*—Close to 1,000 Northern Cheyenne leave Fort Robinson in Nebraska for Indian Territory in Oklahoma.

August 5, 1877: *Northern Cheyenne arrive in Indian Territory*—They join the Southern Cheyenne.

September 5, 1877: *Crazy Horse is killed.*

September 9, 1878: *The Cheyenne flight north begins*—About 300 Northern Cheyenne, under the leadership of Little Wolf and Dull Knife, flee Indian Territory to journey home to the north, pursued by the army.

October, 1878: *Northern Cheyenne reach Nebraska.*

Mid-October, 1878: *The parting*—Dull Knife leads about 150 to Red Cloud Reservation to seek sanctuary. Little Wolf leads his followers to Lost Chokecherry Creek in the Sand Hills of Nebraska.

October 23, 1878: *The capture*—Dull Knife and his group captured and taken to Fort Robinson.

January 9, 1879: *Fort Robinson outbreak*—Dull Knife and his group attempt to escape.

Late winter, 1879: *Little Wolf leads his followers north to the Yellowstone River country.*

March 25, 1879: *Little Wolf and his followers are captured and brought to Fort Keogh in Montana.*

November 16, 1884: *President Chester A. Arthur signs an Executive Order*—A reservation is established for the Northern Cheyenne in Montana.

GLOSSARY

MONTHS

While there is no standard set of names that the Cheyenne agree to, these are some of the most commonly used by the Cheyenne and Lakota:

Moon of the Frost in the Lodges .... January
Moon of the Snowblind Eyes .... February
Moon of the Light Snows .... March
Moon of the Greening Grass .... April
Moon of the Strawberries .... May
Moon of the Ripening Juneberries .... June
Moon of the Reddening Cherries .... July
Moon of the Ripe Plums .... August
Moon of the Yellow Leaves .... September
Moon When the Water Freezes at the Edges . .October
Moon of the Fallen Leaves .... November
Moon of the Big Freeze .... December

RIVERS

Antelope Pit River .... Little Missouri River
Arrowpoint River .... Arkansas River
Blue Earth Creek .... Beaver Creek
Bull River .... Cimarron River
Bunch of Trees River .... Smoky Hill River

Elk River .... Yellowstone River
Fat River .... South Platte River
Fork Creek ... East Fork of the Little Powder River
Great Medicine Dance Creek .... Reno Creek
Moon Shell River .... North Platte River
Red Shield River .... Republican River
Sudden River .... Niobrara River
White Water River .... White River
Wolf River .... North Canadian River

COUNTRY

Grandmother's Country .... Canada

ARMY PERSONNEL

Bad Hand .... Colonel Ranald MacKenzie
Bearcoat .... Colonel Nelson A. Miles
Big Leggins .... Johnny Brughiere
Long Hair ...... General George Armstrong Custer
Red Face .... Captain Joseph Rendlebrock
Tall White Man ...... Lieutenant Henry W. Lawton
Three Stars .... General George Crook
White Hat .... Lieutenant William P. Clark

CHARACTERS

Bear–warrior
Bear Rope–father of Comes in Sight Woman
Bear Shield–warrior
Bear Walks on Ridge–warrior
Big Crow–warrior
Big Foot–warrior
Big Horse–warrior
Bighead–aunt of Noisy Walking
Black Coyote–husband of Buffalo Calf Road
Black Crane–peacemaker of the Cheyenne
Black Hairy Dog–keeper of the Sacred Arrows
Black Horse–warrior, Southern Cheyenne
Black Sun–warrior
Box Elder–prophet of the Cheyenne people
Braided Locks–warrior
Brave One–friend of Buffalo Calf Road
Bridge–healer
Broad Faced One–young woman
Buffalo Calf Road–warrior woman, originally
   Southern Cheyenne, raised among the Northern
   Cheyenne, married to Black Coyote
Bull Hump–son of Dull Knife, married to Leaf
Bullet Proof–warrior
Chicken Woman–sister of Black Coyote, married to
   Whetstone
Coal Bear–keeper of the Sacred Hat

369

Comes in Sight–brother of Buffalo Calf Road, Southern Cheyenne

Comes in Sight Woman–daughter of Bear Rope

Crane Woman–daughter of Lame White Man and Twin Woman

Crazy Horse–Chief of the Oglala Lakota

Crooked Nose–sister of Wooden Leg, Little Hawk's intended

Crow Split Nose–Chief of the Elk Warrior Society

Cut Belly–warrior

Dirty Moccasins–old man chief

Dull Knife–old man chief

Feather on Head–wife of Little Wolf

Finger Woman–daughter of Sweet Taste Woman

Fist–warrior

Gathering His Medicine–oldest son of Iron Teeth and Red Pipe

Great Eyes–keeper of the Sacred Shield, father of Leaf

Growing Dog–warrior

High Forehead–mother of Runs Ahead

Hog's Daughter–daughter of Wild Hog

Hog's Wife–wife of Wild Hog

Hump Nose–warrior

Iron Shirt–father of Pemmican Road

Iron Teeth–wife of Red Pipe, mother of five

Lame White Man–Southern Cheyenne, married to Twin Woman

Last Bull–Chief of the Kit Fox Warriors

Leaf–daughter of Great Eyes, married to Bull Hump

Left Alone–widow, Southern Cheyenne
Left Hand–warrior
Limber Hand–warrior
Limpy–warrior
Little Finger Nail–artist of the Cheyenne, suitor of Singing Cloud
Little Hawk–warrior, suitor of Crooked Nose
Little Heart–sister of Brave One
Little Hog–son of Wild Hog
Little Hump–son of Dull Knife
Little Red Hood–daughter of Lame White Man and Twin Woman
Little Seeker–daughter of Buffalo Calf Road
Little Shield–warrior
Little Wolf–old man chief
Long Feathers–wife of Many Colored Braids
Many Colored Braids–warrior, husband of Long Feathers
Medicine Top–son of Box Elder
Medicine Wolf–warrior
Medicine Woman–healer
Moving Robe–Lakota, sister of One Hawk
Noisy Walking–warrior
Oak–father of Great Eyes
Old Bear–old man chief
Old Crier–messenger of the Cheyenne
Old Grandmother–grandmother of Spotted Deer
One Hawk–Lakota warrior, brother of Moving Robe
Pawnee–son of Little Wolf
Pawnee Woman–wife of Dull Knife

Pemmican Road–sister-in-law of Buffalo Calf Road, married to Comes in Sight

Pretty Walker–daughter of Little Wolf

Pug Nose–warrior

Quiet One–wife of Little Wolf

Red Bird–nephew of Great Eyes

Red Cloud–Oglala Lakota chief

Red Pipe–husband of Iron Teeth

Ridge Walker–Buffalo Calf Road's aunt, married to Vanishing Heart

Rising Sun–son of Iron Shirt, brother of Pemmican Road

Roman Nose–warrior

Runs Ahead–friend of Little Seeker, daughter of High Forehead

Scabby–warrior

Short One–wife of Dull Knife

Singing Cloud–young woman, Helper of the Healers

Sitting Bull–Chief of the Hunkpapa Lakota

Spotted Deer–young grandson of Old Grandmother

Spotted Eagle–Chief of the Arrows All Gone Lakota

Spotted Tail–Chief of the Brule Lakota

Standing Elk–warrior

Swallow–Buffalo Calf Road's cousin, daughter of Ridge Walker and Vanishing Heart

Sweet Taste Woman–mother of Finger Woman

Tangle Hair–Chief of the Dog Warrior Society

The Princesses–three daughters of Dull Knife

Touch the Clouds–Chief of the Minniconjou Lakota

Twin Woman–married to Lame White Man, Southern Cheyenne

Two Moons–warrior
Vanishing Heart–Buffalo Calf Road's uncle, married
  to Ridge Walker
White Bird–warrior
White Bull–father of Noisy Walking, Holy man
White Shield–warrior
Wild Hog–Chief of the Elk Warrior Society
Wooden Leg–warrior, brother of Crooked Nose and
  Yellow Hair
Woodenthigh–son of Little Wolf
Yellow Bead–young woman
Yellow Eagle–warrior
Yellow Hair–warrior, brother of Wooden Leg and
  Crooked Nose
Yellow Woman–widow, mother of Pug Nose,
  Southern Cheyenne
Young Eagle–player of the Medicine Flute
Young Elk–warrior
Young Magpie–warrior

OLD MEN CHIEFS

Old Bear
Dirty Moccasins
Little Wolf
Dull Knife

FAMILIES

Buffalo Calf Road
Black Coyote–husband
Little Seeker–daughter
Infant–son
Comes in Sight–brother
Pemmican Road–sister-in-law, married to Comes in
  Sight
Chicken Woman–sister-in-law, sister of Black
  Coyote, married to Whetstone
Whetstone–brother-in-law, married to Chicken
  Woman
Ridge Walker–aunt, married to Vanishing Heart
Vanishing Heart–married to Ridge Walker
Swallow–cousin, daughter of Ridge Walker and
  Vanishing Heart

Bear Rope
Comes in Sight Woman–daughter

Box Elder
Medicine Top–son

Brave One
Little Heart–sister

374

Dull Knife
Pawnee Woman–wife
Short One–wife
Bull Hump–son, married to Leaf
Leaf–daughter-in-law, married to Bull Hump
The Princesses–three daughters
Little Hump–son

Great Eyes
Oak–father
Leaf–daughter, married to Bull Hump
Bull Hump–son-in-law
Red Bird–nephew

High Forehead
Runs Ahead–daughter

Iron Shirt
Pemmican Road–daughter, married to Comes in
  Sight (Buffalo Calf Road's brother)
Rising Sun–son

Iron Teeth
Red Pipe–husband
Gathering His Medicine–oldest son

Lame White Man
Twin Woman–wife
Crane Woman–daughter
Little Red Hood–daughter

Little Wolf
Feather on Head–wife
Quiet One–wife
Pretty Walker–daughter
Woodenthigh–son
Pawnee–son

Many Colored Braids
Long Feathers–wife

Noisy Walking
White Bull–father, Medicine man
Bighead–aunt

Old Grandmother
Spotted Deer–grandson

Sweet Taste Woman
Finger Woman–daughter

Wild Hog
Hog's Wife–wife
Hog's Daughter–daughter
Little Hog–son

Wooden Leg
Crooked Nose–sister, Little Hawk's intended
Yellow Hair–brother

BIBLIOGRAPHY

Bad Heart Bull, Amos, *A Pictographic History of the Oglala Sioux*. Lincoln: University of Nebraska Press, 1967.

Bent, George, *Bent Papers*. Beinecke Rare Book and Manuscript Library, Yale University.

Bighead, Kate, *She Watched Custer's Last Battle* recorded by Thomas B. Marquis. Hardin, Montana: By the Author, 1933.

Bismark Tribune, accounts of the capture and trial of Black Coyote, April 26, 1879, p.1; June 7, 1879, p. 4; July 19, 1879, p. 1.

Boye, Alan, *Holding Stone Hands: On the Trail of the Cheyenne Exodus*. Lincoln: University of Nebraska Press, 1999.

Brown, Dee, *Bury My Heart at Wounded Knee*. New York: Bantam Books, 1972.

Connell, Evan S., *Son of the Morning Star: Custer and the Little Bighorn*. San Francisco: North Point Press, 1984.

Graham, Colonel W. A., *The Custer Myth: A Source Book of Custeriana*. New York: Bonanza Books, 1953.

Grinnell, George Bird, *The Cheyenne Indians: Their History and Ways of Life*. 2 Vol. Lincoln: University of Nebraska Press, 1972.

————, *The Fighting Cheyennes*. Norman: University of Oklahoma Press, 1956.

Hardorff (ed.), Richard, *Cheyenne Memories of the Custer Fight*. Lincoln: University of Nebraska Press, 1998.

————, *Lakota Recollections of the Custer Fight*. Lincoln: University of Nebraska Press, 1997.

Hoebel, E. Adamson, *The Cheyennes*. New York: Holt, Rinehart and Winston, 1960.

Hyde, George E., *The Life of George Bent*. Norman: University of Oklahoma Press, 1968.

Iron Teeth, *Iron Teeth: A Cheyenne Old Woman* in *Cheyenne and Sioux*, recorded by Thomas B. Marquis. Stockton, California: University of the Pacific, 1973.

"Billy Jackson's Capture by the Cheyenne," *Forest and Stream*, August 7, 1897, pp. 102–103.

Linderman, Frank B., *Pretty Shield: Medicine Woman of the Crows.* New York: The John Day Co., 1972.

Little Finger Nail, *Sketchbook*, Department of Anthropology Archives, Catalog Number 50.1/6619, American Museum of Natural History, New York.

Little Wolf Papers, Special File, Box 10, Military Division of the Missouri, Records of the United States Army Commands, Record Group 393, National Archives.

Llewellyn, K. N., and Hoebel, E. Adamson, *The Cheyenne Way.* Norman: University of Oklahoma Press, 1941.

Marquis, Thomas B., *The Cheyennes of Montana.* Algonac, Michigan: Reference Publications, 1978.

Truman Michelson's narratives of the history and military exploits of the Northern Cheyenne. MS. 2811, MS. 2822, MS. 2828, MS. 3218, National Anthropological Archives, Smithsonian Institution.

Monnett, John H., *Tell Them We Are Going Home: The Odyssey of the Northern Cheyennes*. Norman: University of Oklahoma Press, 2001.

Niethammer, Carolyn, *Daughters of the Earth*. New York: Collier Books, 1977.

Powell, Peter J., *Sweet Medicine*. 2 Vol. Norman: University of Oklahoma Press, 1969.

————, *People of the Sacred Mountain*. 2 Vol. San Francisco: Harper and Row, 1981.

Judge Eli S. Ricker Collection, Nebraska State Historical Society.

Sandoz, Mari, *Cheyenne Autumn*. New York: McGraw Hill, 1953.

————, *Sandoz Papers*, University of Nebraska Library at Lincoln.

Secretary of War, *Annual Report*, 1879.

Sheridan, Lieutenant-General Philip H., *Record of Engagements with Hostile Indians Within the Military Division of the Missouri from 1868 to 1882*. Washington, D.C.: Government Printing Office, 1882.

Stands in Timber, John and Liberty, Margot, *Cheyenne Memories*. Lincoln: University of Nebraska Press, 1972.

United States Senate, 46th Congress, 2nd Session, *Testimony and Report on the Removal of the Northern Cheyenne to Indian Territory*, Report Number 708, 1880.

Weist, Tom, *A History of the Cheyenne People*. Billings: Montana Council for Indian Education, 1977.

White Man, Wesley, Interview, Lame Deer, Montana, Summer 1980.

Wooden Leg, *Wooden Leg: A Warrior Who Fought Custer*. Lincoln: University of Nebraska Press, Reprint of 1931 edition by Midwest Co.

Wooden Leg, John, Telephone interview, Summer 1980.

Yellow Nose–Spotted Wolf, *Ledger Book*, Catalog Number 166,032 in the National Anthropological Archives, Smithsonian Institution.

ABOUT THE AUTHORS

Rosemary Agonito is the author of five books and many articles and has lectured widely on women's history and issues.

Joseph Agonito is a specialist in the Plains Indians and has been honored for his original research on Native Americans. The Agonitos have traveled extensively in the West, visiting sites of Cheyenne history depicted in this book.

The Agonitos live in Syracuse, New York.

Center Point Publishing
600 Brooks Road • PO Box 1
Thorndike ME 04986-0001 USA

(207) 568-3717

US & Canada:
1 800 929-9108